The Complete Female Warriors

The Complete Female Warriors

A History of Outstanding Military Women
Through the Ages

Two Volumes in One Special Edition

Ellen C. Clayton

(Mrs. Needham)

LEONAUR

The Complete Female Warriors
A History of Outstanding Military Women Through the Ages
by Ellen C. Clayton (Mrs. Needham)

FIRST EDITION

First published in two volumes under the titles
Female Warriors Volume 1 & 2

Leonaur is an imprint of Oakpast Ltd

ISBN: 978-1-78282-710-8 (hardcover)
ISBN: 978-1-78282-711-5 (softcover)

http://www.leonaur.com

Publisher's Notes

Contents

CHAPTER 1

Mythology to More Modern Tribes of Amazons

Were it not for fear of Mrs. Grundy whose awful visage is to the modern Briton what the Gorgon's head was to the ancient Greeks it might be said that Popular Prejudice is the deaf, deformed sister of Justice. Popular Prejudice makes up her mind on certain subjects, and is grandly unconscious of any fault within herself; ignorant that she is deaf, and that she is morally blind, although able to see every petty object that passes within her range.

Popular Prejudice, like her stately cousin, Mrs. Grundy, arranges fixed rules of etiquette, of conduct, even of feeling, and never pardons the slightest infringement of the lines she marks out. A man may lay down his life for "an idea," but if it be outside the ramparts of Popular Prejudice, he does so as a rebel, maybe a fool. A man may have high aspirations, but if by the breadth of a hair's line they run not parallel with the views of Popular Prejudice, let him be anathema maranatha, let him be bound in chains, away with him to outer darkness, to the company of the few who share his—"crotchets."

Whisper it not in Gath that a woman should dare ever to transgress the lines laid down by Popular Prejudice. A woman is a subordinate accident in Creation, quite an afterthought, a supplementary notion, a postscript, though Humour might laughingly say, much like the famous postscript to a lady's letter. Man (though he is permitted to include in his superb all-comprehensive identity, Woman) is big, strong, noble, intellectual: a Being. Woman is small, weak, seldom noble, and ought not to be conscious of the significance of the word Intellectual.

The exception is supposed to prove the rule. A woman may be forgiven for defying Popular Prejudice, if she is very pretty, very silly, and very wicked. Popular Prejudice has the natural instinct of yielding to any little weakness that may be imagined to flatter a Man. But Popular Prejudice is superbly angry with a woman who is perhaps not pretty, yet ventures to claim good sense and personal will, and who may be innately good. Popular Prejudice is the fast friend of lean-faced Envy; and woe betide the woman (or even the man) who would presume to sit down at the board of these allies uninvited.

Popular Prejudice, having decided that woman is a poor, weak creature, credulous, easily influenced, holds that she is of necessity timid; that if she were allowed as much as a voice in the government of her native country, she would stand appalled if war were even hinted at. If it be proved by hard facts that woman is not a poor, weak creature, then she must be reprimanded as being masculine. To brand a woman as being masculine, is supposed to be quite sufficient to drive her cowering back to her 'broidery-frame and her lute.

Popular Prejudice abhors hard facts, and rarely reads history. Yet nobody can deny that facts are stubborn things, or that the world rolls calmly round even when wars, rumours of wars, revolutions, and counter-revolutions, are raging in every quarter and subdivision of its surface.

War is, undoubtedly, a horrid alternative to the average woman, and she shrinks from it—as the average man shrinks. But, walking down the serried ranks of history, we find strange records of feminine bravery; as we might discover singular instances of masculine cowardice, if we searched far enough.

As argumentation is unpleasant and unprofitable, be it counted only idle pastime gathering a handful of memories from the playground of history.

Opinion among the ancients on all subjects was as fairly divided as it has been among moderns. Naturally, however, in that uncivilised stage of the world's development, men and women inclined more towards brute force than they now do. Plato, the Athenian philosopher, lamented that the lives of women should be wasted in domestic, and sometimes servile, duties; arguing that if the girls were trained like the boys, in athletic sports and warlike exercises, and were taught to endure fatigue, they would soon cease to be the weaker sex, and could not only fight as well as their lords and masters, but might take the command of armies and fleets.

But though the counsels of the great Athenian were followed in many things, they were entirely declined on this question. His countrymen, even in cases of the direst necessity, were loath to swell their ranks with female recruits; and it was only during the degenerate days of the Empire that Rome publicly authorised the combats of women in the amphitheatre.

Very few people deny that woman did, occasionally, fight in olden times. All nations, from the rudest barbarians to those most advanced in civilisation, hold this belief. An old Chinese tradition says that but for the wisdom of certain *mandarins* in days gone by, the weaker sex might possibly be now the stronger in the Celestial Empire. Once upon a time, so the story runs, the Chinese women, discontented with the unequal share accorded to them in the government, rose in rebellion. The revolt so very nearly became a revolution that the emperor and his ministers, to prevent a recurrence of the danger, decreed that henceforth the feet of girls throughout China should be bandaged in such a way as to put it out of their power ever again to take the field as warriors. And thus, says the fable, originated the famous Golden Lilies.

The ancients were all familiar with the idea of women sometimes exchanging the spindle and distaff for the spear and shield. Not only did they believe their goddesses to take part occasionally in the battles of mortals, but the supreme direction of military affairs was assigned to a female, as Goddess of War; and this deity, combining wisdom and courage, frequently proved more than a match for the brutal if not blundering God of Battles. Pope observes:

> Which, indeed, is no more than just, since wisdom is generally averse to entering into warlike contests at all; yet when engaged, it is likely to triumph over brute force, and to bear off the laurels of the day.

No general amongst the ancients would have dared to enter an enemy's country, besiege a city, or risk an engagement without first sacrificing to the Goddess of War.

All nations alike held the same belief. The Egyptians offered sacrifices to Neith, the Goddess of War, Philosophy, and Wisdom, to whom lions were subject, and whose fitting emblem was the vulture. The Greeks and Romans adored Minerva, the Thunderer's armour-clad daughter: and Bellona, sister, or perhaps wife of Mars, whose chariot she was said to drive through the din and tumult of the fight, lashing the foaming horses with a bloody scourge.

And Victoria, whose name denotes her office, was so greatly honoured both in Greece and Rome, that Hiero, King of Syracuse, to flatter the Romans, once sent them an idol figure of this goddess, three hundred and twenty pounds in weight, made of solid gold; while the Egyptians, who worshipped her under the name of Naphte, represented her in the form of an eagle, because that bird is the strongest of aerial warriors, and invariably victorious over all the feathered race.

The Brahmins, who claim an antiquity as great as, or greater than, Egypt, worshipped, and still worship, Durga, or Katyayini, whose ten arms and hands, each of which grasps a warlike weapon or emblem, prove how formidable a foe she is believed to have been. Our ancient British forefathers prayed to Andate, or Andraste, Goddess of Victory, and called upon her in their hour of need. The northern races, Goths, Vandals, Germans, who over-ran Europe during the decline of the Roman Empire, assigned a somewhat analogous place in their mythology to the Valkyrias, or Disas—

Those dread maids, whose hideous yell
Maddens the battle's bloody swell.

These beautiful women were believed to take a leading part in every battle fought on earth. Mounted on swift steeds, armed with helmets and mail, drawn swords in their hands, they rode wildly over the field to select those heroes destined by Odin for the slaughter, and lead them to Valhalla, the Paradise of the Brave.

Nor is the belief in warlike goddesses confined to the Old World. When Cortez entered Mexico, he found the subjects of Montezuma worshipping, amongst other deities, all more or less repulsive to the eye, a horrid basalt monster named Teoyamiqui, Goddess of War. She was supposed to be wife of the equally terrible Huitzilopochtli, or Tlacahuepancuexcotzin, the Mexican Mars. Like the Valkyrias, her chief duty was to conduct those warriors who fell in defence of the gods to the house of the Sun, the Elysium or Valhalla of the Mexicans, where she transformed them into humming-birds.

The present age is a decidedly sceptical one.

It is the fashion nowadays, (1879), to sneer at the traditions venerated by our grandfathers. Those chapters in the world's history which have not been *proved* by *facts*, have passed, in the opinion of many well educated people, into the category of fable and nursery-rhyme. The early histories of Greece and Rome, and of our own country too, are now taken, if taken at all, *cum grano salis*. King Arthur, Hengist and Horsa, and many another hero of whom we were once so proud, have been cast, by most matter-of-fact writers, on the same dusty shelf with

Achilles and Hector, Romulus and Remus, side by side with Jupiter and Mercury, Jack the Giant-Killer and Blue Beard. Scarcely anybody in our days is so credulous as to believe that the Amazons ever existed. Gibbon observes:

> Amongst barbarous nations, women have often combated by the side of their husbands; but it is almost impossible that a society of Amazons could have existed in the old or new world.

His opinion has been endorsed by most subsequent writers, some of whom are even more positive in their expressions of incredulity.

Ancient writers are divided on the question. Strabo denies that there ever was or could have been such a community, and adds, to believe in their existence we must suppose "in those days the women were men and the men women." Plutarch, more moderate, half believes they did exist, but doubts most of their marvellous achievements, which, he thinks, "clearly resemble fable and fiction." Amongst those who speak for the defence, Herodotus, Diodorus Siculus, Justin, and Quintus Curtius stand prominently forward.

Their origin, as related by Justin, though curious, is far from being impossible or even improbable in the remote days when they lived. Some years previous to the reign of Ninus, King of Assyria, two young princes of the Scythian blood-royal, Hylinos and Scolopitos, being driven from their native country by a faction of the nobility, induced several hundred young men and women to emigrate with them. After a toilsome march through barren wilds they settled at last in Cappadocia, on the rugged banks of the Thermodon. This little river, which now bears the name of Termeh or Karmili, falls into the Black Sea, between Trebisond and Sinope.

For a number of years, the newcomers carried on a species of border warfare with the natives of the Themiscyrean plains—stealing their cattle, tearing up their corn, destroying their homes by fire and sword. At last the aborigines surprised and massacred the male settlers, by means of an ambush. The wives of the latter, having now no one to whom they could look for protection, armed themselves and expelled the foe from their territory.

From this time, they laid aside all thoughts of marriage, "calling it slavery and not matrimony." And, to enforce this law, it is said, they murdered a few men who had escaped the fury of the natives in the general massacre. The Amazons were thenceforth forbidden even to speak to men, save during certain days in the year. At the appointed time, throwing aside their military character, they visited the surrounding nations, and were permitted, by special treaties, to depart again unmolested. Justin says they strangled all their male children directly they were born; Diodorus, that they distorted their limbs; while Philastratus and others affirm that they sent them back, uninjured, to the fathers.

The girls were bred, like their mothers, "not in idleness, nor spinning, but in exercises of war, such as hunting and riding." In early childhood the right breast was burnt off, that they might, when grown up, be more easily able to bend the bow and hurl the. dart. From whence, some say, they derived the name of Amazon, which is formed of two Greek words, signifying "wanting a breast." Bryant, the antiquarian, rejects this theory, and suggests, though with less probability, that the name comes from Zon, the Sun, which was the national object of worship.

The bow was their favourite weapon, and from constant practice they acquired such proficiency as to equal, if not surpass the Scythians and Parthians, who were the most skilful archers of ancient times. With the Greeks and Romans it was not uncommon to speak of a very superior bow or quiver as "Amazonian."

The nation soon became formidable, and in due time grew famous throughout the world. At one time the dominion of the Amazons extended over the entire of Asia Minor and Ionia, besides a great part of Italy. So renowned did they at last become, that Jobates, King of Lycia, commanded Bellerophon to effect their subjugation, feeling certain that the hero would never return; great indeed was his astonishment to see the redoubtable conqueror of the Chimera return victorious, and he no longer hesitated to confess the divine origin of the hero. It is said that Cadmus, the founder of Thebes, was married to an Amazon named Sphynx when he carried letters from Egypt to Greece, about 1550 B.C.

Lampedo and Marpesia were the first Amazon queens whose names became known beyond their own dominions. To give greater *éclat* to their numerous victories, they claimed to be daughters of the God Mars—a common expedient in the olden times. Taking it in turn to defend the frontier and invade foreign countries, they speedily conquered Iberia (Georgia), Colchis (Mingrelia), Albania, the Tauric Chersonese (the Crimea), and a great part of Asia.

To commemorate the achievements of Queen Marpesia during her passage over the craggy and snow-capped Caucasus, when every peak, every ridge was bravely defended by hordes of desperate mountaineers, the name of Mount Marpesia was bestowed upon one of the loftiest rocks.

It was Marpesia who founded Themiscyra, the capital of the Amazons, on the banks of the Thermodon. She adorned this city with many stately buildings, conspicuous amongst which was the royal palace. Many cities in Asia Minor owed their origin to the same queen—amongst others, Ephesus, Thyatira, Smyrna, and Magnesia.

On the death of Marpesia, who was surrounded by the barbarians during an expedition into Asia, and, together with her entire army, put to the sword, Orithya, Orseria, or Sinope, and her sister Antiope, or Hippolyte, ascended the throne. Orithya, the most famous of all the Amazon queens, inherited the beauty, together with the military skill of her mother, Marpesia. Under her rule the nation became so renowned, that Eurystheus, fancying he had at last found a task beyond the powers of Hercules, commanded the hero, as his ninth labour, to bring him the girdle of the Amazon queen. The hero succeeded, however.

Hercules, accompanied by Theseus, Castor and Pollux, and most of the young princes of Greece, sailed to the Euxine with a fleet of nine ships, landed at the mouth of the Thermodon, during the temporary absence of Orithya with the best part of the army, and gained an easy victory over Antiope, whose sister Menalippe he made prisoner; restoring her to liberty in exchange for a suit of the royal armour, including, of course, the girdle.

Historians differ as to the expedition of Theseus. Some say he took away Hippolyte or Antiope, at the same time that Hercules captured her sister; others, however, relate that he undertook a separate voyage many years after that of Hercules, and carried Antiope to Greece, where he made her his queen. Plutarch, in his life of Theseus, gives many details of this latter expedition.

When Orithya heard of the invasion, and of the part which the Athenian prince had acted in it, she vowed not to rest till she was revenged. Calling her subjects together, she soon found herself at the head of many thousand warriors. At her entreaty, Sagillus, king of Scythia, furnished a squadron of horse, commanded by his nephew, Panasagorus. Passing through Colchis, over Mount Caucasus, and crossing an arm of the Cimmerian Bosphorus, which, tradition says, was frozen, the Amazons marched victoriously through Taurica, Thrace, Thessaly, Macedonia, Attica, and entered the city of Athens.

A hard-fought battle in the streets—described in detail by old Plutarch—ended by the total rout of the Amazons, who were compelled to take refuge in the camp of the Scythians—the latter, in consequence of a quarrel, having taken no part in the engagement. The fate of Orithya is unknown, and historians differ as to that of Antiope. Some say she fell in the battle by the hand of an Amazon, while fighting in the Athenian ranks, side by side with Theseus; but according to others, it was her mediation which brought about a treaty of peace some four months later.

Theseus and the Amazon queen had a son named Hippolytus, or Demophoon, who afterwards ascended the throne of Athens.

That the Amazons survived this defeat is evident, since, years after this, we find the Phrygians imploring aid of Priam, king of Troy, against Myrene, queen of the Amazons. Little is known about this war, save that the queen lost her life, and was succeeded by the beautiful Penthesilea, who not only made peace with Priam, but led a chosen band of Amazons to the assistance of Troy when it was besieged by the Greeks. She arrived shortly after the death of Hector, and, some declare, seemed, in the eyes of the old king, destined to take the place of the deceased hero.

New life was infused into the dejected Trojans. But, alas! their joy was short-lived. The morning after her arrival Penthesilea fell by the hand of the invincible Achilles, who, struck by her exquisite beauty, repented too late of what he had done. The sarcastic Thersites jeered and derided, as usual, till the hero, in a fury, turned on the sneering old wretch and slew him. Diomedes, enraged at the death of his mocking old comrade, dragged the corpse of the Amazon queen from the camp, and flung it into the Scamander.

Pliny ascribes the invention of the battle-axe to this queen.

After the death of Penthesilea we learn nothing of the Amazons until the days of Alexander the Great. When that conqueror arrived at Zadracarta, the capital of Hyrcania, about the year B.C. 330, he is said to have been visited by an Amazon queen named Minithya, or Thalestris, who—like another Queen of Sheba—having heard of his mighty achievements, travelled through many lands to see him, followed by an army of female warriors. After staying thirteen days, she returned home, greatly disappointed with the personal appearance of the Macedonian king, who, contrary to her expectations, proved, 'tis said, to be a little man.

This is the last we ever hear of the great female nation. Some Roman authors affirm that the Amazons, in alliance with the Albanians, fought most valiantly in a battle against Pompey the Great, B.C. 66. But the only ground for this assertion consisted in the fact that some painted shields and buskins were found on the battlefield.

If we may believe Herodotus, the Sauromatae, or Sarmatians, in Scythia, were descended from the Amazons. This historian relates how, after a victory gained by the Greeks over the Amazons near the Thermodon, the victors distributed their prisoners into three ships, and set sail for Greece. Once upon the open sea, the captives rose upon their guards and put them to death. Being totally ignorant of navigation and the management of sails, oars, or rudder, they resigned themselves to the mercy of winds and waves. They were carried to the Palus Maeotis (the Sea of Azof), where the liberated Amazons resumed their arms, sprang on shore, and meeting a stud of horses, mounted them, and commenced plundering the natives.

The people, ignorant alike of the dress, the language, or the country of the invaders, supposed them to be a body of young men. A sanguinary battle, however, led to mutual explanations. The Amazons consented to accept an equal number of young Scythians as husbands; but afraid that their habits would never assimilate with those of the mothers and sisters of their husbands,—for the Scythian women, so far from going to battle, passed their days in the wagons—resolved to seek out some desert land where they would be free to follow their own manners and customs. Crossing the Tanais (the Don), they travelled six days' journey east and north, and set up their homes in an uninhabited country. The nation increased greatly in the course of two or three centuries, and, even in the days of Herodotus, retained the habits of their progenitors. The women pursued the chase on horseback, sometimes with, sometimes without their husbands, and, dressed like men, they fought in battle.

No maiden was permitted to marry till she had first killed an enemy; the historian adds:

"It sometimes, therefore, happens, quaintly, that many women die single at an advanced age."

Hippocrates says they were condemned to single-blessedness till they had slain at least *three* enemies.

Yet, in spite of this, there was only one Sarmatian queen who became famous for her deeds on the battlefield. This was Amagia, whose husband. King Medosac, having given himself up to indolence and luxury, permitted the affairs of the nation to fall into disorder. At last

Amagia took the reins of government into her own hands, received ambassadors, took the command of the army, went in person to reinforce the frontiers with troops, and not only repelled several invasions but even made some incursions into foreign countries to assist such of her allies as were in peril. Very soon she became an important personage, and was more than once chosen as mediatrix by the various petty monarchs of the Chersonese.

As a ruler, Queen Amagia had not her equal in those days throughout Scythia. Her judgments were sound; and both as a general and as a governor, she was respected by all. Her justice was severe and unbending, and untempered with mercy.

The African Amazons, who are said to have existed for some centuries prior to those of Thermodon, were not, like the latter, a community of women only, but the men were kept in close subjection to their better-halves, by whom they were treated as women are usually treated in barbarous countries. While the women conducted the government, or fought with their neighbours, the men stayed at home, attending to the household duties. They were not permitted, under any circumstances, to serve as soldiers or hold any public office. The girls were not allowed to marry till they had served a certain number of years in the army; and, like the Asiatic Amazons, one breast was burnt off.

This nation, Diodorus tells us, originally dwelt on a large island called Hesperia, on the western coast of Africa. This isle, which, the historian says, abounded "with all sorts of fruit trees," is supposed to have been one of the Canaries. The climate was then, as now, delicious, the soil more than ordinarily fertile, and the natives possessed "many herds of cattle and flocks of sheep and goats."

The Amazons, more warlike than their neighbours, speedily conquered the entire island; and, crossing into Africa, subdued great part of Numidia and founded a large city named Chersonesus, in the Tritonis Morass. This gigantic fen was situated near the Atlantic Ocean, under the shadow of the lofty Mount Atlas.

When Queen Merina ascended the throne, she determined to accomplish mightier deeds than her ancestors. Assembling an army of thirty thousand foot and two thousand horse, dressed in coats of mail made from the skins of large serpents, she passed into Africa, conquered the Atlantides, the Gorgons, and many another nation, and formed an alliance with Orus, King of Egypt, the son of Isis. After making war successfully on the Arabians she conquered Syria and Cilicia, and the tribes around Mount Taurus, who, says Diodorus, "were both men of strong bodies and stout hearts"; marched through Phrygia, and passed along the shores of the Mediterranean, founding several cities, one of which she named after herself, and the others after her principal captains. Crossing to the Greek Archipelago, where she conquered Lesbos and other isles, Merina founded the city of Mitylene, and named it after her sister, who accompanied the expedition.

Shortly after the return of the Amazons to Africa, Mompsus, a refugee from the court of Lycurgus, king of Thrace, and Sipylus, a banished Scythian, invaded the dominions of Merina. The queen was slain in the first battle, together with many thousand Amazons; and the rest of her subjects, after bravely contending in several engagements with the invaders, retired, it is said, into Lybia.

We also read that Egee, another queen of the African Amazons, also raised a large army, with which she invaded Asia. Being opposed by Laomedon, King of Troy (who was afterwards conquered by Hercules), she defeated his troops in several actions, and took a quantity of valuable plunder. While re-passing the sea a storm arose, and Egee perished with her entire army.

The nation was finally extirpated by Hercules when he undertook his journey into Africa, and erected the famous Pillars.

Herodotus mentions two Libyan tribes, the Machlyes and Auses, dwelling on the shores of Lake Tritonis, who trained their girls to the use of arms. Once a year, at the festival of Minerva, their patron-goddess, the maidens of each tribe formed themselves into two hostile armies, and attacked each other before the temple with sticks and stones, contending for the victory with the most desperate valour. On the conclusion of this *sham* fight, the most beautiful of the survivors was presented with a magnificent suit of armour and a sword, and, amidst the noisiest acclamations from the spectators, escorted in a chariot triumphantly round the lake.

The Zaveces, another African tribe mentioned by the same historian, employed their wives and daughters to drive their war-chariots on the day of battle, thus placing them in the front of the battle.

From what certain modern travellers have reported, it would seem that even as lately as the eighteenth century the legend of the Amazons still held its ground in various parts of Asia and Africa. Father Archangel Lamberti, a Neapolitan monk, who travelled through Mingrelia in the seventeenth century, was told that a warlike and ruthless nation, amongst whom were several female warriors, dwelt somewhere in the neighbourhood of the Caucasus. They were often at war with the Calmuc Tartars and the various tribes living near them. Lamberti was even shown some suits of armour taken from the corpses of these warlike women, together with their bows and arrows and brass-spangled buskins.

The Chevalier Chardin (a Huguenot jeweller, knighted by Charles II. of England), in travelling through Persia, between 1663 and 1680, was told that a powerful nation of Amazons dwelt to the north of the kingdom of Caket. The monarchs of the latter country, which was situated in the neighbourhood of the Caucasus, subjected these Amazons for a time, though they afterwards regained their liberty. The people of the Caucasus, and the Calmucs were always at war with these Amazons, and never sought to make peace or form any treaties, for they knew the warlike women had neither religion, laws, nor honour. Sir John, however, adds that he never met with anybody who had been in their country.

Juan de los Sanctos, an early Portuguese traveller, in speaking of a kingdom named Damut, in Ethiopia, mentions a numerous tribe entirely composed of women, who had adopted (or perhaps retained) the habits of the ancient Amazons. The exercise of arms and the pastime of the chase were their principal occupations in times of peace, but their chief business and pleasure was war. They burnt off the right breast as soon as the girls were old enough to bear it; and, as a rule, they passed their lives in a state of celibacy, the queen setting a rigid example.

Those who married did not rear their male children, but sent them back to the fathers. The neighbouring sovereigns esteemed themselves only too fortunate when they could secure the alliance of this people; and so far from seeking to destroy them, more than once aided them when they were attacked by others. This tribe was finally subjugated, says the Portuguese friar, by the successors of Prester John, the kings of Abyssinia.

Chapter 2

Semiramis, Queen of Assyria to Arsinoe, Queen of Egypt

Semiramis is the earliest female warrior of whose existence there is any certainty. But even her history is intermingled with much of fable and idle tradition. The exact period at which she reigned has never been positively determined. The following dates, assigned to her reign by various historians, ancient and modem, as compared by the anti-quarian Bryant, show the diversity of opinion amongst chronologists upon the subject.

	B.C.
According to Syncellus, she lived	2177
Petavius makes the time	2060
Helvicus	2248
Eusebius	1984
Mr. Jackson	1964
Archbishop Usher	1215
Philo Biblius Sanchoniathan (*apud Euseb.*)	1200
Herodotus (about)	713

The learned Bryant indignantly asked:

What credit can be given to the history of a person, the time of whose life cannot be ascertained within 1535 years?

The early life of this famous woman is enveloped in one of those mythological legends in which the ancients loved to shroud the origin of their heroes and heroines. According to tradition she was the natural daughter of Derceto, a Philistine goddess, and while yet a babe, was left to perish by her cruel mother in a wood near Ascalon, in Syria.

But, as Romulus and Remus were suckled by a wolf, so doves came and fed the future queen. The birds were observed and followed by the neighbouring peasants; and Simma, or Sisona, chief shepherd of the Assyrian king, having no children of his own, adopted the babe, and gave her the name of Semiramis, a Syrian word signifying doves, or pigeons.

At the early age of thirteen or fourteen, Semiramis was married to Menon, one the principal officers of the king, who saw her at the hut of Sisona while inspecting the royal flocks. Captivated by her surpassing beauty and charming conversation, Menon induced her to return with him to Nineveh, the capital. For some months she was kept a close prisoner in her husband's palace; but her influence soon ruled paramount, and all restraints were removed. Two or three years passed thus, during which time Semiramis bore her husband two sons, Hypates and Hydaspes.

When Ninus invaded Media, Semiramis, who only waited for some opportunity to distinguish herself, insisted upon accompanying her husband, who, as one of the principal courtiers, held an important command in the invading army. The campaign was at first an uninterrupted series of successes. One city fell after another before the Assyrian hosts. But the army was suddenly checked in its onward career of victory before the impregnable walls of Bactria. The city was defended with such obstinate bravery that Ninus at last resolved to retreat. But Semiramis presented herself before the assembled council of war, proposed an assault on the citadel, and offered to lead, in person, the storming party.

When the decisive moment arrived, Semiramis proved herself fully equal to the emergency. Amidst volleys of arrows and showers of stones, before which the bravest men turned pale, she led the forlorn hope to the foot of the citadel. Animating all by her courage, shaming cowards by the thought that a young and lovely woman was sharing, nay, braving, the same dangers as themselves, the intrepid heroine rushed up the scaling ladder, and was the first to reach the battlements. A struggle ensued, short, but fierce, and in a few moments the golden standard of Assyria floated from the walls. The capital of Media had fallen.

The king, violently smitten with love for the brave girl, earnestly besought her husband to give her up. He even offered his own royal sister, Sosana, in exchange. But promises and threats were alike vain; and Ninus, in a fury, cast Menon into prison. Here, after being deprived of sight, the wretched husband terminated his existence with his own hands.

Ninus married the young widow; and after their return to Nineveh, she bore him a son called Ninyas.

'Tis said Ninus paid very dear for his marriage. Semiramis, by her profuse liberality, soon attached the leading courtiers to her interest. She then solicited the king, with great importunity, to place the supreme power in her hands for five days. Ninus at last yielded to her entreaties; and, as his reward, was cast into prison, and put to death,—either immediately, or after languishing some years.

To cover the meanness of her origin, and to immortalise her name, Semiramis now applied her mind to great enterprises. If she did not, as some suppose, found Babylon the Great, she adorned it with beautiful and imposing edifices, and made it worthy to be called "the Golden City."

Not satisfied with the vast empire left by Ninus, she enlarged it by successive conquests. Great part of Ethiopia succumbed to her power; and during her stay in this country she consulted the Oracle of Jupiter-Ammon as to how long she had to live. The answer was, that she should not die until conspired against by her son; and that, after her death, part of Asia would pay her divine honours.

Her last and most famous expedition was the war with India. For this campaign she raised an army of more than ordinary dimensions. Ctesias puts down the number at three million foot, fifty thousand horse, and war-chariots in proportion; but this is, no doubt, a slight exaggeration. The chief strength of the. Indians lay in their countless myriads of elephants. Semiramis, unable to procure these animals in sufficient numbers, caused several thousand camels to be accoutred like elephants.

Shahbrohates, King of India, on receiving intelligence of her hostile approach, sent ambassadors to inquire her motive for invading his dominions. She returned a haughty answer; and, on reaching the Indus, she erected a bridge of boats and attempted to cross. The passage was disputed, and although the Indians at last retreated, the victory was more disastrous to the Assyrians than many a defeat.

But Semiramis, carried away by the blind infatuation which guided all her movements in this war, marched into the heart of the country. The king, who fled deceitfully to bring about a second engagement further from the river, faced about, and the two armies again closed in deadly combat. The counterfeit elephants could not long sustain the attack of the genuine animals, who, crushing every obstacle under foot, soon scattered the Assyrian Army. Semiramis performed prodigies of bravery to rally her broken forces, and fought with as little regard for her own safety as though she had been the meanest soldier in the army.

Shahbrohates, perceiving the queen engaged in the thick of the fight, rode forward and twice wounded her. The rout soon became general, and the royal heroine, convinced at last that nothing further could be done, gave the rein to her horse, whose swiftness soon placed her beyond the reach of the enemy.

On reaching the Indus a scene of the most terrible disorder ensued. In the wild terror which possessed the minds of all, officers and soldiers crowded together on to the bridge, without the slightest regard for rank or discipline. Thousands were trampled underfoot, crushed to death, or flung into the river. When Semiramis and all who could save themselves had crossed over, the bridge was destroyed. The Indian king, in obedience to an oracle, ordered his troops not to cross the river in pursuit.

Semiramis was the only sovereign amongst the ancients, except Alexander the Great, who ever carried a war beyond the Indus.

Sometime after her return to Babylon, the queen discovered that her son, Ninyas, was conspiring against her. Remembering now the oracle of Jupiter-Ammon, and believing that her last days were approaching, Semiramis voluntarily abdicated the throne. Some chroniclers give a different version of the story, relating that the queen was slain by her son, and this latter account, though disbelieved by most historians, is the popular story.

Semiramis lived sixty-two years, out of which she reigned forty-two. It is said the Athenians afterwards worshipped her under the form of a dove.

The early lives of Harpalyce and Atalanta, the first known female warriors who were natives of Greece, resemble in some respects that of Semiramis. It appears to have been a favourite custom, during the primitive ages, to have children nursed by birds or beasts. Harpalyce, daughter of Harpalycus, or Lycurgus, king of the Amymnaeans, in Thrace, having lost her mother during infancy, was fed with the milk of cows and horses. Her father trained her in every manly and warlike exercise, riding, racing, hurling the dart, using the bow and arrow. By-and-by she became a mighty huntress; and soon the opportunity came for her to prove herself a brave soldier and a skilful commander. The Getes, or Myrmidones of Thessaly invaded the dominions of King Lycurgus, defeated his best troops and made him prisoner. Directly Harpalyce learned this news she hastily called together an army, placed herself at its head, and falling on the foe, put them to flight and rescued her father.

Lycurgus endeavoured to cure the Thracians of their drunken habits, and caused all the vines in his dominions to be rooted up, whereby he brought about a general insurrection, and was compelled to fly for safety to the isle of Naxos, where he went mad and committed suicide. Harpalyce turned brigand and haunted the forests of Thrace. She was so swift of foot that the fleetest horses could not overtake her once she began running. At last, however, she fell into a snare set by some shepherds, who put the royal bandit to death.

Atalanta, too, was likewise bereft of a mother's care. Her father, Jasus or Jasion, unwilling to rear the babe, yet not sufficiently inhuman to see her slaughtered before his eyes, left her to her fate on Mount Parthenius, the highest mountain in Peloponnesus. Close by was the cave of an old she-bear who had been robbed of her cubs. In place of devouring the babe, the savage brute adopted it, and brought up the girl as her own daughter. Orson-like, the girl learned many of the habits of her shaggy nurse. But, she also, through constant exercise, acquired marvellous dexterity in using the bow and arrow; and with this weapon she once slew the Centaurs Rhoecus and Hylaeus.

Atalanta was one of those brave warriors who sailed in the Argonautic expedition, B.C. 1263; and throughout the voyage she earned the praises of her comrades by her bravery and military skill. After her return to Greece she assisted in the chase of the Calydonian boar, a savage brute of monster size who was ravaging Ætolia. She was the first to wound this beast; hence Meleager awarded her the first prize. His uncles, jealous of the honour thus conferred upon a woman, endeavoured to wrest the trophies from her, and in the scuffle which ensued, Meleager unfortunately slew both his uncles.

This heroine must not be confounded with another Atalanta, daughter of Schoenus, King of Scyrus, famous for her marvellous skill in running, and for the stratagem of the three golden apples by which she was at last defeated.

It would seem that no Grecian or Trojan heroines distinguished themselves during the siege of Troy; though it is not unlikely that many of the Greek soldiers were secretly accompanied by their wives. When Æneas landed in Italy, a few years after the fall of Troy, he found, amongst the sovereigns confederated against him, Camilla, the Amazon Queen of the Volscians, renowned for her high courage, her beauty, and her swiftness in running. Virgil says that she outstripped the winds in speed, and could have skimmed over the topmost stalks of standing corn, or along the surface of the ocean, without leaving a trace of her footsteps.

From childhood she was dedicated by her father. King Metabus, to the service of Diana, and trained in martial exercises. She grew so fond of the chase, that even after the death of her father, she preferred leading the semi-barbarous life of a wild huntress to the prospect of domestic happiness as the wife of a Tuscan noble.

She joined Turnus, King of the Rutulians, with a squadron of horse and a body of foot, equipped in bronze armour. Followed by her retinue of warlike maidens, she bore a prominent part in a battle fought near the walls of Latium. But after spreading death and terror on every side, she was herself slain by a Tuscan chief.

Virgil's description of her death is one of the most beautiful passages in the *Æneid*.

Cyrus, one of the greatest conquerors the world has ever seen, some say met his first and last defeat at the hands of a female general. Many historians describe him as dying peaceably in his bed, surrounded by his family; but others relate that, still thirsting for fresh conquests, he cast his eyes, in an unlucky moment, on the land of the Massagetae, a warlike people governed by Queen Tomyris, a widow, and a woman possessing both courage and energy. Her country extended beyond the broad stream of the Araxes, to the Caucasus. The Massagetae were a savage, hardy race, resembling the Scythians in their mode of like. Agriculture was neglected, and they subsisted entirely upon their cattle and the fish supplied by the Araxes. Though they had nothing to lose by a change, this nation was devotedly attached to its freedom; suffering death rather than the loss of liberty, and resolutely opposing every invader.

It was against this indomitable race that Cyrus marched, at the head of two hundred thousand men, B.C. 529. By means of a stratagem he was at first successful. Knowing the Massagetae to be ignorant of Persian delicacies and the flavour of wine, he spread out a banquet, accompanied with flowing goblets of wine; and, leaving a few hundreds of his worst soldiers to guard the camp, retired to some distance. When the Massagetae, commanded by Spargapises, nephew of Tomyris, had taken the camp, they feasted and drank, till, overcome by drunkenness and sleep, they afforded an easy victory to Cyrus. The greater number, including Spargapises, were made prisoners, or slain.

However, so far from despairing, Tomyris collected the rest of her forces, and having led the Persians into a narrow pass, attacked them with such fury that they were all slain, together with the king. Justin says "there was not one man left to carry the news home;" but as the news *did* somehow find its way home, that fact is doubtful.

The body of Cyrus was discovered after considerable search. Tomyris ordered the head to be cut off and flung into a vessel full of human blood. Exulting over her dead foe she cried:

Satisfy thyself now with blood, which thou didst always thirst after, yet could never satisfy thy appetite.

A few years prior to the invasion of Greece by Xerxes, Cleomenes, King of Lacedaemon, who arrogated to his state the first rank in Greece, went to war with the people of Argos. Having learned from an oracle that he would be victorious, the Spartan king without loss of time invaded the Argeian territories, and routed the enemy in a sanguinary battle at Sepeia. Those Argives who escaped death on the battlefield took refuge in a grove sacred to Argus, their hero; where, however, they were surrounded and burnt alive by the enemy. Upwards of six thousand, the flower and strength of Argos, perished that day. Cleomenes marched direct to the city, which, decimated, almost depopulated though it was, made a gallant defence.

There dwelt in the city a beautiful girl named Telesilla, famous throughout the land as a lyric poetess. Inspired by patriotism, she addressed the Argive women and incited them to defend their homes. The call was responded to with enthusiasm. Armed with weapons from the temples, or from private dwellings, the women of Argos, headed by Telesilla, ascended the walls, and compensated by their courage for the dearth of male warriors.

The Spartans were repulsed; and Cleomenes, afraid of being reproached, even if successful, with fighting against helpless women and timid girls, commanded a retreat.

Demeratus, Cleomenes' partner in the throne, is said by some historians to have accompanied this expedition; and they relate that whilst Cleomenes was besieging the walls, Demeratus attacked the Pamphyliacum, or Citadel, whence he was driven with great loss by Telesilla and her companions. This, however, is acknowledged to be mere tradition, for Herodotus says that the two kings, having quarrelled some years previously, never engaged together in the same war.

Grote, for an even better reason, disbelieves the entire story, which, he says:—

> Is probably a myth, generated by the desire to embody in detail the dictum of the oracle a little before, about 'the female conquering the male.'

Without for a moment denying that the Argeian women could or would have achieved the great deeds ascribed to them, he doubts their having done so, because, says he, the siege never took place at all.

Great honours, so runs the legend, were paid to Telesilla and her brave companions, many of whom fell in the conflict. A statue of the poetess was erected by the grateful citizens and placed in the Temple of Venus.

The terrible danger of the Persian invasion caused all the internal wranglings and disputes of the Greeks to be hushed for a time. In the year B.C. 480, the Great King declared war on the (temporarily) united states of Greece, and sailed thither with a gigantic and overwhelming army and navy. Amongst the tributary sovereigns who followed him in this expedition was Artemisia, Queen of Caria. She was daughter of King Lygdamis, and her husband, the late king, having died while her son was a minor, Artemisia conducted, *pro. tem.*, the government of Halicarnassus, Cos, Nisiras, and Calydne. Though she brought only five ships to the Greek war, they were almost the lightest and best equipped of any in the fleet.

Herodotus says that amongst all the Persian commanders, naval or military, there was not one who gave the king such good advice as this heroine; but King Xerxes was not at that time wise enough to profit by her counsels. She was the only one who had the courage to raise her voice against the proposed sea-fight at Salamis, which Xerxes was resolved to risk.

As the Carian queen foretold, the Persians were defeated. Yet, though she openly disapproved of the battle, Artemisia behaved most gallantly throughout. The Athenians, indignant that a woman should dare to appear in arms against them, offered ten thousand *drachmas* for her capture, alive or dead. The way she escaped displayed great presence of mind, though it also showed how unscrupulous she was in the choice of stratagems. Closely pursued by an Athenian ship (commanded by Aminias of Pallene, the brother of Æschylus), escape seemed impossible. But with her customary decision of mind, the queen hung out Grecian colours, and turned her arms against a Persian vessel. This cost her no feelings of regret, for on board the ship was Damasithymus, King of Calynda, with whom she had some private quarrel. Her pursuers, seeing her send a Persian ship to the bottom of the sea, concluded that she belonged to their navy, and so gave up the pursuit.

Xerxes, from an elevated post on shore, saw the disgraceful flight of his own navy, together with the bravery of Artemisia. When he could no longer doubt that it was she who performed such gallant deeds, he exclaimed, in astonishment, that the men had behaved like women, while the women had displayed the courage of men.

Like most warlike leaders, Artemisia was not at all scrupulous as to the means employed, provided the end answered her expectations. Wishing to possess herself of Latmus, a small city which lay temptingly near to Halicarnassus, she placed her troops in ambush, and under pretence of celebrating the feast of Cybele in a wood consecrated to that goddess, she repaired thither with a grand procession, accompanied by drums and trumpets. The people of Latmus ran out in crowds to witness the show, while Artemisia's troops took possession of the city.

The ultimate fate of Artemisia proves how true it is that "love rules the court, the camp, the grove." She fell violently in love with a native of Abydos, a young man named Dardanus; but her passion was not reciprocated. To punish his disdain, she first put out his eyes, and then took the noted "Lover's Leap" from the promontory Leucas—now Santa Maura.

Artemisia II., who lived more than one hundred and thirty years after the former heroine, has frequently been confounded with her, as both were queens of Caria. The second of that name was daughter of King Hecatomus, and is principally famous for the honours which she paid to the memory of her husband, Mausolus, to whom she erected a magnificent tomb at Halicarnassus, which monument was afterwards reckoned as one of the Seven Wonders of the World.

Most writers represent Artemisia as plunged in tears during her widowhood; but there are some who, on the contrary, declare that she made some important conquests at that time. Vitruvius relates that the Rhodians, indignant that a woman should reign over Caria, despatched a fleet to Halicarnassus to dethrone Artemisia. The queen commanded the citizens to appear on the walls directly the Rhodians came in sight, and to express, by shouts and clapping of hands, their readiness to surrender.

The enemy, falling into the trap, disembarked, and went with all haste to the city, leaving their ships without even one man to guard them Artemisia came out with her squadron from the little port, entered the great harbour, and seized the Rhodian vessels. Putting her own men on board she sailed to Rhodes, where the people, seeing their own ships return adorned with laurel-wreaths, received them with every demonstration of joy. No resistance was offered to the landing; and Artemisia seized the city, putting to death the leaders of the people.

She caused a trophy to be erected, and set up two statues—one representing the city of Rhodes, and the other an image of herself, branding the former figure with a red-hot iron. Vitruvius says the Rhodians were forbidden by their religion to destroy this memorial; so they surrounded it by a lofty building which concealed it from view.

Her death, which took place the same year (B.C. 351) probably reinstated the Rhodians in their liberty.

During the reign of Artaxerxes Nmenon, King of Persia, and brother of Cyrus the younger, the province of Æolia was governed—under the authority of Pharnabasus, *satrap* of Asia Minor—by Zenis the Dardanian. When the latter died. Mania, his widow, went to Pharnabasus with magnificent presents, leading a body of troops, and begged of him not to deprive her of the government. Pharnabasus allowed her to retain the province, and he had no reason to regret it. Mania acquitted herself with all the prudence and energy which could have been expected from the most experienced ruler.

In addition to the customary tributes, she added magnificent presents; and when Pharnabasus visited her province, she entertained him with greater splendour than any of the other governors throughout Asia Minor. She followed him in all his military campaigns, and was of great assistance not only with her troops, but by her advice. She was a regular attendant at all his councils, and her suggestions contributed to the success of more than one enterprise. The *satrap* knew how to estimate her merit; and the Governess of Æolia was treated with greater distinction than any of her fellow-governors.

Her army was in better condition than that of any neighbouring province; she even maintained a body of Greek soldiers in her pay. Not content with the cities committed to her care, she made new conquests; amongst others, Larissa, Amaxita, and Colona, which belonged to the Mysians and Pisidians. In every war she took the command in person, and from her war-chariot decreed rewards and punishments.

The only enemies she possessed were in her own family circle. Midias, her son-in-law, thinking it a reproach on him that a woman should command where he was subordinate, strangled her and her son, B.C. 399, and seized two fortresses in which she had secured her treasures. The other cities of Æolia at once declared against him; and he did not very long enjoy the fruits of his crime. Dercyllidas, commander of the Greek forces in Asia, arrived at this juncture. All the fortresses in the province surrendered, either voluntarily or by compulsion; and Midias was deprived of the possessions for which he had stained his hands in the blood of his relatives.

Cratesipolis was the wife of Alexander, the son of one of Alexander the Great's captains.

On the sudden death of Alexander the Great, his posthumous son and his half-brother were placed on the throne, under the regency of Perdiccas, the most talented of Alexander's captains. However, the generals soon began to quarrel among themselves; two years later, Perdiccas was assassinated, and the regency conferred on Antipater, governor of Macedonia and Greece. The latter, on his deathbed, bestowed the office of regent and the government of the provinces on Polysperchon, the eldest survivor of all the captains who had followed Alexander to India. Cassander, the son of Antipater, indignant at being set aside, went to war with the new regent.

Alexander, the son of Polysperchon, was possessed of great military talent, and his father confided to him the defence of Peloponnesus. Cassander, knowing the abilities of Alexander, offered him the government of Peloponnesus, and the command of the troops stationed there if he would join the faction of the malcontents. The offer was accepted; Alexander established his headquarters at Sicyon.

At the head of his troops he gained several victories. Cratesipolis, his wife, was the idol of the soldiers. They regarded her, and justly, as a woman who possessed the spirit of a hero and the talents of a great general. She interested herself in all their affairs—appeased all their differences, and did not disdain to think of their wants and their pleasures. She consoled those who were sad, relieved those who were in want, and strove to make all happy. Frequently she accompanied Alexander in his expeditions, and was as much respected by the officers as beloved by the privates.

Alexander held his governorship for only a few months. The citizens of Sicyon, furious, and groaning under the yoke imposed upon them, conspired against their rulers. The governor was slain by Alexion and some companions who pretended to be Alexander's friends. The soldiers, who were setting out on an expedition, seized with terror when they saw their leader fall, fled in all directions.

Cratesipolis gave way neither to grief nor despair. Rallying the broken forces, she assumed the command, and soon restored order and discipline. The Sicyonians, who never suspected that a woman could take the command of the army, rose in rebellion, and barred the city gates. Cratesipolis, enraged as much at the insult as at the treachery with which they had slain her husband, laid siege to Sicyon, routed the insurgents in a hotly-contested battle, and took the city by storm (B.C. 317), when, by her command, thirty of the ringleaders were crucified.

Having assuaged her thirst for revenge, Cratesipolis entered Sicyon in triumph, and assumed the government. Appeasing all the troubles caused by the rebellion, she ruled with such wisdom and prudence as to excite the admiration of all. To the last she kept up a large and well-disciplined army, always ready at a moment's notice to set forth on an expedition. The soldiers, whose love and reverence had been increased by the courage with which she had acted during the insurrection, would, any of them, have gladly sacrificed his own life to save hers.

Arsinoe, Queen of Egypt, was the wife of Ptolemy Philopater. She was a brave as well as prudent woman, and accompanied her husband when he invaded Syria, B.C. 217. In the Battle of Raphia she rode up and down through the ranks, exhorting the soldiers to behave manfully during the fight. She remained beside her husband during the heat of the action; and by her presence she greatly contributed to the victory gained by the Egyptians.

CHAPTER 3

Hypsicrates, Queen of Mithridates the Great to Pharandsem, Queen of Armenia

Pontus, in Cappadocia, the *ci-devant* home of the Amazons, passed through many changes and vicissitudes as time rolled on. Under Cyrus and his successors, Cappadocia was divided into two distinct provinces, whose governors made themselves finally independent of Persia, and ruled as kings till the days of Alexander. After the death of the great Macedonian, Pontus was not long regaining its independence: increasing rapidly in power and extent till the days of Mithridates the Great, who made it one of the chief empires of the East.

This ambitious monarch, believing himself a second Alexander, cared for nothing but war; and through his bravery and his obstinacy, he contrived to make himself one of the most formidable rivals Rome ever had to cope with. Hypsicrates was his favourite wife—like most Oriental monarchs, he had more than one; and in respect of personal courage, she was worthy to be the companion of the royal tiger. They were romantically attached to one another; Mithridates, ruthless towards others, was loving and tender to his favourite *sultana*. She accompanied him in many of his perilous expeditions, and fought by his side in more than one battle.

For this reason, her name, properly Hypsicratia, was changed to Hypsicrates; thus, altering it from feminine to masculine, on account of her manly courage. Besides being valiant, she was exceedingly beautiful and highly accomplished, as a queen should be.

After the defeat of Mithridates by Lucullus, the gourmand, on the plains of Cabirae, B.C. 71, the unfortunate monarch sent a messenger to the ladies of his court, enjoining them to die by their own hands rather than fall alive into those of the Romans. All obeyed save Hypsicrates. Though she feared death as little as any among them, yet could she not bear even this temporary separation from her lord. Mounting a swift steed, she overtook the king, after encountering and surmounting innumerable difficulties; and by her presence and counsel she restored to him his former energy and strength of mind.

Five years later (B.C. 66), Mithridates fought a battle with Pompey the Great on the banks of the Euphrates. Hypsicrates appeared in the dress of a Persian soldier, and, mounted on a charger, fought beside the king so long as the action lasted. However, the battle was not of long duration. The barbarians were afraid to await the shock of the iron legions, and fled in wild terror. The Romans ruthlessly slaughtered the fugitives; ten thousand were slain on the field, and the camp fell into the hands of the victors.

Mithridates and his brave queen, placing themselves at the head of eight hundred chosen horsemen, cut their way, sword in hand, through the ranks of the foe. But the eight hundred quickly dispersed, and left the king with only three followers, one of whom was Hypsicrates. She attended him during his flight, grooming his horse, and enduring great hardships through fatigue and want of food. At last they reached a fortress, where lay the royal treasures. Here Mithridates gave to each a dose of strong poison to be taken in case of dire necessity. But whether Hypsicrates finally swallowed the fatal potion, or by what death she passed from the world, historians have not told us.

Cleopatra, the beautiful and ambitious queen of Egypt, was at all times desirous to acquire renown as a great warrior. But she possessed neither the courage nor the prudence necessary for those who seek the laurel-wreath. She was too fond of her ease to take the command of an expedition, unless the occasion was one which rendered her presence absolutely necessary.

She first appeared as a warrior in the year B.C. 48, when her brother Ptolemy deprived her of her share in the throne. She withdrew to Syria, raised troops there, and re-entered Egypt at the head of her forces shortly after the Battle of Pharsalia. Pompey, routed by Caesar, fled to Egypt, where he was assassinated by order of the king. Scarcely had he breathed his last, when Caesar landed. He assumed the right to arbitrate between Ptolemy and Cleopatra. The former refused to accept him as referee, and for several weeks the great Caesar had to contend with the soldiers of the king as well as with the infuriated citizens of Alexandria. However, the war was soon terminated by the defeat and death of Ptolemy; and the crown was bestowed upon Cleopatra.

After the assassination of Julius Caesar, Cleopatra declared for the *Triumvirs*, Antony, Octavius, and Lepidus. She prepared a powerful fleet, designing to take the command, and sail to the assistance of Caesar's avengers. Violent storms prevented the squadron from setting out; but some time subsequently the queen sailed with a well-equipped fleet to join the *Triumvirs*. Again, she was frustrated by the elements. A terrible storm arose, wrecked many vessels, threw the queen on a bed of sickness, and compelled the fleet to put back to Alexandria.

This love of warlike display finally caused her ruin and that of Antony. Against the advice of the most practised Roman officers, she insisted upon taking an active part in the war against Octavius. Before the decisive Battle of Actium, Antony was counselled not to hazard a sea-fight; but the haughty Egyptian queen, like Xerxes of old, insisted upon it. So, her advice was followed in preference to that of old and experienced generals.

The battle was fought on the 2nd September, B.C. 31, at the mouth of the Ambracian Gulf, within sight of the opposing land armies who were encamped on each shore anxiously watching the struggle. A more magnificent sight could not have been seen than the fleet of Antony; and the most splendid object in it was the galley of Cleopatra, blazing with gilding and bright colours, its sails of purple, flags and streamers floating in the wind. Victory inclined to neither side till the flight of the Egyptian queen.

Terrified by the horrid din of the fight, though in no personal danger, she fled from the scene of action, her example being followed by nearly all the Egyptian fleet, which numbered sixty ships. Antony, when he saw the queen's galley take to flight, forgot everything but her, and precipitately followed. And thus, he yielded to Caesar not merely the victory, but the Sovereignty of the World.

About the time that Cleopatra sat on the throne of Egypt, the neighbouring kingdom of Ethiopia was ruled over by another warlike queen, Candace, whose kingdom comprised that part of the Nile valley, which, under the name of Meroe, contained numberless towns and cities in a high state of civilization. Very little is known concerning this queen, save what we glean from Strabo. The year before the Battle of Actium, Candace invaded Egypt, and compelled the Roman garrisons of Syene, Elephantine, and Philae to surrender. Caius Petronius, Roman *prefect* of Egypt, marched against the Ethiopians, and routed Candace near Pselcha, after which the victor ravaged great part of Ethiopia.

When Petronius left the country, Candace attacked the garrison he had left in Premnis. But directly the prefect heard of this he returned hastily to Meroe, again defeated the Ethiopians, and imposed a heavy tribute on the kingdom. Candace sent an embassy to Octavius, who was then at Samos, suing for peace. The dictator not only granted her prayer, but remitted the tribute levied by Petronius.

The next female sovereign who defied Rome on the battle-field was of a very different stamp from Cleopatra, or even Candace. This was Boadicea, the "British Warrior Queen," the story of whose wrongs and bravery was for centuries a favourite subject with po-ets. Her name, which has been variously written Boadicea, Boudicea, Bonduca, Vonduca, Voadicea, or Woda, signified "the Woman of the Sword," and in the ancient British or Welsh language is equivalent to Victoria. She was the daughter of Cadalla, King of the Brigantes; and, through her mother, Europeia, daughter of Evanus, King of Scot-land, she claimed descent from the kings of Troy and the Ptolemies of Egypt.

Boadicea's career was a sad and a stormy one from first to last. At an early age she was compelled by her stepmother, the wicked, am-bitious, Cartismandua, to marry Arviragus, son of that queen by her first husband. King Cymbeline. Arviragus was King of the Iceni, who possessed a great part of Essex, Norfolk, and Cambridgeshire. They are said by Tacitus to have been a rich and powerful nation. After the queen had presented her lord with a son and two daughters, the Emperor Claudius came to Britain. Arviragus, having suffered several defeats, was compelled to divorce Boadicea, and marry Gwenissa, the emperor's daughter.

A general insurrection of the Britons was the result; and the na-tives, led at first by the famous Caractacus, brother of Boadicea, and ultimately joined by Arviragus himself, were defeated again, and again by the Romans. Weary at last of the never-ending struggle, Arviragus and Boadicea accepted very humiliating terms from Vespasian, and were permitted to retain their dominions.

Towards the close of his life Arviragus appears, for some unex-plained reason, to have changed his name to Prasutagus. Dreading the rapacity of the Romans, he thought to secure their protection for Boadicea and her two daughters (her son died long before), by mak-ing the emperor Nero joint-heir to his dominions. He died *A.D.* 61.

Scarcely had he ceased to breathe, when Catus, the Roman procurator, who commanded in the absence of Suetonius Paulinus, Governor of Britain, annexed the country of the Iceni, seized the personal effects of the deceased monarch, treated all his relations as prisoners of war, despoiled the wealthier Iceni, imposed heavy taxes upon the poor, and demanded from Boadicea the payment of large sums which her father, Cadalla, had bestowed upon the Romans. Unable to pay, the queen was publicly whipped, and her daughters were treated even more shamefully.

Burning for revenge, Boadicea raised the standard of revolt. She was soon joined by patriots from all parts of Britain. Eighty thousand men, headed by the queen, rushed down like wild beasts on the colonies of Camulodunum (Malden), Colchester, and Verulam (St. Alban's), putting to death, in the first-named city, with every torture they could devise, more than seventy thousand persons of every age and sex.

Shortly after the destruction of Camulodunum, Boadicea was joined by her brother Corbred, king of Scots. Together they marched to the attack on Colchester, Petilius Cerialis, the conqueror of Batavia, marched out from Verulam at the head of the ninth *legion* to oppose the victorious Britons. He had lately received from Germany reinforcements, amounting to eight auxiliary cohorts of one thousand horse. A furious battle ensued, resulting in the total defeat of the Romans. Upwards of six thousand Romans and three thousand confederate Britons (their allies) were slain.

Petilius fled with his broken *cohorts*—for, it is said, not even one foot-soldier escaped the carnage—to his entrenched camp. Catus Decianus, the procurator, was severely wounded in the engagement, and, struck with terror, he continued his precipitate flight over sea into Gaul.

Suetonius Paulinus, absent at the time on that expedition which concluded with the massacre of the Druids in Mona (the Isle of Anglesea), hastened back to South Britain. With ten thousand men, he entered London; but, despite the prayers of the people, he deserted it at once, and encamped at a short distance north of the city. Scarcely had he departed, when Boadicea marched directly on London, captured it after a slight resistance, and put the inhabitants to the sword.

For some time, Suetonius was afraid to venture on a battle against a victorious queen commanding a force so immeasurably superior to his own, amounting, according to Tacitus, to one hundred thousand, while Dio Cassius raises the number as high as two hundred and thirty thousand; while the Romans could muster scarcely ten thousand. At last an engagement took place on a wild spot, guarded in the rear by a dense forest.

Before the battle, Boadicea passed up and down in her chariot, exhorting the warriors to avenge her wrongs and those of her daughters. Dio Cassius has described the British queen, as she appeared on that memorable day. She was a woman of lofty stature, with a noble, severe expression, and a dazzlingly fair complexion, remarkable even amongst the British women, who were famous for the whiteness of their skin. Her long yellow hair, floating in the wind, reached almost to the ground. She wore a tunic of various colours, hanging in folds, and over this was a shorter one, confined at the waist by a chain of gold. Round her alabaster neck was a magnificent "*torques*," or collar of twisted gold-wire. Her hands and arms were uncovered, save for the rings and bracelets which adorned them. A large British mantle surmounted, but did not conceal the rest of her attire.

Suetonius on his side used all his powers of oratory to excite the Romans to do their best, telling them to "despise the savage uproar, the shouts and yells of undisciplined barbarians," amongst whom, he said, "the women out-numbered the men."

The battle was long and obstinately contested; but the steady order of the iron legions triumphed over the savage onslaught of the Britons. The latter were routed with terrible slaughter, leaving, Tacitus says, upwards of eighty thousand dead on the field. The Romans lost only five hundred. Tacitus adds:—

The glory won on this day, was equal to that of the most renowned victories of the ancient Romans.

The exact scene of this engagement has been variously placed by different writers. Some decide that Battle-Bridge, King's Cross, marks the spot; while by others it has been settled as identical with the ancient camp called Ambresbury Banks, near Epping. Some even place it at Winchester.

Boadicea, rather than let herself be taken alive, put an end to her own existence by poison. She was afterwards interred with due honours by her faithful adherents.

The two daughters of Boadicea, completely armed, fought most valiantly in the battle; and even during the rout of their countrymen they strove wildly for victory. At last they were made prisoners, and brought into the presence of Suetonius, who expressed deep sympathy for them, and spoke with indignation of their oppressors.

The elder princess, by the intervention of Suetonius, was married, some months later, to Marius, also styled Westmer, son of Arviragus and Gwenissa. This prince was acknowledged by the Romans as King of the Iceni, over whom he ruled for many years. His son Coel was the father of Lucius, the first Christian king of Britain. Boadicea, the younger daughter, inherited not only her mother's name, but her bold, dauntless spirit, and her relentless hatred of the Romans. Marius, fearing her influence over the Iceni, banished her from his court. She raised a formidable army of Brigantes and Picts, and sailed to Galloway, which was occupied by the Romans. Marching in the dead of the night, she fell on the encampment of the foe and slew several hundred men. The entire Roman Army would probably have been put to the sword had not Petilius, the general, ordered his men to light torches. The Britons were driven off, and next morning Boadicea was attacked and defeated in her own camp.

Next day Boadicea marched to Epiake, the Roman headquarters in that district, and setting it on fire, destroyed the garrison. Shortly after this she was captured in an ambuscade. It is said by some that the young princess, expecting a horrible death, followed the example of her mother, and took poison. Others, however, declare that she was brought alive into the presence of the Roman commander, who interrogated her respecting the object of her invasion, when Boadicea, making a spirited answer, was slain by his guards.

The bravery of Boadicea and her daughters was not so strange in those days as it might now be. The British and Caledonian women were, as a rule, brave and warlike, and invariably followed their husbands to battle. More than five thousand women enlisted under the banners of Boadicea, and fought, many of them, as bravely as the men. Women, even far advanced in years, marched with their male relations to the defence of king or country; and those who did not fight hand to hand with the foe, peppered him well from a distance with volleys of stones. To render themselves competent to share the perils and dangers of the battlefield, the women, in times of peace, practised the use of arms, and inured themselves to fatigue and hardship; as Holinshed says:—

Never refusing to undergo any labour or fatigue assigned them
by their leader.

The women of Caledonia were equally warlike. In a curious old book of engravings published in London during the last century, entitled a *Collection of Dresses of Different Nations, Ancient and Modern,* there are three plates, one of which represents a Caledonian woman, after De Brii, dressed in a short garment, and armed with masculine weapons; the other two represent the wife and daughter of a Pict. The woman Pict is entirely naked, and is tattooed and painted with stars, rays, and various similar devices. In one hand she grasps a lance and in the other two darts. The girl differs from the mother only in being painted with divers floral ornaments in lieu of the astronomical adornments.

The Gallic and German women also, joined frequently in the battles between rival tribes. Philostratus, probably for this reason, speaks of Amazons living on the shores of the Danube; and in Lucius Flaccus we also read of German Amazons. The Allemanni, the Marcomanni, the Quadi, and the other warlike tribes who dwelt beyond the Rhine were always accompanied by their wives and daughters whenever they set out on an expedition. During the battle, such of the women as took no share in the action, stood on the outskirts, cheering and encouraging the warriors. More than once a beaten army of Germans was stopped in its flight by the women, and obliged, through very shame, to turn again and confront the enemy. If their side was defeated the German women almost invariably committed suicide on the corpses of their friends. During the wars of Marcus Aurelius with the Marcomanni and Quadi, several women were found amongst the slain, many clad in armour.

Under the patronage of the emperors the combats of Roman matrons in the amphitheatre afforded intense gratification to a pleasure-seeking public. Juvenal, the satirist, regards these female duels from a ludicrous point of view, he says:

"What a fine business it would be, for a man to cry out at an auction of his wife's equipment, 'Who bids up for my wife's boots? Who'll give most for her corselet, helmet, and gauntlet?'" The Romans, however, often tried to raise amateur corps of female warriors, in imitation of the ancient Amazons, whose warlike deeds were much admired in the imperial city. Suetonius tells us that Nero, when he learned the news of Galba's revolt, dressed up the women of his *seraglio* as Amazons, arming them with battle-axes and small bucklers, and intending to march at their head against the rebels.

In the third century the Roman Empire was in a state of dire confusion. So many governors of provinces and commanders of legions had assumed the purple, with more or less success, in various parts of the world, that at last the emperor, who was recognised by the senate at Rome, though nominally sovereign of the universe, was, in fact, very little more than ruler of Italy. One of the first to dispute the imperial dignity in Europe was Posthumus, commander of the legions in Gaul. He so far acquired the affections of his soldiers that they proclaimed him Emperor of the West, *A.D.*, 257. His dominion, the capital of which was Cologne, extended over Gaul, Spain, and Britain.

There dwelt in Cologne a noble Roman lady named Victoria. Some say she was the sister of Posthumus. Be that as it may, she persuaded the emperor to raise her son, Victorinus, to the throne, as his colleague; and when Posthumus was murdered by the soldiers, three years later, Victorinus remained sole emperor of the West. He was a brave soldier and an able general, and reigned over Gaul for about a year longer, when he was slain by the troops, *A.D.* 269. His eldest son, named after himself, was now proclaimed emperor; but in a few days, he, too, fell a victim to the fury of the legions.

An ordinary mind would have sunk beneath this double misfortune; but the "Heroine of the West" was cast in a very different mould from most women. Exceedingly ambitious, she possessed both the courage and the ability to carry out her schemes. Even when her son was living, she held the reins of government. So great was her influence over the legions, they obeyed her behests in everything without a murmur. She passed much of her time amongst them, and received thence the title of *Mater Castrorum*,—"Mother of the Camp." When her son became emperor, she, as his mother, received the title of Augusta.

Victoria bestowed the vacant throne first on Marius, a distinguished general, who was slain in a few days, and next on Tetricus, the chief noble in Aquitaine, a distant relative of her own. During his absence in Spain she continued to govern the Gallic provinces. Placing herself at the head of the troops, she maintained the authority she had seized against all the armies sent from Rome. Even during the early days of Aurelian's reign, she opposed the imperial forces with the same bold and undaunted spirit, and with equal success.

Very soon Tetricus grew weary of being subordinate to Victoria. The empress, stung by his ingratitude, would have hurled him from the throne to which she had raised him; but Tetricus took care to prevent this by causing Victoria to be poisoned, *A.D.* 269, a few months after his own accession.

Since the days of Semiramis no female ruler in ancient times attained so high a pinnacle of greatness throughout the East as Zenobia. For more than five years, unaided, she set the Roman emperors at defiance, defeated their armies, and laughed equally at their threats and their underhand machinations.

Septimia Zenobia was an Arab princess, and while some writers assert that she was a Jewess, the heroine herself claimed descent, through her father Amru, from the Ptolemies of Egypt. Truly she was as beautiful as any Egyptian queen—even the handsome Cleopatra. By some writers she has been cited as the loveliest woman of her age. An olive complexion, pearly teeth, large, brilliant, black eyes, which sparkled alternately with the fire of the heroine and the sweetness of the loving wife—such were the charms of her face. Her voice was rich and musical. She was conversant with Greek, Latin, Syriac, and Egyptian; and compiled for her own reading an epitome of Homer. Her tutor in philosophy was the famous Greek, Cassius Longinus.

Zenobia was a widow, and the mother of a son, Vhaballathus, when she wedded Odenathus, Prince of Palmyra. The latter, however, was a widower, and also the father of a son—Ouarodes, or Herod, a weak and effeminate youth.

Septimius Odenathus, who raised himself by his own genius and the fortune of war, to the sovereignty of the East, was, like his wife, an Arab. He was chief prince of the wild Saracen tribes who dwelt in the Syrian deserts, on the shores of the Euphrates. Odenathus early learned the rudiments of war in the exciting chase of wild beasts—a pastime which, to the last, he never wearied of, and in which he was joined with equal ardour by Zenobia. Together the royal pair, during the intervals of peace, hunted lions, panthers, or bears, through the woods and deserts of Syria.

When the emperor Valerian was captured and flayed alive by Sapor, King of Persia, *A.D.* 260, Odenathus marched, at the head of an Arab host, against the Persians, defeated them near Antioch, compelled them to retreat, beat them again on the banks of the Euphrates, and finally drove them across the river; capturing, in the first battle, the greater part of the wives and treasures of Sapor.

Zenobia accompanied her husband in this, as in all his subsequent expeditions, and bravely seconded his efforts. She proved herself as good a soldier as any, and endured, with the utmost fortitude, the same hardships as the meanest there. Disdaining the use of a covered carriage, she frequently marched several miles at the head of the troops.

Pursued closely by Odenathus and Zenobia, Sapor fled through Mesopotamia, suffering many defeats, losing towns and cities, and at last took refuge in Ctesiphon, his capital, where the victors besieged him for some months.

The Roman senate recognised the deeds of Odenathus by granting him the title of Augustus, A.D. 263. In the following year the royal pair undertook a second expedition against Sapor. New triumphs were added to the glories of the last campaign. The Persian king was once more forced to take refuge in Ctesiphon, which would no doubt have fallen had not the incursion of a horde of Scythian Goths into Syria compelled Odenathus to raise the siege.

Surrounding nations soon learned to respect the brave prince of Palmyra and his no less warlike consort. Even Sapor, humiliated though he had been, was glad, not merely to make peace, but to join in close alliance with his conquerors, who were threatened by the underhand machinations of the contemptible emperor Gallienus. But the brilliant career of Odenathus was unexpectedly brought to a close by the hand of his nephew, who, believing himself insulted by the monarch, assassinated him, together with his son Herod, at a banquet in the city of Emesa, A.D. 267.

The murderer gained nothing but the empty pleasure of revenge. Scarcely had he assumed the title of Augustus ere he was sacrificed by the royal widow to the memory of her husband, though some historians have accused her of being an accomplice in the double murder. Zenobia was proclaimed queen; and, passing over Timolaus and Herennius, her sons by Odenathus, she arrayed Vhaballathus in the purple, and showed him to the troops as their emperor.

With the death of Odenathus ceased that authority granted him as a personal favour by the emperor and senate of Rome; and Gallienus despatched an army to dethrone Zenobia. But the queen soon compelled the Roman general to retreat into Europe with the loss of both army and reputation. Zenobia governed the East for more than five years; and by successive conquests she extended her dominions from the Euphrates to the Mediterranean and the borders of Bithynia; and added, besides, the land of the Ptolemies. Her power became so great that the warlike Claudius II., who succeeded Gallienus, was satisfied that while he was occupied in the defence of Italy from the Goths and Germans, Zenobia should assert the dignity of the Roman power in the East.

Palmyra, the capital of the warrior queen, almost rivalled the Eternal City in the magnificence of its temples, its mansions, its public monuments, and the luxury of its citizens. It became the great centre of commerce between Europe and India, and its merchants grew wealthy through the trade of East and West. Arcades of lofty palms shadowed its streets of marble palaces; purling fountains, fed by icy springs, rendered it a perfect Elysium in the midst of burning arid sands. Schools, museums, libraries, fostered by the care of Zenobia, encouraged and aided the arts and literature.

At last the stern, the inflexible Aurelian ascended the throne of the Caesars. Firmly resolved to rid the empire of every usurper, great or small, he began by re-conquering Gaul and making prisoner the Western usurper, Tetricus. He then passed into Asia, *A.D.* 272, when his presence alone was sufficient to bring back Bithynia to its allegiance. Of course, Zenobia did not indolently permit an invader to approach within a hundred miles of her capital without taking measures to arrest his progress. She marched with all her forces to oppose him; but was signally defeated in two battles, the first near Antioch, the second near Emesa. In both engagements the queen animated the soldiers by her presence, though the actual command devolved on Zabdas, the conqueror of Egypt. The latter, Zenobia's principal general, has been by many supposed to have been Zabba, the queen's sister; this, however, is mere surmise.

After the second defeat, Zenobia was unable to raise a third army. She retired within the walls of her capital, prepared to make a gallant defence, and boldly declared that her reign and her life should end together.

Aurelian arrived before Palmyra, after a toilsome march over the sandy desert which separated the city from Antioch. His proposals being rejected with scorn, he was obliged to begin the siege; and, while superintending the operations, he was wounded by a dart.

He wrote in a letter:

The Roman people speak with contempt of the war which I am waging against a woman. They are ignorant both of the character and of the power of Zenobia. It is impossible to enumerate her warlike preparations of stones, of arrows, and of every species of missile weapons. Every part of the walls is provided with two or three *balistae*, and artificial fires are thrown from her military engines. The fear of punishment has armed her with a desperate courage.

Zenobia was at first supported in her determined resistance by the hope that the Roman Army, having no means of getting provisions, would soon be compelled to retreat, and also by the expectation that Persia would come to her aid. Disappointed in both calculations, she mounted her swiftest dromedary and fled towards the Euphrates. But the Roman light cavalry pursued, and soon overtook the queen, who was brought back prisoner. Palmyra surrendered almost immediately after, and was treated with unexpected clemency by the victor.

The courage of Zenobia entirely deserted her when she heard the angry cries of the soldiers, who clamoured for her immediate execution. She threw the entire guilt of her obstinate resistance upon her friends and counsellors, and the celebrated Longinus, amongst others, fell a victim to the emperor's rage.

Vhaballathus, the only surviving son of Zenobia, withdrew into Armenia, where he ruled over a small principality granted him by Aurelian.

When the emperor returned to Rome, in the following year (*A.D.* 274), he celebrated, after the manner of Roman conquerors, a magnificent triumph in honour of his many victories over the Goths, the Alemanni, Tetricus, and Zenobia. Elephants, royal tigers, panthers, bears, armed gladiators, military standards, and war-chariots passed in succession. But the great object of attention was the Eastern queen, who, completely laden with golden fetters, a gold chain, supported by a slave, round her neck, her limbs bending beneath the weight of the jewels with which she was decked, was compelled to precede, on foot, the triumphal car in which, not many months previously, she had hoped to enter the gates of Rome as a conqueror.

After the conclusion of his triumph, Aurelian presented Zenobia with an elegant villa at Tibur (or Tivoli), about twenty miles from the capital; and here she passed the rest of her days as a Roman matron. She died about the year 300. Her daughters married into wealthy and noble families; some say, indeed, that Aurelian espoused one of them; and the family was not extinct even in the fifth century. Baronius supposes Zenobius, Bishop of Florence, in the days of Saint Ambrose, to have been one of the great queen's descendants.

Amongst the numberless captives—Sarmatians, Alemanni, Goths, Vandals, Gauls, Franks, Dacians, Syrians, Arabs, Egyptians—who unwillingly graced the triumph of Aurelian, were ten Gothic women, captured in a battle between the Goths and Romans when the emperor was driving the barbarians out of Italy. Each party was distinguished in the procession by its own, or by some fancy name; these Gothic females were designated "Amazons." Besides these prisoners, many Gothic women and girls, in male attire, had been found dead on the field of battle.

Hunila, or Hunilda, one of these Gothic women, was afterwards married to Bonosus, a wealthy and influential Roman general, Governor of Rhaetia. She was admired and distinguished amongst her new friends for her beauty, wit, and virtue. But the *ci-devant* Amazon kept up communications with her own countrymen; and Bonosus, promised assistance by his wife's relations, assumed the purple. For a few months his authority extended over Gaul, Spain and Britain; but at last he was conquered by the Emperor Probus. To avoid falling into the hands of the victor, he put an end to his own life by hanging; whereupon some wit, alluding to his favourite vice (for Bonosus, they say, could drink as much as ten strong men) remarked that "there hung a bottle, not a man."

Probus spared the life of Hunila, and granted her an annual pension for the rest of her days; he permitted her sons to enjoy their paternal estate.

Mavia, Queen of Pharan, another of those troublesome women who defied the Roman emperors, was by birth a Roman, and by education a Christian. When very young she was carried away by a troop of Arabs, who brought her to their prince, Obedien, King of Pharan. The latter, who was himself a Christian, charmed by the beauty of his captive, made her his wife. At his death Mavia became sole ruler of Pharan. Placing herself at the head of a numerous army, *A.D.* 373, she invaded Palestine, and advancing as far as Phoenicia, defeated the forces of the emperors Valentinian, Valens, and Gratian in a series of battles extending over some months.

The Roman governor of Phoenicia, unable to make head against the invader, was compelled to seek assistance of the general commanding the Eastern emperor's forces. The latter came speedily to his aid, and after bragging much and loudly of what he would do, engaged in battle with Mavia. He was signally beaten, his army cut to pieces, and he had to fly ignominiously.

After this victory the Queen of Pharan gained many another battle, and she proved herself so dangerous an opponent that the Romans were compelled to sue for peace. Peace was at last concluded, on the condition (dictated by Mavia) that the anchorite Moses should be sent as bishop to Pharan. Having thus destroyed idolatry in Pharan, the queen remained for the rest of her days in friendly relationship with the Romans, to one of whom, Count Victor, she gave her daughter in marriage.

Towards the close of the fourth century, one of the Sapors, King of Persia, invaded Armenia, which for many years previously had maintained its independence. He was resolutely opposed by King Tiranus and his wife Pharandsem, or Olympias; but after valiantly defending his throne for nearly four years, Tiranus was deserted by his nobles and compelled to surrender.

Armenia was once more reduced into a Persian province, and divided between two of Sapor's favourites. The city of Artogerassa was the only stronghold which still dared to resist the Persians. It was defended by Pharandsem. The Persians were surprised and routed under the walls by a bold and concerted sortie of the besieged; but the former were constantly reinforced, while the latter steadily diminished in numbers, through famine and disease, rather than by the weapons of the foe. After a siege of fourteen months the city was compelled to surrender. Pharandsem, with her own hand, flung open the gates, when she was seized by the victors, and, by order of Sapor, impaled.

CHAPTER 4

The Arabs

The Arabs; even in "the days of their ignorance," were always a brave, warlike people. Their liberty, almost the only wealth they possessed, was jealously guarded with such courage and determination, that the greatest nations of antiquity were unable to subdue them. With the preaching of Mohammed began the glorious days of Arabia. Their semi-obscurity as a nation, hitherto, had been due solely to the want of some common bond of union, some link to bind together the princes of the various tribes. But when there was one leader to rally round, one faith to propagate, one Paradise for those who fell in conquering the heathen, the wild children of the desert proved that they could conquer foreign countries as well as defend their native sands. During the early days of Islamism, a vast number of women, many belonging to the highest rank, followed their relatives to battle, and fought for or against the *Koran* as bravely as the men—nay, more than once it was the valour of the Arab women that retrieved the fortunes of the day.

The Prophet had many obstacles to overcome before converting the great majority of his countrymen to the new faith. Scarcely had he promulgated his new doctrines, and gathered round him a few faithful adherents, when the neighbouring chiefs rose up, sword in hand, to stifle the new movement, ere it attained more dangerous dimensions. His principal opponent during the first few years of the Hegira was Abu Sofian, chief of the Koreishites, who were, to a man, idolaters.

The first military exploit of the Islamites was despoiling a wealthy caravan, led by that great chieftain, in the valley of Bedar. Abu Sofian, with three thousand soldiers, avenged this insult on Mount Ohud, where the Prophet, who had only nine hundred and fifty men, was defeated and wounded; barely escaping with his life. In this action, fought in the third year of the Hegira (*A.D.* 611), Henda, the wife of Abu Sofian, commanded the reserve of the Koreishites. She was accompanied by fifteen other women, of high rank. By exhortation and singing they animated the men to fight well. Indeed, the ultimate success of Abu Sofian was due, in a great measure, to their presence.

Another of Mohammed's early opponents was Forka, an Arab lady possessing a castle and immense wealth. She was a kind of feudal peeress, and retained a body of soldiers to defend her domain. For some years she defied the Islamites; but at last Zeid, one of the principal Moslem leaders, was despatched to seize her castle. Forka defended herself for some time with obstinacy and resolution; but, after a troublesome and lengthy siege, the fortress was taken by storm, and Forka was slain, together with the best part of the garrison. Her daughter, with all her wealth, became the prey of the victors.

The rapid success of Mohammed induced many Arabs to take up the prophetic office on their own account; imitators arose in various parts of Arabia, sometimes achieving a temporary success almost rivalling that of Mohammed. The most successful was named Mosseylemah, whose headquarters were the city and suburbs of Yemaumah. During the life-time of Mohammed, little notice was taken of this rival by the "true believers;" but after the death of the Prophet, *A.D.* 632, the Caliph Abubeker despatched Khaled, "the Sword of God," with a large force to capture Yemaumah. Mosseylemah and nearly all his followers were slain in a fierce action fought near the city.

Mujaia, one of the impostor's principal officers, who had been made prisoner before the battle, wishing to save his fellow-citizens from total extermination, told Khaled that the city was still crowded with brave warriors ready to shed the last drop of blood in defence of their homes; and he recommended the Arab general to open negotiations at once. Leaving the latter to consider his advice, Mujaia found means to communicate with the inhabitants, whom he sent word to arm all the women and girls in helmets and mail, and to distribute them, armed with spears and swords, on the walls.

Khaled perceiving the ramparts bristling with arms, began to fear that an assault on a stronghold so well defended might become an enterprise of some magnitude. So—though contrary to his pet war cry, "No quarter given, and none received,"—the ruthless Islamite thought it best to accept a capitulation on comparatively mild terms.

On entering Yemaumah, Khaled soon saw the deception practised upon him. But, with a generosity of which he was not often guilty, he permitted the people to enjoy the benefits of the treaty.

During the siege of Damascus by Khaled, *A.D.* 633, several instances occurred of female heroism, both on the side of the Arabs and that of the Greeks. One day the governor of Damascus marched out to dislodge the besiegers; the latter, pretending to fly, led the Greeks to a considerable distance from the city. Then turning upon the foe, they assailed him on every side. Seffwaun the Salmian, a distinguished Moslem chief, seeing a Greek officer conspicuous for the splendour of his armour, knocked him down with a blow of his mace. He was about to strip the fallen chief, when he found himself fiercely attacked by the widow, who had accompanied her husband into battle, and whose death she now prepared to avenge. Seffwaun, wishing to avoid the dishonour of shedding the blood of a woman, contrived by dexterous manipulation of his sword to frighten his frail antagonist without wounding her or being himself wounded. She was soon compelled to retire for safety behind the swords and spears of her friends.

Another day some Arab women were captured by the Greeks during one of the skirmishes. While the Greeks were carousing in their tents, a girl named Khaullah, one of the prisoners, urged her sisters in captivity to arm themselves with tent-poles, and brain anybody who approached them. She set the example by shattering the skull of a Greek soldier who was so imprudent as to venture within reach of her arm. A general conflict ensued; ending by Khaled and several Arab horsemen coming to the rescue and carrying off the Islamite damsels.

Either this heroine, or another of the same name afterwards turned the fortunes of the day in the Battle of Yermouks, which decided the fate of Syria. The Arabs, far outnumbered by the Greeks, fled to their tents, and refused to stir, despite the alternate taunts or encouraging words of the women. The latter at last, in despair, armed themselves, and withstood the foe till night closed in to end the combat. Next day, led by Khaullah, sister of one of their principal commanders, the women again marched to the attack.

In leading the van, Khaullah was struck down by a Greek; but Wafeira, her principal female friend, ran to her aid and cut off the soldier's head. The Arabs, shamed into their former courage by the noble conduct of the women, attacked the Christians with such fury that the latter were speedily routed, with a loss, it is said, of one hundred and fifty thousand slain and about fifty thousand made prisoners.

Khaullah, the leading heroine of this fight, was afterwards married to the ill-starred Caliph Ali.

In the year 647, Abdallah, the Moslem governor of Alexandria, crossed the Libyan Desert and appeared before the walls of Tripoli, at that time the most important city on the Coast of Barbary. After surprising and cutting to pieces several thousand Greeks who were marching to reinforce the garrison, the Arabs, frustrated in an attempt to storm the massive fortifications, prepared to lay formal siege. The city was strengthened very soon by Gregorius, the Greek *prefect*, who arrived at the head of one hundred and twenty thousand men. He rejected indignantly the option of the *Koran* or tribute. For several days both armies engaged in deadly combat, from dawn till the hour of noon, when, from fatigue and thirst caused by the blazing sun, they were compelled to seek shelter and refreshment.

The daughter of Gregorius, a young girl of great beauty, fought by her father's side throughout every engagement. She had been trained from early youth to excel in warlike exercises; and by the splendour of her arms and apparel she was conspicuous amidst the dust and confusion of the fight. Gregorius, to excite his soldiers to deeds of bravery, offered her hand and one hundred thousand pieces of gold to the man who brought him the head of Abdallah, the Moslem general. When the Arabs heard this they compelled their leader to withdraw from the field.

The Moslems, discouraged by the absence of their chief, were rapidly giving way; but the counsels of Zobeir, a brave Arab warrior, turned the fortunes of the day, he cried:

Retort on the *infidels* their ungenerous attempts. Proclaim throughout the ranks that the head of Gregorius will be repaid with his captive daughter, and the equal sum of one hundred thousand pieces of gold.

This was accordingly proclaimed. At the same time Zobeir resorted to a stratagem which took the Greeks completely by surprise, and gained an easy victory for the Arabs. The contending armies having, as usual, separated after the engagement, were retiring to their respective camps overcome by fatigue, when the two Moslem chiefs, who had placed themselves in ambush with fresh troops, rushed out upon the exhausted Greeks and routed them with fearful slaughter. The *prefect* himself was slain by the hand of Zobeir; his daughter, while seeking revenge or death in the thick of the fight, was surrounded and captured.

Ayesha, daughter of Caliph Abubeker, was the favourite wife of the Prophet. After the death of her husband she lived in retirement, for twenty years, at Medina. But she possessed a restless, ambitious spirit, and had no inclination for a life of repose and obscurity. After the sudden murder of Caliph Othman, in 654, when Ali was elected, she refused to acknowledge the latter, and declared her belief that he had a share in the murder of his predecessor. The nation, divided into opposing factions, was soon plunged into civil war. The malcontents, headed by Ayesha, assembled in thousands at Mecca, and marched thence to Bassorah, where they expected to find warm support.

Arrived before Bassorah they were astounded to find the gates shut against them. Ayesha, mounted on a camel, advanced to the walls and harangued those assembled on the battlements. But she was old and crabbed, with sharp features and a shrill voice—rendered even more shrill by the rapidity with which she spoke,—so the people only laughed at her. The louder they laughed, the shriller her accents grew. They reproached her for riding forth, bare-faced, to foment dissension among the Faithful; and they jeered at her followers for bringing their old grandmother in place of their young and handsome wives.

However, a number of the citizens were secretly in favour of the malcontents; and the friends of Ayesha seized the palace one dark night, *bastinadoed* the governor, plucked out his beard, and sent him back to his master. Great, however, was the dismay of Ayesha when the *Caliph* encamped one morning before Bassorah; but, resolved not to give way, she rejected the proposals of Ali, and plunged both armies into a fierce engagement before very well knowing what she was about. But terrified at the horrors of war, to which until this day she was almost a stranger, the old woman besought Kaub, who led her camel, to throw himself between the combatants. In trying to obey her command he was slain.

The large white camel of Ayesha soon became the rallying-point of the insurgents, around which the fury of the battle concentrated. The reins were held alternately by the Modian Arabs, who chanted pieces of poetry; and it is said that out of the tribe of Benni Beiauziah alone not less than *two hundred and eighty* lost a hand on this occasion. The *howdah*, pierced all over with arrows, had something the appearance of a porcupine or a giant pincushion.

After the battle had raged for several hours, the *Caliph*, seeing plainly that it would go on so long as the camel remained alive, ordered his chiefs to direct all their efforts towards cutting down the beast. First one leg was cut off; but the camel maintained its erect position. Another leg was cut off; yet the animal remained immovable. For a moment the soldiers of Ali thought the camel was a sorcerer or a genie. But a third leg was cut off, and the camel sank to the ground.

The battle soon ended; all resistance ceased when the insurgents knew that their leader was taken. Ali treated his prisoner with that true chivalry which had already sprung up amongst the Arabs. He sent her home to Medina, escorted by female attendants disguised as soldiers, and while he lived she was not permitted to meddle in politics. After the murder of Ali, she resumed her former position. Many years after, when Moawyah wished to make the *Caliphate* hereditary in his family, he purchased the influence of Ayesha by the gift of a pair of bracelets valued at one hundred and fifty thousand *dinars*, or nearly seventy thousand pounds.

The "Battle of the Camel," as it is generally styled by Oriental historians, was fought in December, *A.D.* 656, (*A.H.* 36.)

During the reign of Caliph Abdul Malek the Islamites in northern Africa found a most formidable opponent in Cahina the sorceress, Queen of the Berbers. Under the lead of this pseudo-prophetess, the original natives of Barbary made a determined stand for many years against the *Koran*.

Cahina directed her followers to lay waste the lands that lay between Egypt and her dominions, telling them that it was the fruitfulness of those districts which caused the Arab invasions. Her commands were only too faithfully executed. Cities, towns, and villages were destroyed; fields desolated, trees cut down, and the entire face of the land changed from a beautiful garden planted with waving palms and lovely flowers, into an arid waste with scarcely a tree or blade of grass to be seen.

But this scheme ultimately proved the ruin of Cahina. The natives of the ruined districts joyfully welcomed the Moslems on their next invasion. Cahina again took the field with all her forces; but her ranks this time were thinned by desertion. She was speedily defeated and made prisoner with her principal advisers. Rejecting the proposals of the Arab general—the *Koran* or tribute—her head was cut off, put in a camphor-scented casket of great price, and sent to the *Caliph*.

Although Persia was one of the earliest conquests effected by the followers of Islam, scarcely two centuries had elapsed before it was divided into a number of independent states, ruled by Arab, Turkish, or Persian princes. Towards the close of the tenth century. Queen Seidet, widow of one of these independent monarchs, governed the state as regent for her son, who was a minor. She ruled with so much wisdom, and under her guidance the kingdom flourished so greatly, that she had every reason to be offended when her son, grown old enough to take the reins of government, appointed Avicenna, the family physician, to be his Grand Vizier, and committed everything into his hands. Avicenna treated the queen with so little respect that the latter retired from court, raised troops, and marched against her son, whose forces she easily routed. Not wishing, however, to deprive him of the throne, she merely acted as his chief adviser, and aided him with salutary counsels so long as she lived.

Sultan Mahmoud, founder of the Gaznevide dynasty, held Seidet in the deepest respect. While she lived he refrained from attacking her son's dominions; but after her death he annexed them without scruple.

In these days few persons, save students of Oriental history, have even so much as heard of Kharezmé, in Tartary; yet in the eleventh and twelfth centuries it was considered by surrounding nations as the most powerful state in Asia, and its court the most magnificent. At the beginning of the thirteenth century, it was actually, although not nominally, governed by Turkhan Khatun, mother of the reigning *Sultan*. In those days the Mongols, under the irresistible Jenghiz Khan, were advancing with rapid strides towards Europe. It was not long before they besieged the capital of Kharezmé.

The city held out for twelve months against the Mongol hordes commanded by the three sons of Jenghiz Khan. The inhabitants, male and female, made a defence worthy of their ancient fame. Even the women aided in the numberless sorties made from the city. But at last, despite their bravery, the place was taken by storm. Men and women alike fought hand to hand with the Mongols, and retired from street to street, till scarcely any remained alive.

According to the lowest computation more than one hundred thousand Kharezmians were slain during the siege. The valour displayed by the women became so famous throughout Asia, that many Oriental historians, by way of accounting for it, gravely assert that the people of Kharezmé were descended from the Amazons.

Mr. Palgrave, who travelled through Arabia in 1862-3, says that it is customary amongst the Bedouin Arabs, when they go into battle, to have their army preceded by a maiden of good family, styled a *Hadee'yah*, who rides on a camel into the midst of the fight, encouraging the men to fight bravely by reciting pieces of extempore poetry, satirical or heroic, as best suits the occasion. Very frequently the

Hadee'yah is slain.

Such was the fate of a brave girl, noted for her eloquence and gigantic stature, who led on the Amjan Bedouins at Koweyt rather more than twenty years ago, (as at 1879), against Abd-Allah, heir to the throne of Nejed. This "Arabian *Bellona*" was slain by the lance of a Nejdean warrior, and her death is said to have been the principal cause of the final rout of the Amjan Army.

CHAPTER 5

Libyssa and Valasca, Queens of Bohemia to Richilda, Countess of Hainault

Europe, during the two or three centuries after the downfall of the Roman Empire, bears a strong resemblance to Greece during the heroic age. In the *Nibelungen*, the *Iliad* of those days, we read of god-like heroes, Herculean warriors, giant princes, and Amazon queens. That was an age when might constituted right, when rulers led their own armies in the field, where the lead was given to the strongest or the most daring.

The Salique law seems in those days to have been very generally disregarded—if indeed it had been introduced as yet; for we read of more than one queen who ruled alone over the more or less barbarous kingdoms of Europe, Æneas Sylvius narrates how a warlike queen named Libyssa ascended the throne of Bohemia on the death of her father, King Crocus. Her husband, Przemislas, whom she espoused in 632, being originally only a peasant, was probably a humble, weak-minded individual, ruled by his wife; for the queen proceeded to enrol the greater number of her female subjects into a species of militia.

They were trained, like the Amazons, to the use of arms and to ride on horseback. After the death of Libyssa, the narrator further says that the principal favourite of the queen, Valasca, with the assistance of the female troops, seized the throne, and held it until her death, which occurred seven years later. Resolved to form a nation of Amazons, Valasca passed a law that all male children should have their right eyes put out and their thumbs cut off, to keep them from using bow and arrows. And this barbarous order was rigorously enforced while

Valasca lived, the men not daring to raise any complaint. The demise of this Amazon-queen soon restored everything to its natural order.

Wanda, the first Queen-Regnant of Poland, was unanimously elected by the people on the death of her father, Cracus, about the year 700. She was a talented woman, and esteemed herself fully capable of conducting the government without the assistance of a husband. To the numerous offers of marriage, she received, a refusal was the invariable answer. At last Rudiger, a German prince, hoping to bring about a happy union by force of arms, invaded Poland with a great army.

Wanda raised troops, and advanced to meet the invaders. When the opposing armies came in sight, Rudiger, believing that his warlike preparations must needs have terrified the queen, besought her to accept him, and thus save the lives of their soldiers. Wanda answered that no man should ever share her throne, because he would love her kingdom better than herself. When this spirited answer was spread amongst Rudiger's officers, they refused to fight against so heroic a queen. Surrounding the prince, they endeavoured to dissuade him from risking a battle; but finding their remonstrances vain, they refused to second his efforts, and Rudiger, in despair, flung himself on his sword.

Wanda returned in triumph to Cracow. She never received another proposal of marriage.

In the year 711 the Moors, commanded by Tarik, crossed the Straits of Gibraltar and invaded Spain. Even after the defeat and death of their king, the Goths disputed every foot of ground before giving way to the *Infidels*. The latter, impeded at every step, were glad to grant peace on almost any terms. One of the principal Gothic leaders was Theodomir, or Tudmir Ben Gobdas, a Spanish noble belonging to one of the most honourable families in the land. He possessed large estates in the South, and his authority over them was so great that not only was the district named after him, the Land of Tudmir, but he was styled king. Having been totally routed in a battle, when the greater number of his soldiers were slain, he escaped to the fortified citadel of Tudmir, where he was soon besieged by the Moors.

Finding his position grow daily more and more untenable, Theodomir resorted to an expedient, already practised by the people of Yemaumah when besieged by Khaled. He commanded all the women to put on male attire, to tie their hair under their chin (to imitate long beards), and to appear, armed with bows and arrows, lances, swords, and shields, on the towers and battlements, in sight of the Moors. He himself, with his few remaining soldiers, stood in front, to conceal as much as possible these feminine guards. The Moors, overrating the strength of the garrison, offered Theodomir advantageous terms, which he accepted. Although they afterwards discovered the fraud, the *infidels* scrupulously observed the treaty.

The women of Tortosa distinguished themselves so highly in some skirmishes with the Moors, that a military Order of Knighthood was conferred upon them.

The word "Infantry" is said to owe its origin to one of the Spanish *Infantas*, who, hearing that her father had been defeated by the Moors, raised a body of foot-soldiers, and placing herself at their head, defeated the *infidels*. In memory of her bravery, foot-soldiers were henceforth styled Infantry.

The Moors never could obtain a footing north of the Pyrenees; yet, despite the invariable want of success attending their attempts, they made constant incursions into France, besieging towns, burning villages, and ravaging the open country. Amongst other cities besieged by them was Carcassonne, situated on the banks of the River Aude, governed in those days by Queen Carcas, famous for her military prowess. When Charlemagne, a few years previously, besieged the city, it was defended so courageously that he permitted the queen to retain the sovereignty.

The Saracens, ridiculing the notion of a female warrior, declared that, in place of fighting, she ought to be spinning. This contemptuous speech, spoken immediately under the city walls, was overheard by queen Carcas. Arming herself with a lance, to which, as if it had been a distaff, she attached a quantity of hemp, she set the hemp on fire, and rushed into the midst of the Saracens, who fled, terrified, in all directions.

The shield and lance of queen Carcas may yet be seen at Carcassonne. Over the city gate there is an effigy of the royal heroine, with the inscription "*Carcas sum.*"

While the South of Europe was overrun by the Saracens, England, Ireland, and Scotland were harassed by the terrible Danes, who for several centuries kept these islands in constant terror. The most powerful opponent of the Danes in England was, as everyone knows, King Alfred the Great. During the latter years of his reign, the land was tolerably secure from invasion; but after his death the Vikings and their wild followers came swarming over the country again, burning, plundering, massacring, just as they had done before Alfred drove them away.

Elfrida, the eldest daughter of King Alfred, inherited all her father's courage and warlike spirit, and, like him, proved an implacable foe to the Danes. She was married early to Ethelred, Earl of Mercia; and on his death the government of the province devolved upon the widow. And nobly did she fulfil her trust. Mercia was greatly harassed by the Danes—as, indeed, was the entire country in those days. The Welsh joined in alliance with the invaders, and would have marched to their aid but for the promptitude of Elfrida, who entered Wales, 916, at the head of an army, and took Brecknock by storm, capturing therein Queen Anghared and many of her attendants. The "Lady of Mercia" had another motive in this invasion, which rendered Wales tributary to the Saxons; and this motive was the desire to avenge the death of the good Abbot Egbert, whom the Welsh had slain.

King Owen fled to Derby, where he was kindly received by the Danes. When Elfrida learned this she marched thither, and captured the city "before Lammas," 918. So reckless was she of her own safety on this memorable day, that it had almost proved to be her last. Pressing at the head of her troops through the narrow gateway where a vast multitude of Danes barred the way, many of her principal officers were struck down, and four of her guards were slain by the hand of the Welsh king. Gwynne, Lord of Ely, and steward of Elfrida, perceiving the danger of the princess, set the gates on fire, and rushed furiously upon the Welsh and Danes, who gave way before his onslaught.

Owen, unable to escape, preferred to fall by his own hand than yield himself prisoner to a woman.

Two years later, in 920, Elfrida recaptured Leicester and York from the Danes; and besides repairing the fortifications of the former city, encompassed it with a massive wall of such strength that Matthew Paris styles it *indissoluble*.

Shortly after this, and before the war was over, Elfrida died at Tamworth, in Staffordshire, leaving an unmarried daughter named Elswina. She was buried at Gloucester, in the porch of St. Peter's monastery, a building erected at her own expense.

This heroine has been praised by all the old historians for her prudence, courage, and talent for governing. Ingulphus says that considering the great actions of her life, the cities she built, the castles she fortified, and the armies she raised, Elfrida "might have been thought a man." She was generally styled queen by the Mercians, who regarded themselves as her subjects.

According to tradition it was the same wild Vikings, the terror of our land, who founded the mighty Russian Empire; and their successors, the Grand Dukes and *Czars*, have ever since retained that thirst for conquest which distinguished the roving Normans. The Grand Duke Igor was one of the first among the successors of Rurik who caused the Russian standard to be feared by surrounding states. After subduing most of the neighbouring towns, his victorious career was suddenly brought to a close in 945, during an expedition against the Drevlians, by whom he was surrounded, and put to the sword with all his troops.

Igor was succeeded by his son Sviatoslaf, the first Christian sovereign of Russia. The prince being too young to conduct the government, his mother, Olga, undertook the regency. The Drevlians, fancying the royal widow would be easily intimidated, sent to demand her in marriage for their prince. But Olga, after causing their ambassadors to be slain (by various quaint stratagems which Nestor has preserved) called out her troops, placed herself at their head, and marched against the Drevlians, taking her son with her to teach him the art of war. After destroying all the towns and villages of the enemy, she laid siege to Karosten, their capital, which was built entirely of wood—the very name signifying "wall of bark."

Finding the city too strong and too well defended, she made proposals of peace to the inhabitants, declaring that she would be satisfied with three sparrows and a pigeon from each house, as tribute. The people joyfully complied, and sent the birds to the Russian camp. Olga caused the birds to be let loose, with lighted torches tied to their tails; they, of course, flew back to their nests in the house-eaves of Karosten. The town was soon in a blaze from end to end. The terrified inhabitants, flying to escape the flames, were met by the swords and lances of the Russians. The Drevlian prince and his court perished in the massacre, as indeed, did nearly everyone in the city, save the dregs of the population.

Having glutted her thirst for revenge, Olga made a progress through Russia, taking Sviatoslaf with her. Towns and villages arose at her command, taxation was regulated on a better footing; and by various measures highly beneficial to the prosperity of the country, the Grand Duchess proved herself a most able ruler. In 955 she went to Constantinople to be baptised a Christian, and in the course of a few years the Greek faith spread through the land, and paganism was abolished.

When Sviatoslaf grew old enough to rule his own dominions, Olga resigned the reins of government. She lived in retirement for several years, and died in 968 at an advanced age.

In the Middle Ages, chemistry and mathematics were things known to few people except the monks; any man who studied the sciences was styled an alchemist, and suspected of being in league with the Evil One. When it was a woman who gave herself up to learned studies, the people could scarcely be withheld from tearing "the sorceress" to pieces.

Occasionally, however, despite what the world said, noble ladies, especially on the Continent, did apply their minds to what in those days went by the name of the Black Art. Amongst these was Richilda, Countess of Hainault, who married Baldwin the Good, eldest son of Baldwin, Marquis of Flanders, one of whose daughters, Matilda, became the wife of William the Conqueror, and another of Tosti God-winsson, son of the powerful Earl Godwin.

The fame of Richilda as a wicked sorceress caused her to be anything but a favourite in the country; and when her husband died, Robert le Prison, Count of Friesland, and brother of the deceased, endeavoured to wrest Flanders from her young son Arnulf, or Arnoul, who was little more than a boy. William the Conqueror espoused the cause of Richilda, and sent over Fitz-Osbern, Earl of Hereford, the tyrant of the Welsh, to her aid. The countess also implored the assistance of her liege lord, the King of France.

A battle took place on St. Peter's Day, 1071, at Bavinchorum, near Cassel; Richilda and Fitz-Osbern commanded their troops in person. The left wing of the foe was routed, and Robert le Prison made prisoner and sent to St. Omer. But this success was counterbalanced by the death of Fitz-Osbern and young Arnoul. Richilda's forces fled in confusion, and the heroine was made prisoner.

An exchange was effected, by which Richilda and the Frisson regained their liberty. The countess immediately set about raising fresh troops to avenge the death of her boy. The contending armies met again; this time at Broqueroi, near Mons, where the troops of Richilda were routed with so terrible a slaughter that the scene of the conflict was afterwards known under the name of "the Hedges of Death." All hope now fled the breast of Richilda. Escaping from the field, she took refuge in a convent, where the rest of her days were passed under the severest penances—to atone, as folks said, for her past dealings with the Prince of Darkness.

CHAPTER 6

The Crusades

It would be difficult at the present day to appreciate the wild enthusiasm spread throughout Europe by the preaching of Peter the Hermit. Thousands from all classes—kings, princes, nobles, priests, peasants, beggars, all alike impelled by the same blind impulse, many amongst them scarcely knowing where they were going or for what they went to fight,—hastened to take up arms against the *Infidel*.

The enthusiasm was not, as it would probably in our days, confined to one, nor even to three or four nations. Robert of Gloucester says "There were men":—

Of Normandy, of Denmark, of Norway, of Bretagne,
Of Wales, and of Ireland, of Gascony, of Spain,
Of Provence, of Saxony, and of Allemayne,
Of Scotland, and of Greece, of Rome and Aquitaine.

Ay, and women too. The first Crusading armies which set out in the spring of 1096, commanded by Peter the Hermit, Gaultier-sans-Avoir, and other leaders of less reputation, comprised nearly as many women as men. Even where they did not contend hand to hand with the Saracens, these heroines cheered the warriors by marching with them in the ranks, by carrying food and ammunition to the battle-field, by speaking with enthusiasm of the cause for which they had armed. It was, indeed, owing as much to the courage and endurance of the women, who suffered without a murmur the miseries of cold, hunger, and want of clothing, as to their own indomitable bravery that the Templars owed the capture of Antioch. William of Tyre, speaking of the grand review held before Nice in 1099, says that exclusive of the cavalry, who, to the number of one hundred thousand were well armed in helmets and mail, there were found six hundred thousand

Crusaders of both sexes, many of them little children.

When the second Crusade was preached, many ladies, especially in France and Germany, formed themselves into squadrons and regiments of Amazons, and assumed the arms and armour of the Templars. The commander of the German Amazons, who, says Michaud, was more admired for her dress than her courage, received the title of the "Golden Footed Dame," or the "Lady with the Golden Legs," on account of her magnificent gilded buskins and spurs. She enrolled her troop under the banner of the emperor Conrad, who started for the East 1147. The French Amazons were commanded by their queen, Eleonora of Aquitaine (afterwards wife of Henry II. of England). Forming themselves into a squadron of light cavalry, they went through a regular course of military training, and, by constant exercise, they acquired tolerable proficiency in the use of arms.

Mezerai, speaking of these "squadrons of females," declares that by their valour they "rendered credible all that has been said of the prowess of the Amazons;" but, *certes*, those who followed King Louis to the Holy Land rendered themselves more notable for rashness and folly than manly courage. They set out in the year 1147, with the bold determination to share all the fatigues and brave all the dangers incident to a crusade; but their first essay in the presence of the enemy proved sufficient to put an end to their gallant resolutions and cover their leader with ridicule.

The corps of Amazons, escorted by a band of sterner warriors commanded by a distinguished knight, had been sent on in advance, with strict orders from the king to encamp on the heights of Laodicea, and there await his arrival. They reached the spot as the sun was setting, and the black, dreary rocks appeared to the romantic, but inexperienced eye of Eleonora, an exceedingly uninviting situation for a resting place. With the haughty imperiousness of her nature, she insisted on turning aside to a beautiful valley watered by cool streams, and overshadowed by lofty palms, where, despite the warnings and expostulations of the brave captain who led her escort, she encamped.

In this charming but unprotected dale they were soon attacked by a party of Saracens. King Louis arrived barely in time to save the corps of Amazons from capture. Compelled to hazard an engagement under peculiarly disadvantageous circumstances against an enemy who received reinforcements from moment to moment, Louis was so near being made prisoner as to be obliged to seek refuge in a tree. The Christians were victorious, but it was with heavy losses. Eleonora and her followers retired to the court of her cousin Raymond, Prince of Antioch, and there passed the rest of the season.

While the Crusades lasted, ladies continued to accompany husbands and lovers to the East. In the arsenal of the palace at Genoa there are, or were some few years since, several light cuirasses, made for a band of Genoese ladies, who, towards the close of the thirteenth century, wished to join in a crusade against the Turks. However, by the entreaties of Pope Boniface VIII., who wrote an autograph letter for the purpose, they were persuaded to relinquish their design.

Pierre Gentien, an old French poet, who flourished at the latter end of the thirteenth century, has left a species of epic in rhyme, wherein he describes a tournament held by certain noble dames who were about departing with the knights beyond the seas. In this poem the author, describing how the combatants, to acquire proficiency in the use of arms, disputed the prize of valour with all the courage and enthusiasm of the knights of those days, takes the opportunity to name forty or fifty, the most beautiful ladies of their time. His poem has been therefore admired rather as being a memoir of the old French families than for the excellence of the poetry.

The somewhat ridiculous termination to her first essay in presence of the foe did not entirely quench the military ardour of Eleonora of Aquitaine. After she had been for some years the wife of King Henry II., she stirred up her sons, Richard and John, to rebellion against their father; and went so far as to appear in masculine attire, at the head of their forces in Aquitaine. And thus clad, she was made prisoner.

When Prince Arthur was prosecuting his claims on the English crown, Philip Augustus, the French king, sent him with a military retinue into Normandy, then in the hands of the English. The French barons laid siege to Mirebeau, a fortified town near Poitiers. It was defended for King John by Eleonora, who, though she had then attained the age of fourscore, was as active as ever, and had only just returned from a journey into Spain—a matter of some difficulty in those days. When the French had captured the town, the veteran Amazon threw herself into a strong tower which served as a sort of citadel; and here she held out bravely till the arrival of John with reinforcements, on the night between July 31st and August 1, 1202; when the besiegers were compelled to surrender.

During the wars between the Empress Maud and Stephen, the latter was ably seconded by his queen, Matilda of Boulogne. For the first five years of his usurpation, the king was disturbed only by the revolt of Baldwin, Earl of Exeter, and the invasion of David, King of Scotland. Matilda showed herself to be an able politician and a brave soldier. In June, 1137, she laid siege to Dover Castle, which had been seized by the rebels, and, at the same time, sent orders to her Boulogne subjects to blockade the fortress by sea.

In July, 1139, the empress, escorted by her brother Robert, Earl of Gloucester, landed in England. After several battles, of which little is known, she defeated and captured King Stephen near Lincoln, 1141. The empress was at once proclaimed queen of England, and after sending Stephen in irons to Bristol, she entered London. Matilda made humble suit for the liberty of her lord, and offered, in his name, to resign all claim to the crown; but the empress refused, save on the petitioner also surrendering her inheritance of Boulogne. The queen refused; and with the assistance of William of Ypres, Stephen's talented but unpopular minister, she raised the standard of the king in Surrey and Kent, where a large party were in favour of the royal captive.

Miss Strickland remarks:

> In the pages of superficially-written histories, much is said of the prowess and military skill displayed by Prince Eustace at this period; but Eustace was scarcely seven years old at the time when these efforts were made for the deliverance of his royal sire; therefore it is plain to those who reflect on the evidence of dates, that it was the high-minded and prudent queen, his mother, who avoided all Amazonian display by acting under the name of her son.

The empress, being warned that the Londoners, weary of her insolence, had a mind to serve her as she had served Stephen, fled from the city by night, and laid siege to Winchester Castle. The men of London and Kent, headed by Matilda, Eustace, and William of Ypres, were soon at the city gates, and Maud was closely invested for several days in her palace. To escape the horrors of a city in flames, the empress feigned herself dead, and her body was conveyed to Gloucester. Robert, her brother, was made prisoner, and his liberty was purchased by the release of Stephen.

From this time the fortunes of the empress rapidly declined. She was so closely invested in Oxford during the inclement Weather of 1142, that she was compelled to dress herself and her attendants in white, which, as the ground was covered with snow, more readily escaped observation, and so steal away from the town. The war continued to rage with the utmost fury for the next five years; but Maud, weary at last of the miserable struggle, returned to Normandy in 1147.

Queen Matilda died at Henningham Castle, in Essex, on May 3rd, 1151, a little more than three years before her husband. The empress outlived both her rivals, and died abroad, September 10th, 1167.

The famous contest between the Guelfs and the Ghibelines, which for nearly three hundred years devastated Italy, broke out early in the twelfth century. The struggle was at first hardly more than a feud between two powerful families; but it soon developed into an obstinate war between two political parties—the Guelfs, who formed the papal and Italian party, and the Ghibelines, who favoured the German Emperors.

One of the leading events of this war was the siege of Ancona, in 1172, by the Archbishop of Mentz, Frederic Barbarossa's deputy in Italy, backed by all the power of Ghibeline Tuscany. The citizens, reduced to the direst extremities, applied for aid to William degli Adelardi, a noble and influential citizen of Ferrara, and to the Countess de Bertinoro. Aldrude, the countess, who belonged to the illustrious house of Frangipani, has been immortalised by the Italian writers of those days, on account of her personal beauty, her generosity, and the magnificence of her court, which was the favourite resort of Italian chivalry, poetry, and art. She was married young to the Count de Bertinoro, who died, and left her a widow in the bloom of youth.

The Countess and Adelardi, with their combined forces, hastened to the relief of the beleaguered city, near which they arrived at sunset. Having pitched their camp on a hill overlooking the Ghibeline tents, the soldiers were assembled, and harangued with exciting speeches, which they received with loud applause, mingled with the clashing of arms. However, they gained a bloodless victory. The besiegers, alarmed at the strength of the foe, struck their tents, and retired under cover of night.

The famished Anconians, relieved from the presence of the imperial army, received a fresh stock of provisions. They came out to thank the countess and her ally, and offered them magnificent presents.

On her homeward march, the countess fell in with a party of retreating Ghibelines. Numerous skirmishes took place, in which the troops of Aldrude were uniformly victorious.

The date of this heroine's death is unknown.

The designs of the Hohenstaufen on the throne of Sicily drew their attention for a time from Lombardy. Henry VI., who ascended the imperial throne of Germany on the death of his father, Frederick Barbarossa, established a claim on the crown of the Two Sicilies in right of his wife, the daughter of King Roger. Constantia became the rightful queen of Sicily on the death of William the Good in 1189; but the throne was usurped by Tancred, her natural brother. Henry invaded the Neapolitan states in 1191; but though successful at first, a terrible mortality in his camp compelled him to raise the siege of Naples and retire from the country.

After the death of Tancred, his widow resigned all claim to the crown; stipulating that her infant son, William, should be left in possession of Tarentum, But the cruel and perfidious emperor, who had failed in all his attempts on Naples and Sicily during the lifetime of the king, cast the boy into prison, after putting out his eyes, imprisoned the queen and the princesses in a convent, and carried the royal treasures to Germany.

When the emperor returned to his own land, Naples and Sicily rose against his tyranny. Hastening back with a mighty army, Henry defeated the rebels, and commanded that the leaders should suffer the most excruciating tortures. Constantia, shocked at his barbarity, quarrelled with her husband, cast off her allegiance, and stirred up the Sicilians to a fresh rebellion. Thousands flocked to her standard, and the empress, at this time fifty years old, led them against the German troops. Henry, who had sent away most of his soldiers to the Holy Land, was defeated, and compelled to submit to the terms dictated by Constantia.

The emperor died at Messina in 1197, shortly after the conclusion of the treaty, and his wife has been accused of administering poison, to rid her people of a cruel and vindictive tyrant. After his death, Constantia lived peacefully in Sicily as regent of the island and guardian of her infant son, the Emperor Frederick II. She died three years later, in the year 1200.

Returning to England, we find Dame Nichola de Camville, a noted heroine of those days, personally engaged on the royal side during the Barons' wars. Nichola de Hara, widow of Gerard, Lord Camville was co-sheriff for the county of Lincolnshire. She held the Castle of Lincoln for King John against Gilbert de Gaunt, who had captured the city; and after the death of John she defended it for his son, Henry III.

Shortly after the death of King John, the Count de la Perche, a French knight commanding the Confederate Barons, marched to Lincoln at the head of six hundred knights and twenty thousand soldiers, and besieged the castle. It was defended by Dame Nichola till the arrival of the Earl of Pembroke in May, 1217, when the battle, afterwards known as "Lincoln Fair," quelled for a time the rebellion of the English barons, and established Henry III. on the throne.

Turn which way we will, we see nothing but civil wars and struggles for supremacy between crowned heads and nobles. Crossing to France, some nine or ten years later, we find the great vassals of the throne conspiring to deprive Queen Blanche of the regency. However, Blanche of Castille was not a woman easily intimidated. At the head of a large army, she went with the young king (her son) to Brittany, the seat of the conspiracy. The malcontent nobles, not being prepared to meet the royal forces in the field, submitted for a time.

In the following year, 1227, the royal troops defeated and captured Raymond, Count of Toulouse, leader of the Albigeois, and the queen treated her noble captive so harshly that the French lords again took up arms, led by the Duke of Brittany. Despite the severity of the winter, the queen-regent and her son marched into Brittany; and after surmounting terrible obstacles from the cold, and from the snow and ice, which stopped both roads and rivers, laid siege to the stronghold of Bellesme. This fortress which from the thickness of its walls, was supposed to be impregnable, had a garrison of Bretons, supported by a body of English auxiliaries.

The besieged were in hopes that the royal army, horribly decimated by the severe weather, would be compelled soon to retire. But the queen was not the one to yield when she had once resolved on anything. To preserve her soldiers, hundreds of whom perished from the bitter cold, she caused immense fires to be kept constantly blazing, and offered high rewards to all who brought wood into camp. To encourage the men, she slept in the open air by the bivouac fires, conversed with the troops, and encouraged officers and privates alike by her affability and condescension.

Queen Blanche pressed the siege with unyielding determination. After two assaults had been made the great tower was dismantled, and the garrison surrendered. The Duke of Brittany was made prisoner, though, through motives of policy, he was speedily set at liberty. The queen next took Nantes and Acenis; and the revolt was brought to a close in 1230 by the surrender of the Count de Marche.

From the courage and military tact displayed by the queen during the siege of Bellesme, she received the complimentary title of "the

Great Captain."

The regency of Blanche ended in 1235, and Louis IX. took the government into his own hands; but she again took up the regency in 1248, when her son set forth on his crusade. She died in 1252, before St. Louis came home from his ill-starred expedition.

So deep was the respect entertained for the memory of Blanche of Castille, that many of the queen-dowagers of France assumed the surname of Blanche, as the Roman emperors took the title of Augustus.

Until the thirteenth century, Prussia was inhabited by heathen barbarians. In 1226, Conrad of Masovia gave the Teutonic Knights a strip of land on the Vistula, that they might protect Poland from the Prussian savages. For more than half a century the knights carried on a war of extermination against the natives; again, and again were the Prussian tribes vanquished, again and again they rebelled. In 1240 a general insurrection of greater magnitude burst forth, and nearly all the knights were massacred.

Those who escaped—principally the Knights of the Cross—took refuge in the castles of Thorn, Reden, and Culm, where they were soon beleaguered by the Prussians. The knights in Culm were induced by a stratagem to come out, when they fell into an ambuscade, and were all slain. The city would have fallen had not the women closed the gates, clad themselves in mail, and mounted the walls with spears in their hands. The Prussians, deceived by this stratagem, withdrew their forces, believing that Culm was still strongly garrisoned by sturdy knights.

Prussia was at last converted to Christianity, and adopted the manners and customs of Germany, of which it is now the leading State.

The contests between the Guelfs and Ghibelines proved fatal to Italian liberty. Might became right, tyrants arose on every side, and either by open force or by fraud, possessed themselves of the sovereign power in some one of the Lombardian cities and the adjacent territories. The various military leaders, whether Italians or Germans, were mere freebooters, accountable to no one for their acts, permitting the utmost license to themselves and their followers. One of the most infamous of these mercenaries was Acciolin, who was not a brutal and rapacious robber, but a man of refined cruelty. His favourite mode of torture was to fasten his prisoners to half-putrefied corpses, and leave the living and the dead to rot away together. In 1253, this fiend in human shape captured Bassano by storm, after a tiresome siege. The garrison was commanded by John Baptista de Porta, who was either governor or lord of the place.

Blanche de Rossi, his wife, a native of Padua, put on armour, mounted the ramparts, and fought by the side of her husband. When the town fell the governor was slain, and Blanche, after making a desperate resistance, was made prisoner and led in triumph before Acciolin. Directly the villain set eyes upon his beautiful captive, he was seized with a violent passion for her; and to escape him, she sprang, clad as she was in armour, through a window. But in place of death, she only met with a sprained shoulder. Directly she recovered from her swoon the tyrant sent for her again, and finding his renewed protestations were repulsed with loathing, he obtained by force what was denied to his prayers. Blanche then withdrew to the place where her husband's body had been thrown, and flinging herself into the open grave, was crushed to death by the falling earth and stones.

In the year 1333, King Edward III., espousing the cause of Edward Baliol, invaded Scotland. The Battle of Hallidon Hill, July 29th, in which the Regent Douglas was defeated, placed Baliol on the throne; and Edward, carried away by his ambitious designs upon the French throne, left his army in charge of the Earls of Arundel and Salisbury, and returned to England. Montague, Earl of Salisbury, laid siege to the castle of Dunbar, a place of great importance, esteemed as the key of Scotland, on the south-east border.

It had been fortified very recently; and in the absence of the Earl of March, was defended by the countess, who, from the dark colour of her complexion, was popularly styled "Black Agnes." She was the daughter of Randolph, Earl of Moray, and inherited from her father a fierce, intrepid spirit. During the five months' siege she performed all the duties of a bold and skilful commander, and the garrison had the utmost confidence in her abilities. Constantly on the ramparts, she derided the English with biting sarcasms. When the battering-engines hurled stones against the walls, she scornfully told one of her female attendants to wipe off the dust with her handkerchief.

The Earl of Salisbury knew well the kind of foe he had to deal with. One day he was superintending the siege operations, when an arrow from the castle whizzed past and struck a knight who stood by, piercing through his chain-mail haubergeon, and killing him on the spot.

"There comes one of my lady's tire-pins," exclaimed the Earl. "Agnes's love-shafts go straight to the heart!"

A monster called the "sow," a huge engine covered with hides, somewhat resembling the *testudo* of the Romans, was at last rolled to the foot of the walls. When the countess saw this ponderous machine coming, she cried in a loud, mocking voice:—

"Montague, beware! your sow shall soon cast her pigs!"

She quickly verified her words by hurling an immense piece of rock upon the "sow," crushing both it and its occupants to pieces.

Salisbury finding he could not succeed by fair means, bribed the gate-keeper to leave the gates open on the following night. The porter disclosed this to the countess, who directed him to keep to his bargain and say nothing about it. The earl, who commanded the party that were to seize the castle, rode through the darkness at the head of his soldiers, found the gates open according to agreement, and was about to enter, when one of his men, John Copeland, passed in front of him. The portcullis was suddenly dropped; Copeland, mistaken for his master, remained a prisoner. The earl was saved by his men, who dragged him back just in time. Agnes, from a high turret, saw that the general had escaped.

"Farewell, Montague!" she cried. "I intended that you should have supped with us tonight, and assisted in defending the fortress against the English."

Salisbury, despairing of being able to take the place, either by treachery or by storm, turned the siege into a blockade, closely investing the castle by sea and land, and tried to starve the garrison out into a surrender. Alexander Ramsay, hearing of the extremities to which Black Agnes was reduced, embarked with a party of forty resolute men, eluded the vigilance of the English, and entered the castle, under cover of night, by a postern next the sea. Sallying out again, they attacked and dispersed the advanced guard of the besiegers. Salisbury, disheartened by so many reverses, withdrew his forces, after having remained before Dunbar for nineteen weeks.

About this time the duchy of Brittany was the subject of contention between two rivals, John, Count de Montfort, son of the late duke, and Charles of Blois, who had married the duke's granddaughter. Philip de Valois, King of France, decided the dispute in favour of Charles, and despatched a large army to establish him in the capital. Edward III., of England, at once declared for the Count de Montfort, as an enemy to the house of Valois, which he—King Edward—wished to drive from the throne of France.

The count was betrayed into the hands of his rival by some malcontent nobles. But Jane, the brave countess, sustained his sinking fortunes "with the courage of a man and the heart of a lion." Directly the news of her husband's capture arrived at Rennes, where she resided, the countess assembled the citizens, showed them her infant son, and entreated them not to desert the last male heir of their ancient dukes. Her eloquence, beauty, and courage produced a magical effect. The people swore to defend her and her son to the last extremity.

The countess next visited all the strongholds throughout Brittany, and excited the people to resist the French, and to adopt the requisite measures of defence. Then, sending her boy to England, she shut herself up in Hennebonne, and there awaited the reinforcements promised by King Edward.

Charles of Blois entered Brittany, captured Rennes, and despatched a force, commanded by Prince Louis of Spain, to besiege Hennebonne. The garrison, animated by the presence of the valiant countess, made a resolute defence. Jane herself performed prodigies of valour. Clad in armour from head to foot, she stood foremost in the breach, sustaining every attack of the foe with the utmost *sang froid*, or ran from post to post, according as the troops required encouragement or reinforcement.

One day the besiegers, engaged in an attack on the town, left their camp totally unprotected. The countess, perceiving their neglect, sallied forth by a postern-gate at the head of five hundred picked men, set fire to the enemy's baggage and magazines, and created such universal alarm that the besiegers gave over their assault on the town to intercept her return. Jane, seeing that her retreat was cut off that way, galloped towards Arrai, where she arrived in safety. In five days she returned, cut her way through the camp of Charles, and re-entered the town.

By this time, however, the breaches in the walls had grown so numerous that the place was deemed untenable. The bishop of Léon, despite the entreaties, the prayers of Jane, resolved to capitulate, and opened negotiations with the enemy. Jane mounted the highest turret and turned her eyes towards the sea, with a last hope of seeing her deliverers. She descried some small specks far away in the distance. Rushing down into the street, she cried, with transports of joy:—

Succours! Succours! The English succours! No capitulation!

The English fleet soon entered the harbour, and a small but valiant body of English, headed by the chivalrous Sir Walter Manny, cast themselves into the town. The negotiations were at once broken off, and the besiegers, balked of their prey, renewed the attack with more determined vigour than ever.

Sir Walter and his companions were at dinner with the countess when a huge mass of stone crashed through the roof of an adjoining house, terrifying the ladies assembled in the castle hall. Starting from his seat. Sir Walter vowed to destroy the terrible engine which had thrown this missile. In a few moments the English sallied forth, hewed the monster catapult in pieces, burned the sow, and threw the enemy's camp into confusion. The foe, recovering from their first astonishment, tried to surround the returning warriors; but the English knights stood their ground till the archers and men-at-arms had recrossed the ditch. Then driving back their assailants they crossed the draw-bridge, and were received with acclamations by the townspeople, while the countess herself "came down from the castle to meet them, and with a most cheerful countenance kissed Sir Walter and all his companions, one after another, like a noble and valiant dame."

Prince Louis abandoned his camp the same evening, and retired to that of Prince Charles before the Castle of Arrai.

Charles, though unsuccessful in his attack on Hennebonne, soon became master of nearly the whole of Brittany. During the truce between England and France, the Countess de Montfort came to London, and asked King Edward to grant her further assistance. He commanded Robert of Artois to return with her, accompanied by a strong force, to Brittany. They encountered the French fleet near Guernsey; and during the engagement Jane displayed her accustomed bravery. The contending fleets were at last separated by a storm, and the English sailed to Brittany, took Vannes by storm, and massacred, not only the garrison, but even the townspeople. The French soon recaptured the town, when Robert of Artois was slain.

Edward III. landed in Brittany in 1345, with twelve thousand men, but was not at first very successful. In June he was obliged to conclude a short truce with France, during which the Count de Montfort was set at liberty; but he died of a fever on Sept. 20th, when his son John was proclaimed duke. At the end of July, 1346, the English invaded Normandy. The Countess de Montfort, assisted by an English force under Sir Thomas Dagworth, defeated Charles of Blois, who was made prisoner.

Charles was set free in May, 1360, when peace was concluded between France and England. The treaty, though it did not interfere with Brittany, brought about an arrangement some months later, by which the duchy was divided between the rival claimants.

But Charles broke faith, and renewed hostilities with the assistance of France. The struggle was at last decided in favour of the Count de Montfort, by the death of Charles and his son John, both of whom were slain in the Battle of Arrai, gained by the English, September 20th, 1364, the same day of the month on which his rival died.

The French heroine of this war was Julia du Guesclin, sister of the great Constable. When the English invaded Brittany to support the Count de Montfort, Julia, who was living with her sisters in a convent, was obliged to take refuge in the fortress of Pontsorel, which was soon besieged by the English. The garrison was small and the besiegers were many, but Julia, with a courage worthy of her brother Bertrand, persuaded the French not to surrender.

Clad in a coat of mail (one of her brother's) she stood on the ramparts and hurled back all who attempted to scale the walls. Animated by her courage, the French made so sturdy a defence that the English were compelled to retire, discomfited. Julia then commanded the garrison to throw open the gates and pursue the foe. The retreating army, confronted unexpectedly by a strong force commanded by the Constable himself, who was returning to Pontsorel, and surrounded on all sides, were nearly all slain, while their commander was made prisoner.

When the war was over, Julia returned to her convent, where she passed the rest of her days.

Another heroine of this war was Jane de Belleville. Her husband, Oliver, Lord of Clisson, was accused of holding secret intelligence with the English; and in 1343 Philip de Valois, without waiting till the evidence should be well substantiated, caused him to be decapitated. The widow, burning for revenge, sold her jewels, and with the proceeds equipped three vessels. After sending her son, a lad of twelve, to England, to ensure his safety, Jane cruised about the coast of Normandy, attacking every French ship which came in her way, and ravaging the country for a mile or so inland. This female *corsair* was frequently seen, with a sword in one hand and a torch in the other, amidst the smoking ruins of a castle, or the smouldering heaps of a destroyed village, directing with inhuman exultation the ferocious cruelties suggested by her thirst for vengeance.

While King Edward and Philip de Valois were devastating France in their contests for the crown, the Romagna was the scene of a fierce struggle between the Pope, the Visconti, and the various nobles and cities of Italy. After having lost a great part of his territories, Innocent II.

reconquered the States of the Church by means of the Cardinal Legate Egidius Albornez. But the Papal governors were so tyrannical that the nobles of the Romagna, with few exceptions, fought desperately to maintain their independence. Francesco d'Ordelaffi, lord of Forli, was the last to give way. He was ably seconded in his brave resistance by Marzia, his wife, a member of the house of Ubaldini.

While he was defending Forli, he entrusted the town of Cesena to his wife, and in the beginning of 1357 the husband and wife separated. Marzia took up her station in Cesena, with a garrison of two hundred knights and an equal number of common soldiers. She was accompanied by her son and daughter, and by Sgariglino de Petragudula, the wise counsellor of the Ordelaffi family.

The town was soon invested by a force ten times as numerous as the garrison. At the end of April some terrified burgesses opened the gates of the lower town. But Marzia, recollecting the words of her husband, who declared that unless the Pope offered him honourable terms he would sustain a siege in every one of his castles, that when they were all taken he would defend Forli, the walls, the streets, his own palace, even to the last tower of his palace, before surrendering his rights, retreated to the upper town with those soldiers and townspeople who remained faithful. Sgariglino having proved to be a traitor, she caused him to be executed; his reeking head was flung from the battlements amongst the besiegers.

Marzia took upon herself all the duties of governor and military commander. She wore her helmet and *cuirass* day and night, and scarcely closed her eyes at all. At last she was compelled to retire into the citadel with four hundred soldiers and citizens who swore to stand by her to the death. But the citadel, undermined by the Papal engineers, almost hung in the air. Marzia's father, permitted by the legate, entered Cesena and besought her to surrender. Her answer was firm and simple. Her husband gave her a duty to perform, and she must obey implicitly.

At last the people began to murmur. Marzia was compelled to surrender. She conducted the negotiations herself; and so skilfully did she manage, that the Legate, afraid of driving her to despair, consented that her soldiers should return home unmolested, with their arms and accoutrements. On the 21st of June she opened the gate of the citadel.

She had disdained to make terms for herself, so the legate cast Marzia and her children into prison.

It is curious to note that there are now no remains of Cesena to commemorate the heroic valour of Marzia.

The illustrious northern heroine, Margaret, whose military achievements gained for her the title of "Semiramis of the North," was daughter of Waldemar, King of Denmark, and was born at Copenhagen in 1353. On the death of her father, Margaret, through her exceeding popularity with the people, succeeded in placing Olaus, her son, on the throne. Haquin, King of Norway, Margaret's husband, died in 1380, and Olaus in 1387. The election of a female sovereign was not yet authorised by custom; but Margaret's superior talents, her beauty, and her profuse liberality prevailed, and she was chosen Queen of Denmark, and, soon after, she was elected Queen of Norway.

By taking advantage of the internal dissensions in the kingdom of Sweden, Margaret gained over a faction of the nobility, who offered her the crown. She marched into Sweden with a large army, and after a war of seven years defeated and captured King Albert at Falkoeping. She kept him a prisoner seven years longer, at the expiration of which he resigned all claim to the Swedish crown.

To effect a permanent union of the three Scandinavian crowns, Queen Margaret concluded the famous Union of Calmar, 1397. She restored tranquillity at home, and was successful against all her enemies abroad; but her latter years were disturbed by the ingratitude of Eric, whom she had chosen as her successor. She died in 1412.

According to Border tradition, a Scottish maiden named Lilliard fought at the Battle of Otterburn ("Chevy Chase") on the 19th of August, 1388, and displayed the same style of valour attributed to the gallant Witherington, who fell in the same battle. It is said that the following inscription was, till within a few years ago, to be seen on her tombstone:—

Fair Maiden Lilliard lies under this stane,
Little was her stature, but great was her fame,
On the English lads she laid many thumps,
And when her legs were off, she fought upon her stumps.

One of the most faithful adherents of Henry Bolingbroke in his days of adversity was Sir John de Pelham, who had been squire to old John of Gaunt. When Lancaster was banished by King Richard, Pelham followed him abroad, leaving Pevensey Castle in charge of his wife, Lady Joan. Sir John was one of the fifteen lances who disembarked at Ravenspur, in July, 1399, with Henry; and on the 4th of the same month, while he was sharing the fatigues and perils of what seemed then a rash enterprise, the partisans of Richard II. laid siege to Pevensey castle. Lady Joan, a noble and spirited woman, took upon herself the conduct of the defence, and directed all the efforts of the garrison with such prudence and decision that the besiegers were forced to retire.

When the Duke of Lancaster ascended the throne as Henry IV., he remembered the services of his faithful adherents. Sir John de Pelham was created a Knight of the Bath, and appointed royal sword-bearer, treasurer-at-war, and chief butler to the king. The king further displayed his confidence in Sir John by sending James I. of Scotland as a prisoner to Pevensey castle. The courage of Lady Joan was also publicly recognised and applauded.

Eric, Margaret's successor on the Scandinavian throne, proved to be a very inferior ruler to his illustrious aunt. Nearly all his reign was taken up with an inglorious war for the Duchy of Schleswig. The quarrel was decided in favour of Denmark by the Emperor Sigismund; but the Count of Holstein refused to accept the imperial decree, and the war waxed fiercer every day. The Hanseatic League, whose fleet then ruled the Baltic, joined the alliance against Denmark; and in 1428 a powerful armament, commanded by Count Gerard of Holstein, invested Copenhagen. The city would doubtless have fallen but for the courage of Eric's queen, Philippa, who was the daughter of Henry IV. of England. Throwing herself into the city, the queen, by her exhortations and example, inspired the garrison with such enthusiasm and patriotic fervour, that the foe were compelled to retire discomfited.

Elated by her success, Philippa now resolved to carry the war into the enemy's country. So, while Eric was endeavouring to gather reinforcements of men and money in Sweden, the queen, with a fleet of seventy-five sail, invested Stralsund. But this time fortune was against the heroine. The Danish Navy was almost entirely destroyed in a great sea-fight. Eric, without reflecting that he had himself suffered many a worse defeat, flew into a rage when he heard of this disaster; and carried away by his blind fury, he even struck the queen. The high-spirited Philippa, unable to forgive this brutality, retired to a convent, where she died shortly after.

Chapter 7

Jeanne d'Arc, the Maid of Orleans to Caterina Sforza

At the beginning of the fifteenth century there dwelt in the little village of Domremy, on the banks of the Meuse, Jacques d'Arc, or Darc, a peasant, and Isabeau Romie, his wife. Though comparatively poor, they had the respect of their neighbours as being a hardworking, honest couple. They had three sons and two daughters, all of whom were bred, like their parents, to humble occupations. Joan, Jeanne, or Jehanne was born according to different writers, in 1402, 1410, or 1412.

She was exceedingly beautiful, with fine expressive features, and jet-black hair. She was about the middle height, with a delicately moulded frame. Her education was the same as that of most peasant-girls, French or English, in those days—spinning, sewing, and repeating her Paternoster and Ave Maria. From her infancy Jeanne was employed in various duties, the chief of which was driving the cattle to and from pasture. She was of a religious, imaginative disposition, and as early as her thirteenth year began to indulge those superstitious reveries which afterwards made her famous.

Although her gentleness caused her to be universally beloved, she shunned girls of her own age, and took but little interest in the amusements of others. While her young friends were playing under the "Fairies' Tree" near the fountain of Domremy, Jeanne was dancing and singing by herself in pious fervour, or weaving garlands for the Holy Virgin in the small chapel of Notre Dame de Bellemont.

The villagers of Domremy were, without exception, staunch Royalists, while those of the neighbouring hamlet were zealous Burgundians. A very bitter hostility prevailed between the rival parties. On one occasion a band of troopers invaded Domremy and drove all the people from their homes. The family of Jeanne found shelter for a few days at an inn; whence arose the mistake of the English chroniclers, who state that the maiden was in early life an innkeeper's servant.

For a quarter of a century, France had been torn by civil war, and the death of Charles VI. in 1422 plunged the country into hopeless confusion and anarchy. According to the Treaty of Troyes (concluded in 1420), Henry VI. of England was proclaimed King of France, which his uncle, the Duke of Bedford, governed as regent. Queen Isabella and the Duke of Burgundy joined England; and the *Dauphin*, abandoned by his own mother, had a very small party indeed. The English Army was commanded by several brave and talented warriors—the Earls of Salisbury, Somerset, Warwick, Suffolk, Shrewsbury, Arundel, and many gallant knights.

The *Dauphin*, at the age of nineteen, was crowned at Poitiers, as Charles VII. On the 12th of October, 1428, the Earl of Salisbury laid siege to Orleans, the last stronghold of any importance held by the Royalists. It was bravely defended by Glaucour, Lahyre, and Dunois. Repeated messages were sent to the king imploring assistance. The city was naturally strong, and well-garrisoned, but the English commenced an elaborate system of counter-fortification, and cut off the supplies of the besieged.

Jeanne d'Arc watched with eager anxiety the siege of Orleans. Even as a child she had learned to detest the English; and now she felt herself commanded by frequent visions and supernatural admonitions, to undertake the deliverance of her king and country. Believing firmly that Heaven destined her to save France, she refused more than one advantageous offer of marriage. In February, 1429, being then, according to the most reliable authorities, barely eighteen, she was commanded by a vision of Our Lady to raise the siege of Orleans, and afterwards conduct Charles to Rheims to be crowned in state.

She presented herself before Robert de Baudricourt, governor of Vaucoulour, a town situated a few miles from Domremy, and related her mission. Believing her to be insane, the governor twice sent her away, threatening the second time to box her ears; but when she returned a third time he thought it best to send her with letters of recommendation to the *Dauphin*, at Chinon, in Touraine.

The fame of Jeanne d'Arc preceded her; and the king awaited with impatience the arrival of his extraordinary visitor. Although Charles disguised himself and mixed with his courtiers, Jeanne singled him out at once, and addressed him as king of France.

After being subjected to the most severe examination during three weeks, by divines, counsellors of parliament and learned men, the king was satisfied that her story was true, and consented to accept her aid. She was furnished with a suit of armour, and armed with a sword marked on the blade with five crosses, taken by her directions from the tomb of an old warrior in the church of St. Catherine at Fierbois. In company with several nobles she was sent to the camp at Blois, thirty-five miles from Orleans. Her presence produced the most miraculous effect upon the drooping spirits of the soldiers.

The French generals resolved now to make some great effort for the relief of Orleans; and ten thousand men, commanded by St. Severre, Lahyre, and the veteran Dunois were despatched to its aid. Most of the soldiers retreated in dismay when they saw the strong towers of the besiegers, but La Pucelle, followed by a small party, forced her way through the English camp, and entered Orleans on the 29th of April, 1429. She was clad in armour and mounted on a snow-white horse; her head was bare, and the long raven tresses, parted across her forehead, were tied at the back with ribbon. In her right hand she grasped a lance; by her side hung the consecrated sword and a small battle-axe.

On the 4th of May a sortie was made against the English bastille of St. Loup, but the French were driven back with great slaughter. Jeanne, hearing the noise of the fight, mounted her horse and galloped to the spot, when she rode into the midst of the battle. The French, re-animated by her presence, again charged the English, drove them back, and captured the bastille.

After this first success the rest was comparatively easy. On the 6th and 7th the remaining bastilles on the south bank of the Loire were carried by storm. The most important, that at the head of the bridge, defended by Sir William Gladsdale with five thousand picked men, yielded after an attack of fourteen hours. During the attack on this tower, Jeanne, having placed a ladder against the walls, was attempting to scale the battlements, when she was struck in the neck by an arrow. She plucked out the weapon immediately, but the loss of blood compelled her to leave the field. However, when she heard that her absence dispirited the soldiers, she insisted upon returning to the scene of action.

The Earl of Salisbury died during the siege; and the Earl of Suffolk, who succeeded to the command, raised the siege on the 8th of May, and beat a hasty retreat.

Jeanne d'Arc, the "Heaven-sent Maid," had now fully entered upon her extraordinary career of victory. The universal belief in her elevated mission—as much amongst the English as the French—produced marvellous results. Resolute and chivalrous, pious and gentle, she won the hearts of all,—even the roughest and most sceptical veterans. However, it was only in matters of moral discipline that she was implicitly obeyed; oaths or foul language were severely censured when they reached her ears. She compelled the entire army, generals and soldiers alike, to attend regularly at confession; and at every halt she ordered an altar to be established and the Holy Sacrament administered. But the generals, while they skilfully employed her to animate the soldiers, did not implicitly follow her counsels in military matters.

Her tactics were very simple, she said:

I used to say to them 'go boldly in among the English,' and then
I used to go boldly in myself.

Her duties were chiefly confined to bearing at the head of the army the consecrated sword and the sacred banner—the latter made of white satin, *semée* with *fleurs-de-lis*, with the words "Jesus Maria," and a representation of Our Saviour in his glory embroidered on its surface. Her conduct was never stained by unfeminine cruelty. It appears from the documents relative to her trial, that, although she was herself wounded many a time, she never shed the blood of anyone. Some French historians, however, aver that she did sometimes, when hard pressed, use the consecrated sword as a weapon of offence.

When the Earl of Suffolk retired from before Orleans he established his headquarters at Méhun-sur-Loire, and afterwards at Jargeau. Jeanne hastened to Tours, where Charles was residing with his court, and urged him at once to go to Rheims to be crowned. The royal advisers, however, were afraid to venture on such a step when Rheims itself, together with all the intermediate towns, was still held by the English. The French next attacked the towns in possession of the English on the banks of the Loire. During the assault on Jargeau, which was taken by storm, La Pucelle, leading on the French, was seen on the highest step of one of the scaling-ladders, waving her banner over her head. A stone from the English engines struck her so violent a blow on the head, that her helmet was shattered, and she fell heavily to the foot of the wall. Rising on the instant, she cried:—

Amis, amis! sus, sus! Notre Seigneur a condamné les Anglais. Ils sont à nous. Bon courage!

("Friends, friends! sus, sus! Our Lord condemned the English. They are ours. Good luck!)

The Earl of Suffolk was made prisoner during the assault.

Beaugency and Méhun capitulated shortly after the fall of Jargeau; and the English, commanded by Talbot, Earl of Shrewsbury, the "English Achilles," retreated towards Paris. They were pursued and overtaken in April, 1429, at Patai, by the Maid of Orleans. Sir John Fastolfe, one of the bravest knights of his day (whatever Shakespeare may declare to the contrary), advised Talbot to continue his retreat with all speed; but the earl scorned to fly before his enemies, even though, as on this occasion, they were twice as numerous as his own men. The English, struck with a superstitious dread of La Pucelle, fled, after making little resistance; and Talbot, after losing twelve hundred men, was captured. Eight hundred English were slain in the pursuit. Sir John Fastolfe, with a prudence long stigmatised as rank cowardice, continued his retreat to Paris, where he arrived safely without the loss of a man.

Jeanne now insisted that the royal coronation should be no longer delayed. Every obstacle vanished at her approach. Troyes, Chalons, and other cities in rapid succession opened their gates; the people of Rheims expelled the English garrison, and Charles entered in triumph, July 16th, 1429. The consecration took place next day in the cathedral. The Maid stood by the side of Charles, clad in armour; and, taking the office of High Constable, held the sword over the king's head.

Her mission being now concluded, Jeanne d'Arc entreated the king's permission to "return to her father and mother, to keep her flocks and herds as before, and do all things as she was wont to do;" but her presence was considered so necessary to animate the troops, that she was prevailed upon to stay. In September, Jeanne was wounded in an unsuccessful attack on Paris, when she requested, a second time, to be allowed to retire from the war. But she was again overruled. In December, a patent of nobility was conferred upon her; she was first styled Dalis, then Dulis, and finally Dy Lys. Her coat of arms contained two golden lilies and a sword, pointing upwards, bearing a crown. She obtained for the villages of Domremy and Greux an exemption from taxation, which they enjoyed until the equalisation of public imposts in 1789.

In the spring of 1429, the Duke of Burgundy besieged Compiegne. Jeanne d'Arc threw herself into the town on the 21st of May. Believing that her presence now would work the same miracles as of old, she insisted, the evening of her arrival, that the garrison should make a sortie. After some hard fighting the French took to flight. Jeanne took the command of the rear-guard, and tried to rally her countrymen. A Burgundian archer pulled her from her horse; and while lying on the ground she was obliged to surrender to Lyonnel, the Bastard of Vendôme. There is good reason for supposing that Guillaume de Flavy, governor of the fortress, envious of her military renown, betrayed Jeanne into the hands of her enemies.

The English purchased Jeanne from the Duke of Burgundy for ten thousand *livres*; and Henry VI. also settled an annuity of three hundred *francs* upon her captor. Through many weary months the Maid of Orleans dragged out a miserable existence in a dungeon. In place of being treated as a prisoner of war, she was handed over to ecclesiastical justice, charged with heresy and blasphemy. At the instigation of several Frenchmen a process was instituted by the Bishop of Beauvais, in whose diocese she had been captured. The process lasted three months and had sixteen sittings. Jeanne denied resolutely the accusations of sorcery and witchcraft, and named St. Michael, St. Margaret, and St. Catherine as the bearers of the heavenly messages.

The Bishop's Court, representing the Church and the University of Paris, condemned Jeanne d'Arc as a sorceress and a heretic. Charles VII. made little or no efforts to save her; and after four months' imprisonment, the innocent enthusiast was sentenced to be burned alive at Rouen. She was cut off from the Church, and delivered to the secular judges.

On the 24th of May, 1431, she was carried to the stake, which had been erected in the Vieux Marche of Rouen. At sight of the pile her courage deserted her. She submitted to the Church, and confessed that her visions were the work of Satan. Her punishment was commuted to imprisonment for life, but it was not considered expedient to let her live; so, she was condemned as a relapsed heretic, and dragged to the stake. May 30th. She was dressed in female attire; and on her head was a mitre, covered with the words *"Apostate," "Relapse," "Idolâtre," "Hérétique."*

She met her fate this time with terrible calmness. While they were putting the cap on her head, she said to one of the Dominican friars who stood by her side:—

> *Maître, par la grâce de Dieu, je serai ce soir en paradis.*

(Master, by the grace of God, I will be tonight in paradise.)

Falling on her knees, she prayed fervently for a few moments, not for herself only, but for the ungrateful king who had so cruelly deserted her. The judges, even the stern Bishop of Beauvais, were moved to tears. She was burned by a slow fire, and the pile was so high that her agony lasted for a considerable time. Her ashes were gathered together and flung into the Seine.

There is a legend that, as she expired, a white, dove rose from the flames. Another tradition says that after her ashes were removed, the heart was found entire.

The Rouen theatre now occupies that part of the public square on which the stake was erected. It was remarked as a curious coincidence that when Soumet's tragedy of *Jeanne d'Arc* was performed at Rouen, in the autumn of 1865, the last act, which represents the death of the Maid, was played on the identical spot where the real tragedy had been enacted in 1431.

Jeanne's father died of grief at her cruel fate; her mother survived for many years, supported by a pension from the city of Orleans. In 1436 an impostor started up, who pretended to be the Maid of Orleans, giving a plausible account of her escape. She was for some time successful, being acknowledged, even by the brothers, as the heroine herself. Within the last few years this idea of Jeanne's escape has been revived. Many French writers assert that there is ample documentary evidence to prove that the Maid of Orleans lived to be comfortably married, while another girl took her place at the stake. This notion is gaining ground, both in France and England.

Among all the divines who condemned Jeanne, there was only one Englishman—the Bishop of Winchester, Cardinal Beaufort.

In 1450 and 1451 measures were taken to revise the process of condemnation. In 1456 a court, presided over by the Archbishop of Rheims and the Bishops of Paris and Coutance, decided that Jeanne d'Arc was entirely innocent, and declared her to have been falsely condemned.

The citizens of Orleans celebrate the annual Festival of Jeanne d'Arc on the 8th of May; the villagers of Domremy hold an annual *fête* on the 6th of January, the birthday of the heroine. It is said that the girls of the village have so much military esprit that they will hardly deign to look upon a lover who has not served some years in the wars.

The memory of Jeanne d'Arc has been preserved in France by

several monuments. Louis XI. erected a figure of the heroine in front of her father's house; and in September, 1820, another memorial was raised in Domremy, with Jeanne's bust carved in marble. In the market-place of Rouen stands another figure of the Maid. In front of the *Mairie* of Orleans is a statue, modelled by the Princess Marie, daughter of the Citizen King. In April, 1855, a colossal equestrian figure was uncovered in one of the public squares of Orleans, on the exact spot where she animated the French soldiers to attack the foe. It was remarked as a sign of the times that not only the English flag, but also the Turkish crescent stood out prominently from amongst the numberless standards which surrounded the monument.

It has lately been proposed by the Bishop of Orleans, the Cardinal Archbishop of Rouen, and others, to add Jeanne d'Arc to the calendar of French saints. Shakespeare may thus prove once more a prophet; he has put into the mouth of King Charles, the words:—

No longer on Saint Denis will we cry,
But Joan la Pucelle shall be France's saint.

During the fourteenth and fifteenth centuries Italy was terribly harassed by bands of mercenary soldiers, who sought service in every war, and fought neither through patriotism nor for the love of glory, but merely for pay and the opportunity of plunder. These bands, who counted their numbers by hundreds or thousands, according to the reputation of the *Condottiere* (leader) under whom they fought, offered their services to the prince or city that paid them best, without regard to law or justice. Many of the *Condottieri*, such as the Count of Werner, Montreal, Bracchia de Montone, and Francesco Sforza, became famous throughout Italy, not only as able generals, but sometimes even as skilful statesmen; yet, mostly they were ignorant, brutal men, with nothing to recommend them beyond reckless bravery.

Sforza had a sister named Margaret de Attendoli, who shared his warlike spirit and enterprising courage. The family was of humble origin, but through the military genius of Francesco it rose, by rapid strides, to the highest rank and eminence. Before he assumed the sovereignty of Milan, Sforza was grand-constable of Naples; and in this capacity, he was sent to meet the Count de la Marche, the betrothed husband of the Neapolitan queen. The count, dreading the power of Sforza, caused him to be cast into prison, with many of his relations. Sforza's sister was at Tricario with her husband, Michael de Cotignola, when the intelligence of Francesco's arrest reached her.

The relatives speedily assembled an army, Margaret took the command, and a revolt began. According as the Count de la Marche grew more brutal towards his queen and more despotic to her subjects, the insurrection became more general; and at last Count Jaques was besieged in his castle. The besiegers demanded that Sforza should be set at liberty, and that the count should be content with the title of lieutenant-general of the kingdom; but he, knowing the value of his prisoner as a hostage, sent threatening messages to Margaret, demanding that Tricario should be given up, unless she would wish to be the cause of her brother's death. Margaret, indignant at the proposal, took the bold step of imprisoning the deputies, whose families, alarmed for their safety, importuned the count night and day, till he consented to set Sforza at liberty, and reinstate him in all his honours.

Female *Condottieri* were by no means uncommon in those days; and some of the women acquired celebrity, even beyond the Italian borders, for their prowess and military skill. The story of one of these female soldiers is interesting.

About the year 1432, Captain Brunoro, a Parmesan gentleman by birth, and a *Condottiere* by profession, was appointed by Piccinio, the Milanese general (who had just driven the Venetians from Vatellina), to maintain a camp in Morbego, as a central position whence he could command the conquered territory. While thus employed, he occupied his leisure time with hunting, and various open-air amusements. One day, being tired, he stopped to rest in a sylvan grove, where some peasants were celebrating a rustic festival. Doubtless there were many pretty faces there; but one amongst them struck him more than all the rest. He entered into conversation with this pretty girl, who charmed and surprised him by her lively, spirited answers.

On his return home he learned that the pretty peasant was quite a celebrity in the neighbourhood. Her name was Bona Lombardi (or, as some give it, Longobarba), and she was born in 1417, in the little village of Sacco, in Vatellina. She was the only daughter of humble people, of whom little is known except that her father, Gabriel Lombardi, was a private soldier in one of the Italian armies, and died while Bona was a child. Her mother did not long survive; and the little girl was left to the care of her uncle, a poor priest, and her aunt, an industrious countrywoman.

Captain Brunoro remained in Morbego during the summer, and had thus frequent opportunities for meeting with Bona Lombardi. At last he decided that she was the woman of all others to make him happy, and they were married. The marriage was kept secret for some time; but to avoid even a temporary separation. Bona dressed herself in the costume of a *Condottiere*, and accompanied her husband in all his expeditions.

Like all *Condottieri* Brunoro was obliged to adopt various masters; and thus, he very often found himself opposed to one of his former employers. Once he made an enemy of Alexander, King of Naples, who took him prisoner by means of an ambuscade, and cast him into prison. He would probably have ended his days in a Neapolitan dungeon, but for the untiring efforts of his wife. Money, entreaties, threats, all were employed; till at last she procured his release.

Bona learned the art of war to perfection. Her courage and military skill were so highly esteemed by the Venetians that they confided to her and her husband the defence of Negropont, against the Turks, who in those days were dreaded by the Christians as much as the Goths and Vandals were in ancient times. More than once she displayed valour and prudence of a superior order. During the Milanese war, the Venetians having been repulsed in an attack upon the Castle of Provoze, in Brescia, Brunoro was captured. Bona arrived soon after with a small body of fresh troops. Rallying the discomfited Venetians, she led them in person to a second assault on the castle. This time they were successful, and Bona had the pleasure of releasing her husband with the rest of the prisoners.

Brunoro died in 1468, and Bona Lombardi, declaring that she could not survive her husband, built a tomb for the reception of their mutual remains. When it was finished, she sank into a state of languor, from which she never recovered.

Onerata Rodiana, another female *Condottieri*, was, in addition, a celebrated painter. She was born, in the early part of the fifteenth century, at Castelleone, and while yet a girl her reputation as a painter became so great that the Marquis Gabrinio, tyrant of Cremona, engaged her to decorate his palace.

One day, while thus occupied, a dissipated courtier, who happened to see her painting the walls of a room, attempted to take liberties. A struggle ensued, which was terminated by Onerata drawing a stiletto and stabbing her antagonist. She then fled from the palace, disguised herself in male attire, and quitted the city. Meeting with the band of Oldrado Sampuynano, the *Condottiere*, she enlisted under his banner.

The marquis was furious when he discovered the flight of his court-painter, and he despatched soldiers in pursuit. Soon relenting, however, he issued a proclamation, in which he promised full pardon on condition that Onerata would return to her professional labours. But she preferred the life of a soldier, so she remained with her new comrades. By her courage she soon rose to the post of captain; and for thirty years she led the roving life of a free-lance, painting and fighting alternately. When Castelleone, her native town, was besieged by the Venetians in 1472, she hastened with her band to its assistance. She was victorious; but during the action she fell, mortally wounded.

In those days the Grecian isles were a constant subject of contention between Venice and the Turks. The latter, growing stronger every day, soon made their name the terror of southern Europe. A few years after the fall of Constantinople (captured by Mohammed II. in 1453), the Ottomans besieged Coccino, capital of the isle of Lemnos, in the Ægean Sea. The city was defended with the most obstinate bravery by the inhabitants, men and women.

Amongst the bravest of the women was Marulla, a beautiful, noble-looking creature, barely in her twentieth year. Her father, Demetrius, slew such numbers of the Turks that the gateway was half-blocked up with turbaned corpses. At last, pierced with myriad wounds, he fell on the bodies of his foes. Marulla, flying to her father's rescue, was wounded by the same blow which proved fatal to him; but so far from giving way to useless lamentations, she seized his sword, sprang from the walls, and fiercely attacked the Turks. Her fellow-citizens, inspired by her fire, drove the Turks away with terrific slaughter, and compelled them to take refuge in their ships.

When the Venetian admiral arrived next day with the fleet, in place of a beleaguered town he beheld the citizens in their holiday attire, headed by the magistrates in their robes of state, marching in procession to meet him, conducting the heroine Marulla, their deliverer.

To reward her bravery, the Venetian commander ordered each of his soldiers to give her a present, and he promised that she should be adopted by the Republic. He offered her the hand of any one of his captains that she might prefer. But Marulla replied that:

It was not by chance that she should choose a husband; for the virtues of a camp would not make a good master of a family; and the hazard would be too great.

When the Venetian senate received the news of Marulla's bravery, they decreed that various privileges and exemptions from taxes should be settled upon her and her children for evermore.

Henry VI., after losing the crown of France through a female warrior, very nearly saved the crown of England though another; and, what is more remarkable, both were Frenchwomen. But the high-spirited, fierce Margaret of Anjou, though fully as brave, was very different from the peaceful, the angelic Maid of Orleans. However, had the king possessed half the spirit of his wife, the Wars of the Roses might have terminated very differently. When the feeble, almost imbecile king, wishing for peace at any price, publicly acknowledged the Duke of York as heir-apparent to the throne, Margaret refused her consent, and the war was renewed. Henry was made prisoner in the Battle of Northampton; but the queen assembled a formidable army at York, where she awaited her rival.

On the last day of the year 1460, the Battle of Wakefield was fought. Within half-an-hour of the onset, nearly three thousand Yorkists lay dead on the field. This battle, in which Margaret is said to have taken an active part, terminated in a complete victory for the House of Lancaster. The Duke of York, covered with wounds, fell into the hands of the victors. His dying moments were embittered by the taunts of his captors; and afterwards, it is said, his head was cut off by order of the queen, crowned with a paper crown, and placed on one of the gates of York.

The next year, 1461, Margaret defeated the Earl of Warwick in the second Battle of St. Alban's, and recovered the king, who was now merely a passive agent in the hands of friends or foes. She advanced to London; but Edward, Earl of March, son of the Duke of York, having gained a victory at Hereford almost the same day as the Battle of St. Alban's, obliged her to retreat towards the north. He then entered London, where a few days later, March 4th, 1461, he was proclaimed King of England, as Edward IV.

Margaret soon increased her army to sixty thousand men, and Edward was obliged to hasten to the north. At Pontefract he passed in review nearly forty-nine thousand men. The armies met at Towton, in Yorkshire, March 29th, 1461. This was the bloodiest battle fought during the war. No quarter was given or expected on either side. The Lancastrians, routed with fearful slaughter, were intercepted in their flight by the river; and the pursuit of the Yorkists was unrelenting. The slain amounted to thirty or forty thousand. Henry VI. and his brave queen fled to Scotland.

After vainly soliciting aid from the Scottish court, Margaret went over to France, and by promising to give up Calais, obtained ten thousand men. With these she landed in Scotland, where she was speedily joined by many of her partisans, and also by a band of freebooters. With these she entered England, and advanced to Hexham, where she was totally defeated. May 15th, 1464, by Lord Neville.

The unhappy queen, compelled to fly with her son, with difficulty reached the coast, after suffering indignities at the hands of the wild freebooters who infested the kingdom, and sailed for Flanders. The rebellion of Warwick the King-Maker, in 1470, restored Henry VI., for a few short months, to the throne. Edward IV. fled to the Continent; Margaret and her son landed at Weymouth on the very day (April 14th, 1471) that the Earl of Warwick was defeated at Barnet.

When Margaret heard the news of her champion's defeat her courage seemed at first to forsake her. She took refuge with her son in the sanctuary of Beaulieu, in Hampshire. But her undaunted spirit once more led her to the field. She re-assembled her partisans and marched to Tewkesbury, where she was encountered by King Edward on the 4th of May, 1471. The total defeat of the Lancastrians was the result, and Margaret, with her son, was made prisoner. The latter was cruelly murdered, and Margaret was placed in the Tower of London.

After remaining a prisoner for nearly four years. Queen Margaret was ransomed by Louis XI. for fifty thousand crowns. She died in 1482, Voltaire says:

The most unfortunate Queen, wife, and mother, in Europe.

Charles the Bold, Duke of Burgundy, one of the greatest warriors of the Middle Ages, was brother-in-law to Edward IV., whom he assisted, in 1471, with men and arms; the English king promising, in return, to aid Charles against his great enemy, Louis XI. The French King was terribly afraid of the duke; and had not the latter been so rash and the former so crafty, King Louis might have lost his crown. In 1472 Charles crossed the Somme at the head of eighty thousand men, and after capturing Nesle, where he massacred the people and burned the town, he laid siege, in June, to the town of Beauvais, in Picardy. The inhabitants were devoted to Louis XL, and, besides, they knew from the fate of Nesle, where the blood flowed "ankle-deep" in the street, what they might expect in the event of capture. So, the defence was as stout as the attack was fierce.

There dwelt in Beauvais a girl named Jeanne Fourquet, born November 14th, 1454, the daughter of an officer in the king's guards. She was adopted, after her father's death, by a lady named Laisné.

From childhood Jeanne had taken a great interest in tales of warlike valour; she always revered Jeanne d'Arc as a saint. She now displayed her military tendencies in such a way as to save her native town and immortalise her name. Arming herself with a *hachette*, or small axe, she placed herself at the head of a band of women, and led them to the ramparts, where they occupied themselves loading the cannon, pouring hot water, boiling oil, or molten lead on the heads of the besiegers, supplying the archers with arrows, or performing any other service their strength would allow.

The Burgundians at last planted their ladders, and commenced scaling the ramparts; but the first man who planted the flag of Charles was hurled from the battlements by Jeanne Fourquet, who snatched the standard from his hands, and waved it over her head. This deed so animated the defenders of Beauvais, that they gallantly repulsed every assault. After a fierce contest of nine hours, the besieged were reinforced by the garrison of Noyen, and on the two following days by troops and provisions from Amiens, Genlis, and Paris.

Charles battered the walls with heavy guns for nearly a month, and almost destroyed the town with fire-balls. Finding his troops still held at bay, he ordered a general assault on the loth July, at seven in the morning. The attack was fierce, but the defence was resolute. The women, still led by Jeanne, displayed the same courage as before. Thrice the Burgundians scaled the walls, and planted their flag on the battlements; thrice they were repulsed with terrible losses. After the assault had lasted four hours, the Burgundians saw their efforts were fruitless, and sounded a retreat. During the night of the 22nd they broke up their camp, and marched away towards Normandy.

Jeanne Fourquet deposited the flag she had taken in one of the churches of Beauvais—doubtless that of the Jacobins, where it was preserved for many years. It may now be seen at the Hôtel de Ville. Louis XI. granted to her the privilege of bearing this standard at the head of the French Army. Some years after this great event, Jeanne married Collin Pillon, when, not only was she herself exempted from taxation, but the same immunity was granted to her descendants.

It is neither by the name of Fourquet nor Pillon that the heroine is famous. The weapon with which she was armed gave her a more illustrious surname; and since that valiant deed, for which her countrymen must ever remember her with gratitude, she has been known as Jeanne Hachette.

Her portrait may still, (1879), be seen at Beauvais; and in commemoration of her bravery, the anniversary of July 10th is celebrated by an annual procession, in which the women march before the men.

Napoleon III., when President of the French Republic, inaugurated a statue of Jeanne Hachette at Beauvais.

During the civil wars which agitated Castile towards the close of the century, the fortress of Toro was, by a curious coincidence, twice defended by female commanders, the wives of two brothers opposed to one another in politics. In 1475 it was held for Isabel the Catholic by Doña Aldonza de Castillo, wife of the Alcayde, Don Rodrigo de Ulloa, governor of the fortress. After the retreat of Ferdinand, husband of Isabel, she was compelled to surrender. In the following year the fortress was defended against the troops of Ferdinand and Isabel by Doña Maria Sarmiento, wife of Don Juan de Ulloa. All hopes of assistance having been dispelled, she obtained honourable terms of capitulation.

The same year, 1476, Isabel the Catholic having received intelligence that the Portuguese meditated invading her dominions, resolved to superintend in person the defence of the frontiers. Despite the remonstrances of her council, she set out for Estramadura in the summer of 1477, and, after capturing several fortresses, and placing strong garrisons in Badajoz, Ciudad Rodrigo, and other frontier towns, established her headquarters at Seville.

Queen Isabel again displayed her wish to be a warrior during the contest between Ferdinand and the Moors. In 1487 and 1489 she encouraged the Spanish soldiers by her presence in the camp. In 1491 Ferdinand commenced the siege of Granada. Isabel arrived towards the close of May. Attired in a magnificent suit of armour, and mounted on a richly caparisoned horse, she rode through the ranks, greeted on all sides with joyful acclamations.

Wishing to obtain a nearer view of the renowned red towers of the Alhambra, the queen rode forward on the i8th June, escorted by the entire Spanish cavalry, to the village of La Zubia, situated at a short distance from Granada. But her curiosity was very near being the cause of her capture. A large body of Moorish troops sallied out from Granada and attacked the bodyguard of the queen. Matters were growing serious, when the Marquis de Cadix came to the rescue with twelve hundred lances, and put the Moors to flight.

During the conflict Isabel did not display exactly the courage of a heroine. Struck with abject terror, she remained on her knees all the time, praying earnestly; and made a vow that if she escaped she would erect a monastery on the spot.

Most of the great Sforza's immediate descendants were more or less distinguished for military talents. Caterina, or Catherine, the natural daughter of Galeas Sforza, was remarkable for valour, military skill, and also for her personal beauty. She was the wife of Jerome Ricario, Prince of Forli; and sometime after their marriage he was assassinated by Francis Del Orsa, who had revolted against him. Caterina and her children fell into the hands of the assassin, but she soon escaped to Rimini, which still remained faithful. She defended the town, in 1466, with such determination that the besiegers, to frighten her into a surrender, threatened to put her children to death.

Caterina was at last restored to sovereign power, and married John de' Medici, a man of noble family, though not very distinguished for genius or bravery. In 1500 she defended Forli against the talented Caesar Borgia; being compelled to surrender, she was imprisoned in the castle of San Angelo, at Rome. Soon, however, she was restored to liberty; but her dominions were never given back to her. She died shortly after her release.

CHAPTER 8

Spanish Women serving under Cortez to Christina of Sweden

The discovery of America opened up a new field of enterprise for those brave, reckless, ne'er-do-weel soldiers of fortune by whom the Old World was overrun. Adventurers sailed from various ports of Europe, under the command of audacious leaders, such as Balboa and Pizarro, whose daring spirit and enterprising disposition gave them authority over their companions. Numbers of women, imbibing the spirit of the times, accompanied those bands of adventurers—sometimes disguised in male attire, but more frequently in the garments of their own sex.

When Cortez sailed from Cuba, in 1518, on that voyage which terminated in the conquest of Mexico, he was followed by six hundred soldiers, many of whom were accompanied by their wives. These Castilian dames, preferring to endure the hardships of a campaign than be separated from their husbands, and probably feeling curious to see for themselves those marvels of the New World about which all Europe was talking, in no way disgraced the name of Spaniard by any feminine timidity. In the camp before Mexico, which Cortez was besieging, 1521, it was their fortitude which kept up the spirit of the soldiers, who, repulsed in several assaults on the city, and suffering from famine, had become gloomy and despondent.

Several examples have been preserved of the bravery displayed by these Spanish wives. One of them would frequently mount guard to relieve her tired husband; another, seeing the Spaniards repulsed in an attack, hastily donned a soldier's *escaupil*, snatched up a sword and lance, rallied the retreating Christians and led them once more against the Mexicans.

Cortez had requested the women to remain behind, at Tlascala, but they proudly answered him that:

It was the duty of Castilian wives not to abandon their husbands in danger, but to share it with them—and die with them if necessary.

The name of one of these female warriors was Maria d'Estrada, who fought by the side of her husband through every campaign, displaying the same courage as her companions in arms.

Another Spanish-American heroine was Catalina de Erauso, the "*Monja Alferez*," or Nun-Lieutenant. Her life was the most romantic that could be imagined. She has written her own history in pure and classic Spanish, displaying as much literary ability in its composition as, in her warlike career, she had shown heroic valour, mixed with savage cruelty.

She was born in 1592, daughter of a Spanish *hidalgo* of St. Sebastian, Don Miguel de Erauso, an officer in the royal army, and, after the fashion of those days, was destined for the Church. So, at the early age of four, she was sent to the Dominican convent, the prioress of which was her aunt. Here she remained till her fifteenth year; but during all these years she acquired so inveterate a dislike for the cloister that she contrived to make her escape from the convent, shortly before the day on which she was to take the veil. She hid in a chestnut grove for three days, cut her hair short, made her petticoats into male attire, and then started on her travels.

She passed through various romantic adventures in Spain, acting in the different capacities of page, clerk, and servant. Thus disguised, she joined an expedition to South America, where she became a soldier. At different times she assumed one name or another; but that under which she was best known, and was promoted to the rank of lieutenant, was Alonzo Dias. Under this alias she was the victor in several skirmishes. So clear was her judgment that her opinion was frequently asked by the generals at their councils of war.

During the intervals of military duty, Catalina gambled, drank, robbed, assassinated, cursed and swore, and behaved altogether very like an Alsatian bully. She chose for her associates the most desperate and reprobate characters, and seemed to take a fiendish delight in outdoing them. Sometimes she would pay attentions to a simple girl, and when the wedding-day was fixed she would disappear.

One night, in a gambling-house in Chili, she quarrelled with, and stabbed a gentleman of great importance in the city. The relatives made the place so hot for Catalina, that she was compelled to make her escape across the Andes, into another province. Her lawlessness once brought her under the hands of the hangman; and a reprieve arrived just as, with the noose round her neck, she was about to be launched into eternity. She wandered over every part of Spanish America, taking up, at random, the profession of soldier, sailor, or even lawyer.

The discovery of her sex was brought about by a curious accident. Her violent deeds having again provoked the guardians of the law, she was compelled to fly for refuge for sanctuary to a church at Guámango, in Peru. The bishop, a pious man, tried to convert the young criminal, animadverting on the wicked life the latter had been leading, and exhorting her to repentance. The stubborn heart of Catalina, inured to every kind of reproach and harsh language, was touched by the kindness with which the bishop spoke. For a few moments she maintained a dogged silence; then, falling on her knees and bursting into tears:—

"Father," she sobbed. "I am a woman!"

She then told the astounded prelate her extraordinary story. He pitied the unhappy young woman, and by his influence she was pardoned and permitted to return to Spain. She arrived at Cadiz in 1624, whither her fame had preceded her. During her journey through Spain and Italy the streets were crowded by wondering spectators. Pope Urban VIII. allowed her to retain her masculine costume for the rest of her days. It is not known in what year she died; according to an old manuscript preserved in a convent at Vera Cruz, she devoted her latter years to trade, and assumed the name of Antonio de Erauso. Her portrait was taken at Seville by Pacheco, a Spanish painter.

During the early years of the Emperor Charles V.'s reign, the nobles of Castile formed a confederacy called the Holy Junta, and took up arms to recover their traditional rights and privileges. John de Padilla, a young noble, was at the head of this insurrection; but it was his wife. Dona Maria Pacheco, who really conducted the confederacy. She was highly gifted and extremely ambitious, though, like most ambitious people, not at all scrupulous as to the means employed, so long as the event turned out according to her wishes.

The *Junta* soon began to languish for want of money, so Doña Maria persuaded the people to strip the cathedral at Toledo of its plate and jewellery. In 1521 Padilla was captured, and sentenced to death. He wrote to his wife, telling her not to grieve, but rather to consider his death as his deliverance from a weary life. But his capture proved fatal to the confederacy. Toledo, the headquarters of the rebels, was soon invested by the king's troops. Doña Maria used every means to secure her position. She even wrote to the French general on the Spanish frontier, inviting him to invade Navarre. By keeping the death of Padilla fresh in the minds of the citizens, she incited them to make a resolute defence. Sorties attended with varied success were made, sometimes daily, from the garrison.

At last the canons of the cathedral, whom she had offended, worked on the minds of the ignorant, credulous multitude, telling them that Maria's influence over them was due entirely to witchcraft. The loss of three hundred men in a desperate sortie so humbled the citizens that they drove Maria into the Alcazar, and opened the gates to Charles's troops.

Maria defended herself four months longer in the citadel. But at last, reduced to the utmost extremities, she fled into Portugal, where many of her relatives and friends resided, and there passed the remainder of her days in great poverty.

Eleonora of Toledo, the first Grand-Duchess of Tuscany, was a woman possessing great courage and a powerful, ambitious intellect. In 1543 she married Cosmo de'Medici, Duke of Florence. Eleonora took an active part in the wars between her husband and his hereditary enemies, the Strozzi; and in the bloody and terrible battles fought during the struggle, she never left him. Her courage aided greatly to turn the fortune of war.

One day, while riding out with an escort of fifteen horsemen, she encountered Philip Strozzi, commander of her husband's enemies, reconnoitring the Florentine camp. Although he had a guard of forty-five men, Eleonora, with her accustomed bravery, attacked him, slew nearly all his men, and took himself prisoner. Philip, knowing that he could not expect quarter—which had never been granted to prisoners on either side during the war—committed suicide sooner than perish ignominiously on the scaffold. Eleonora was so shocked that she prevailed on her husband to spare the lives of his prisoners henceforth.

Eleonora also took a leading part in the war between Charles V. and Francis I. Together with her husband she was actively engaged in the storming of Sienna. She urged Cosmo to have himself crowned king; but he was unable to carry out her project. Pope Pius V. at length changed his title from Duke of Florence to Grand-Duke of Tuscany.

Eleonora's ambition being now satisfied, she gave up the rest of her life to the encouragement of the fine arts, national education, and founding charitable institutions. The date of her death is unknown.

Under Solyman the Magnificent, the Turks conquered the greater part of Hungary; whose king, Louis II., was routed and slain in the disastrous Battle of Mohacz, 1526. And during the next hundred and fifty years Hungary was the scene of endless strife between the Crescent and the Cross. For a long time, victory inclined to the side of the *infidels*. Women, as usual, took a prominent share in the terrible scenes of bloodshed and carnage. Wherever there was a town to be defended, women immediately took up arms and aided the men to keep off the common enemy.

This female courage showed itself on both sides during these dreary wars. In 1529, during the absence of Solyman, the Christians laid siege to Buda, the capital of Hungary. One day, having overpowered the Turks, they were rushing into the town, when a Jewess tearing a strip of rag from her gown, lighted it, and fired off an immense cannon which the Ottomans in their flight had overlooked. It caused such havoc amongst the Hungarians that they were paralyzed with terror—thus gaining time for the *Janizaries* to rally; and the result was the final repulse of the Christians.

Tradition declares that Solyman, when he heard of this courageous act, ordered the Jewess's gown to be girt with a circle of pure silver.

In 1552 Solyman besieged Temesvar, which was defended by the brave Lasonczy. The wife of the latter led an army to the relief of her husband, and attacked the Turkish camp, but she was soon defeated. The revolt of the German garrison soon after compelled Lasonczy to surrender.

The town of Erlau, besieged at the same time, withstood gallantly the repeated assaults of a numerous army. Its fortifications were of the poorest description, and the garrison small, but the valour, the patriotism of the townspeople supplied every deficiency. Old men and young girls, sword and spear in hand, aided in the defence. One woman was fighting beside her husband when he fell, pierced by a Turkish bullet. Her mother, who was also assisting to defend the wall, now wished to remove the body, and suggested that they should devote themselves to seeing it honourably interred. But the young widow refused to leave the scene of action, she cried:

"May God, never suffer the earth to cover my husband's corpse, till his death has been amply avenged. This is the hour of battle, not a time for funeral and for tears."

She seized the shield and sword of her dead husband, and rushing upon the Turks, refused to leave the breach, till by the slaughter of three *infidels* she had satisfied her thirst for revenge. Then she raised the corpse of her lord, and bore it to the principal church in the town, where she paid to it the last honours with great splendour.

When the Turks were besieging Alba, several women, whose husbands had been slain, volunteered to defend the walls. The Turks were amazed at the cool bravery with which these female warriors defended the various posts assigned to them. For several hours they held a bastion, the possession of which was deemed highly important by both Turks and Christians. Every Turk who endeavoured to scale the bastion had his head struck with a scythe.

For more than three months, thanks to the valour of the women, the town of Valpon set the Mussulman power at defiance, backed though the latter was by all the appliances of war.

The same resistance met them at Agria, not far from Valpon, where the wives and daughters of the citizens carried oil, pitch, boiling water, molten lead, etc., to pour on the heads of the Turks. One woman was struck down by a cannon ball just as she was about to hurl a big stone on the skulls of the *infidels*. Her daughter, seeing her fall, was filled with the thirst for revenge. Rushing to the breach, she fought with the desperate bravery of a lioness deprived of her cubs, slaying and wounding on all sides. At last she was herself slain. One of the citizens fighting on the ramparts observed his son-in-law struck dead by a musket-ball. Turning to his wife, he asked her to carry away the corpse and render to it the last offices.

She replied:

> There is another duty more pressing. That of defending our religion and our country comes before love. To them I will give the last drop of my blood.

During the siege of Szigeth, in 1566, which cost the Turks twenty thousand men, orders were given one day for a general assault. A Hungarian officer, wishing to save his wife from falling into the hands of the *infidels*, took the cruel resolution of putting her to death. But his young wife, less attached to her life than to her husband, declared that she would accompany him to battle, there to receive death or glory. Dressing herself in a suit of his clothes, she armed herself and went with him to the field. No one displayed greater courage than she did. Without once quitting her husband, she slew every Turk who came within reach of her sword. She continued to fight with the same ardour till the close of the engagement, and wherever she was seen a Turkish corpse remained to mark her presence. At last her husband was slain, and she herself, severely wounded by the Turkish arrows, lay on her husband's breast. After receiving the last sacrament, she expired in great agony.

During the siege of Famagosta, in Cyprus, by Mustapha Pacha, in 1571, the noblest Cypriote dames, undismayed by the iron fire of the Turkish batteries, aided to defend the city. Not only did they carry round food and ammunition to the soldiers, but, during the assault, they rolled huge stones on the heads of the Turks assembled in the ditch below or climbing to the attack.

In the annals of French poetry few names stand higher than that of Louise Labé, *La Belle Cordière*. She was born at Lyons in 1526 or 1527. Nature was lavish in her gifts; to personal beauty and an exquisite voice, were added talents for literature and music. Her education included music, languages, riding, and military exercises. The last-named acquirement excited in the mind of Louise a wish to enter the army.

At the age of sixteen she served, under the name of Captain Loys, in the campaign of 1542, which ended in the siege of Perpignan. Some say she followed her father, others her lover to the field; but whatever was the cause of her presence in camp, she earned great praises for her courage. But the French were obliged to raise the siege; and Louise Labé, after sharing in the *fêtes* and tournaments held by the *Dauphin*, gave up the military profession, henceforth devoting her time to music and poetry.

She married Ennemond Perrin, a wealthy ropemaker, and thus acquired the opportunity to follow her literary inclinations. She possessed a valuable library of books in Greek, Latin, Spanish, and Italian, which languages she knew perfectly. Her spacious and tastefully laid-out gardens became the resort of nobles, poets, savants, wits, artists, musicians, and men of genius of every kind; and at these re-unions the musical skill of *La Belle Cordière* showed to advantage. She excited at the same time the admiration of the poets and the envy of the ladies. The street in Lyons where she lived was christened after her. She died in 1566, one year after her husband, who had left her sole heir to his large property.

Her chief works were an *Epistle to Clemence de Bourges*, the *Débat de la Folie et de l'Amour*, a drama in prose, three elegies, and twenty-four sonnets. The first edition of her writings appeared in 1555

Mary of Hungary, wife of the unfortunate Louis II., who was slain in the Battle of Mohacz, was celebrated throughout continental Europe for her military prowess and her love of field-sports. From the latter she acquired the soubriquet of Diana, while from her habit of mixing with the soldiers she was styled (like the Empress Victoria) "Mother of the Camp." She was the daughter of Philip L of Spain, and handsome even for a Spanish princess, majestic in her carriage, yet affable and charming in her manners. Her brother, the Emperor Charles V., had so high an opinion of her political abilities that he entrusted to her charge the government of the Netherlands; and her court soon became famous for the magnificence of its tournaments and spectacles.

Mary commanded during several expeditions against the troops of France; and during the various battles and skirmishes which ensued, she would frequently march on foot, or ride with the soldiers to encourage them by her presence. In 1553, when Charles V. was besieging Metz, which was defended by the Duke of Guise, Mary caused a diversion, by invading Picardy, to prevent Henry II. from succouring the besieged. By this raid she caused terrible havoc, destroying seven or eight hundred villages, and burning Folembrai, a favourite palace of Francis I.

Henry II., in retaliation, burned some of the most populous towns in the Netherlands, together with the royal palace of Bains, which was one of the architectural wonders of the age. Mary vowed that France should repent this deed. She kept her word; and more than once her conduct savoured of gross cruelty. Henry directed his soldiers to try their utmost to make Mary a prisoner; for, said he, he would like to try whether she would retain, in captivity, her haughty, courageous spirit.

Mary resigned the government of the Netherlands in 1555, and returned to Spain, where she died three years afterwards.

Graine-ni-Mhaile, Granu Weal, or Grace O'Malley, a famous Irish heroine who lived during the latter half of the sixteenth century, was daughter of Owen O'Malley, a noted chief who commanded a small navy. He used to make voyages from port to port, partly for commerce, but more especially for piracy. During childhood, Grace frequently accompanied her father on his expeditions. After his death, her brother being a minor, she took command of the galleys, and made several voyages. Her chief rendezvous was at Clare Island, off the coast of Mayo, where she kept her larger vessels moored. Here, too, she had a fortress. Her smaller ships she kept at Carrigahooly Castle, which was her favourite residence, and chief stronghold.

Her piracies at length became so frequent and so daring that a reward of five hundred pounds was offered by the English Government for her apprehension. Troops were sent from Galway to Carrigahooly; but after a siege of more than a fortnight, they were compelled to retire. The people of Connaught relate numerous adventures and extraordinary actions performed on the high seas by Granu Weal.

Her first husband was O'Flaherty, chief of West Connaught. After his death she married Sir Richard Burke, and became reconciled to the English. After her second marriage, she frequently assisted the English with her troops in Connaught; for which Queen Elizabeth wrote her an autograph letter, thanking her and inviting her on a visit to the court, at London. Graine-ni-Mhaile, with several galleys, sailed to London in 1575.

She was received with great distinction by the queen, who offered to make her visitor a countess; but Grace declined this honour, and answered with much spirit, that both of them being princesses, they were equal in rank, and could not therefore confer titles or honours upon each other. But, she said, Her Majesty might confer any rank she pleased on young Burke (son of Grace), who was born on board ship during the voyage to England; named from this circumstance, Tioboid-na-Lung, signifying Theobald of the Ships. Queen Elizabeth, it is said, knighted him under the title of Sir Theobald Burke; he was afterwards created Viscount of Mayo by Charles I.

On her voyage home Granu Weal landed at Howth for provisions. She was greatly surprised to find the gates of the castle closed, because the family were at dinner. Indignant at this dereliction from Irish hospitality, Granu seized a little boy whom she found playing with an attendant near the seashore. Finding that he was the infant heir of Howth, she brought him to Connaught: refusing to restore him till Lord Howth had entered into an agreement that his gates should never again be closed during dinner. The abduction of the infant heir of St. Lawrence forms the subject of a painting at Howth Castle.

Grace O'Malley was buried in a monastery which she had herself endowed, on Clare island. There are yet some remains of her monument to be seen there. Her name has always been familiar in the mouths of Irish peasants; and she is still sung as a heroine in various ballads, English and Irish.

During the fiercely contested wars brought about by the efforts of the Roman Catholic princes to stop the Reformation, women, as usual, took their share of the dangers and privations endured by all for the sake of their faith. They displayed as much courage and fortitude as the men, whether, as the wives and daughters of citizens they aided to defend their homes, or whether as princesses they boldly headed their troops in defence of their religion and their dominions.

Kenan Simonsz Hasselaar was heroine of the famous siege of Haarlem. The revolting cruelty of Spain in her first efforts to stamp out the rebellion in the Netherlands, only stimulated the Dutch to bolder and more desperate efforts for freedom. Haarlem was one of the most important cities; and the Spaniards, resolved to capture it at any price, despatched twelve thousand men, commanded by Frederic of Toledo, to besiege the city in December, 1572. On the 12th, during a severe frost, the place was invested. Bravely did the inhabitants, both soldiers and citizens, resist the Spaniards. Women cheerfully shared in all the toils and dangers, the manifold privations of the defence.

Kenan Simonsz Hasselaar, a widow about fifty years old, of a noble family, raised a troop of three hundred women for the defence of the walls. At the head of her corps she was constantly seen pressing forward to attack the Spaniards, or aiding in the erection of new defences. Even the besiegers, who were repulsed with great slaughter in several assaults, could not help admiring the courage of this Amazon band.

Holland still holds the name of Kenan Hasselaar very dear. One of the ships launched from the government dock-yards every year receives her name. A huge painting suspended in the hall of the Haarlem *Stadthuis* transmits her glorious deeds to posterity; and her portrait hangs in the Treasure Chamber of the Municipality, amongst the commanders of St. John, the relics of the Spanish wars, the town insignia, and the other precious knickknacks and antiquities collected together, accumulated by generations of thrifty and patriotic *burghers*.

The women of Alkmaar (which was besieged by Don Frederic immediately after the fall of Haarlem) displayed the same courage. During the general assault made by the Spaniards on the 18th September, 1573, the women aided the soldiers by hurling down fragments of stones and red-hot iron, and pouring boiling oil, molten pitch, rosin, and lead on the besiegers, of whom a terrible carnage was made.

Mary Queen of Scots, the unfortunate rival of Elizabeth, was a high-spirited, courageous woman, possessing great talents for ruling; and had she lived before the Reformation, she might possibly have been more successful than her ancestors, most of whom came to an untimely end. But the bitter hostility of John Knox was too powerful for the queen, though for some years she contrived to keep her throne. In 1565, shortly before her ill-starred marriage with Darnley, the Congregational citizens of Edinburgh, stirred up to rebellion by the secret machinations of the queen's "base brother, Moray," turned out in hostile array, and encamped at St. Leonard's Crags. Mary, undismayed by the fierce looks and big words of these staunch Protestants, rode to meet them at the head of a mere handful of troops. The rebel leaders fled, and the rest, under promise of pardon, returned to their homes.

In July of the same year the queen wedded Darnley. This was the signal for an open insurrection on the part of the Scottish nobles. Again, Queen Mary showed herself a worthy descendant of the Stuarts. Miss Strickland remarks:

> She acted in this emergency, with energy and spirit indicative of the confidence inspired by her popularity, and showed herself no whit behind the most distinguished of her predecessors in courage and ability.

At the head of five thousand men she left Edinburgh, August 26th, together with her husband, the lords of the council, and her ladies-in-waiting. She was attired in a scarlet and gold-embroidered riding-habit, which, it was said, covered a light suit of armour, while her hood and veil were understood to conceal a steel casque. Pistols hung at her saddle-bow. Darnley, with a vanity inherent in his nature, wore a gorgeous suit of gilded armour.

On the 29th the queen reached Glasgow; and next day the rebels retreated from Paisley towards Hamilton. The queen set out in pursuit. The confederate lords, disappointed in their expectations of a general Protestant rising, were obliged to retreat from place to place before the queen and her army. The bravery and endurance of Mary gained the love and respect of many amongst her subjects.

Mary returned to Edinburgh for a short time; and on the 8th of October she marched again, this time at the head of eighteen thousand men, to renew the war. The rebel lords, terrified at the approach of their royal mistress, fled across the English border, and took refuge in Carlisle.

Queen Mary had no further opportunity of displaying her courage till after the murder of Darnley, in 1567, when the base conduct of Bothwell and the consequent insurrection of nearly all the Scottish nobles forced her once more to take the field in person. When the opposing armies met, June 14th, at Carberry Hill, she rode with her followers to the field, though neither she nor they had broken their fast that morning.

After this followed the captivity of Mary in Loch-Leven Castle. In 1568 she made her escape, and assisted by a few friends, made a last effort to recover her throne. The Earl of Murray (regent during the minority of King James), with a large army intercepted the queen's march at Langside, two miles from Glasgow.

It is not quite clear whether Mary took an active part in the Battle of Langside, which for ever crushed her hopes. Brantôme declares:

> The Queen-Mother of France assured him that Mary mounted her good hackney and rode into the battle like another Zenobia, to encourage her troops to advance, and would fain have led them to the charge in person. But she found them all quarrelling among themselves, and insensible to her eloquence, and more inclined to exchange blows with each other than to attack the rebel host.

According to the popular tradition, however, it was beneath the spreading boughs of a hawthorn, which is still known as "the Queen's thorn," halfway up the green hill behind Castlemilk, that the unfortunate sovereign stood and watched the battle, surrounded by her ladies and a few devoted adherents. Legend also points out another "Queen's thorn" on the hill behind the ruins of Cathcart Castle. According to a local history. Lord Livingstone, at the head of "the bairns of Falkirk," rode with the queen to the battlefield, and afterwards aided her to escape; and this would seem to corroborate what Brantôme has said.

Amongst those heroines who distinguished themselves during the religious wars in France, was Magdalaine de Saint-Nectaire,—also called Se'nectaire, or Sennetaire. She was a staunch Protestant, and after the death of her husband, Gui di Saint Exuperi, she retired to her *château* at Miremont, in Limousin, armed sixty of her retainers, and commenced a series of raids against the Roman Catholics. In 1575, during the reign of the weak and frivolous Henry III., Montal, Lieutenant du Roi, in Limousin, whose soldiers had often been defeated by Magdalaine, resolved to besiege the heroine in her *château*.

With fifteen hundred foot and two hundred horse he arrived before the gates. Magdalaine made a sally, and cut to pieces a detachment of fifty men; but on her return she found that the *château* had been captured. She galloped to Turene, a neighbouring town, to gather reinforcements, returning thence with four companies of mounted arquebusiers. Montal awaited her in a defile of the mountains; but he was vanquished and mortally wounded. His soldiers, discouraged by the fall of their leader, withdrew the same evening to a neighbouring castle, where Montal died four days later.

The year of this heroine's death is not recorded.

Another heroine of these wars was Constance de Cezelli, a loyal supporter of Henry IV. When that monarch, after his accession to the throne, was struggling for supremacy with the League, the troops of the latter, in 1590, besieged the town of Leucates, in Languedoc. It was defended by the Huguenots, under the command of M. de Barri, governor of the place. The latter was captured by means of a pretended conference; but he contrived to write to his wife, Constance de Cezelli, bidding her to take the command and defend the town so long as there was any hope of success.

Constance, according to his commands, maintained order in Leucates, and encouraged the soldiers by frequently appearing on the walls with a pike in her hand. When the Leaguers discovered who it was that commanded the garrison they thought to frighten her into a surrender by threatening to put her husband to death if she did not give up the town. She possessed much private property, which she offered as ransom for her husband; but she declared that she could never purchase his life by an act of treason.

M. de Barri was put to the torture, for the besiegers thought that he would command his wife to open the gates. But he braved all their menaces, and when they were compelled, soon after, to raise the siege the governor of Leucates was strangled.

Although Constance was overwhelmed with grief and horror, she would not allow the soldiers to avenge the death of M. de Barri on some Roman Catholic prisoners.

Henry IV. sent Constance de Cezelli a commission appointing her governor of Leucates, with a reversion in favour of her son. She held this office for twenty-seven years, and proved herself thoroughly competent for the duties of governor.

On the 26th July, 1581, the United Netherlands declared their independence, and invited the Duke of Anjou to rule over them. But, although the prince entered the country with five thousand horse and twelve thousand foot, the military genius of Alexander Farnese, the Spanish governor, together with the vacillating conduct of the Dutch themselves, frustrated all his efforts, and he was compelled to disband his forces and leave the country. The greater number of his soldiers joined the standard of the Prince d'Espinoy, governor of Tournai.

Alexander Farnese laid siege, on the 1st of October, to the important city of Tournai. In the absence of the Prince d'Espinoy, the Princess, Christine de Lalaing, took the command, and conducted the defence in a manner worthy of her distinguished relatives Count Horn and Admiral de Montmorency. The Prince of Parma summoned Tournai to surrender, but Christine gave him a defiant refusal, and set so courageous an example to the soldiers that they made a resolute defence. The princess superintended all the defences in person, and directed all the officers. She appeared daily on the walls; and in one of the assaults was wounded in the arm, though, despite this, she refused to retire till the Spaniards had been repulsed.

After a siege of two months' duration, it became impossible to hold the place any longer. The walls were gradually undermined from without, and the fidelity of the garrison was tampered with by Father Géry, a Dominican friar. The Protestants in the city, not knowing what moment an insurrection would break out amongst the Catholic inhabitants, insisted upon surrendering the place. Christine finding herself deserted by both Protestants and Catholics, obtained honourable terms, and left the city with all the honours of war, carrying all her personal property with her. Farnese, moreover, accepted one hundred thousand crowns in place of sacking the city.

As the princess passed through the gates she was received with an outburst of applause from the Spanish Army, with whom she had acquired a high reputation through her courage. Parma entered the city on November 30th.

In September, 1863, a statue was raised to Christine de Lalaing in the city, which, nearly three centuries before, she had so nobly defended.

In 1588 a panic flew from one end of England to the other on the threatened invasion of the Spanish Armada. As it was supposed that the invaders would attempt to sail up the Thames, several thousand volunteers were assembled at Tilbury, under command of the Earl of Leicester. Richard Hackluyt says:

Vnto the sayd army, came in proper person, the Queen's most roiall Maiestie, representing Tomyris, that Scythian princesse, or rather diuine Pallas her selfe.

On the 8th of August, Queen Elizabeth, mounted on a white charger, a marshal's *bâton* grasped in her hand, rode through the camp, where she was received with enthusiastic acclamations by both volunteers and regulars drawn up on a hill near Tilbury church. Forbidding any of her retinue to follow her, she was attended only by the Earls of Ormonde and Leicester, the latter bearing before her the Sword of State. She was also followed by a page, who had the honour of carrying her "white-plumed regal helmet." The queen's costume was a mixture of the military uniform and the fashionable ladies' attire of the period. Beneath a corselet of polished steel descended observes Miss Strickland:

A farthingale of such monstrous amplitude, that, it is wonderful how her high-mettled war-horse submitted to carry a lady encumbered with a gabardine of so strange a fashion.

Riding bare-headed through the ranks, she addressed the warriors in an oration well calculated to inspire them with enthusiasm. It concluded amidst vociferous and long continued cheering.

After the dispersion of the Invincible Armada, Elizabeth celebrated a triumph, in imitation of the ancient Romans. She rode in a triumphal chariot from her palace to St. Paul's cathedral, where the "enseignes and colours of ye vanquished Spaniards," were displayed to the delighted gaze of the citizens.

During the Border Wars between England and Scotland women had frequent opportunities of local distinction. Holinshed, speaking of a skirmish which took place at Naworth, in 1570, between Lord Hursden and Leonard Dacres, says the latter had in his army " many desperate women, who there gave the adventure of their lives, and fought right stoutly."

The Duchy of Lorraine, or Lothringen, was, for many centuries, a subject of contention between France and Germany. It was for a long time a fief of the German empire; but from the middle of the sixteenth century, the royal family of France became connected with its rulers, and assumed thenceforth a right to interfere in its internal arrangements. During the Thirty Years' War the French drove Duke Charles from his throne, on account of his close connection with Austria.

It was during this war that Madame St. Balmont, who has been styled a second Joan of Arc, performed the gallant deeds for which she became so famous. Barbara of Ernecourt, was born in 1609, at the

Castle of Neuville, situated between Verdun and Bar. She belonged to a good family in Lorraine, and from her earliest childhood she trained herself in military exercises and the use of arms. Her chief delight was hunting, and every kind of field sport, which the Abbé Arnould remarks, "is a kind of war." One day when she was engaging in her favourite pastime, she met with the Count de St. Belmont, and, being mutually charmed, they married shortly after.

Barbara was scarcely more than a girl when she married, and at this time her face was excessively pretty, though it was afterwards spoiled by the smallpox—when, so far from being made unhappy by the loss of her beauty, the Abbé Arnould says:

> She was as pleased, to be marked with it as other women are afflicted on a similar occasion, and said that it would enable her to look more like a man.

Her figure, however, was small and clumsily made; but she was robust, and able to bear a considerable amount of fatigue without being overcome by it.

When the French invaded Lorraine, the Count de St. Belmont, who had always occupied a high place in the estimation of the duke, now actively employed himself resisting the invaders, while Barbara remained as custodian of his castle and estates. Unfortunately, the duke's high opinion of M. de St. Belmont's military talents led the latter into a serious dilemma; for, being given the command of a fortress, he felt himself bound in honour to defend it for several days against the French. In those days there was, it would seem, a rigid code of the military law—doubtless first introduced through humane feelings—by which officers in charge of strongholds refusing to surrender, after all hope of success was gone, were to be punished in the most degrading manner. When this feeble stronghold was taken, the French leaders seriously debated the expediency of hanging their antagonist.

Meanwhile the countess, having been contemptuously treated by a cavalry officer who had taken up his abode on one of her husband's estates, despatched a cartel, signed "Le Chevalier de St. Belmont," purporting to be written by her husband's brother. They crossed swords, and Barbara almost immediately disarmed her opponent; then, picking up his sword and handing it to him with a gracious smile, she said:—

"You thought, sir, I make no doubt, that you were fighting with Le Chevalier de St. Belmont; it is, however Madame de St. Belmont of that name who returns you your sword, and begs you in future to pay more regard to the requests of ladies."

The officer, not caring to show his face in the vicinity, disappeared immediately and was never heard of again.

Barbara's reputation was considerably raised by this duel; several gentlemen in the neighbourhood took refuge in the village and put themselves under her orders. At their head she made frequent raids into those parts of the country occupied by the French. She was always victorious, and almost invariably brought home some trophies in arms or baggage, for, in addition to courage, she possessed great prudence and foresight.

The Peace of Westphalia, in 1648, put an end to the Thirty Years' War, and settled, for a time, the affairs of Lorraine. Barbara laid down the sword and took up the pen, which she wielded quite as skilfully. Her first work, *Les Jumeaux Martyrs*, appeared in 1651; other works of equal merit followed. After the death of her husband she gave herself up entirely to religion, to which she had always been devotedly attached, and retired into a convent. She died before taking the veil. May 22nd, 1660, at the age of fifty-one.

Although there was none of that unfeminine coarseness which so often attaches to women who pass the greater part of their lives in camps, Barbara was always more at her ease in male society than in that of her own sex, in which she felt embarrassed, awkward. While her courage rendered her famous throughout France and Germany, her charity and the zeal which she displayed in the service of the poor, rendered Madame de St. Belmont respected and beloved by persons of every rank who dwelt in the neighbourhood.

Christina of Sweden, daughter of Gustavus Adolphus, the great Protestant hero of the Thirty Years' War, inherited her father's native love for battles, soldiers, even the smell of powder—all, in fact, that pertains to a warrior's life. When she was about two years old, her father took her to Calmar. The governor did not know whether to give the customary salute, afraid lest the child might be frightened by the noise of the cannon. But Gustavus, whom he consulted, replied, after a moment's hesitation:—

Fire! The girl is the daughter of a soldier, and should be accustomed to it early.

The salute was therefore given. Christina clapped her hands in delight.

"More! More!" she cried.

Pleased to see her evident predilection for the taste of gunpowder, Gustavus Adolphus took his daughter, soon after, to see a grand review. She displayed even greater delight than before, and Gustavus said, with a smile:—

Very well; you shall go, I am resolved, where you shall have enough of this.

However, the early death of Gustavus Adolphus hindered him from ever fulfilling this promise; and Christina, in her memoirs, regrets that she was not permitted to learn the art of war under so illustrious a master.

In 1647, at the age of twenty-nine, Christina resigned the crown of Sweden. Passing through Denmark and Germany, she proceeded to Belgium; and from Innspruck she went to Rome, which she entered in state, attired in the costume of an Amazon, and mounted on a war-horse.

CHAPTER 9

The Amazons in South America

Down from the lofty Andes rolls the majestic Amazon, the largest river in the world. From its sources to the Atlantic the length is upwards of four thousand miles. The banks are clothed with immense impenetrable forests of pine, cedar, red-wood, holly, and cinnamon, affording a haunt to savage jaguars, bears, leopards, tigers, wild boars, and a great variety of venomous serpents; and abounding, too, in birds of the most beautiful plumage, and apes of the most fantastic appearance. The waters swarm with alligators, turtles, and almost every description of fish. The shores and islands were formerly peopled by numerous tribes of Indians, who have either become extinct or retired further up the mountains.

This majestic river was first explored in 1540-41, by Francisco Orellana, a Spanish adventurer. Gonzalo Pizarro, brother of the Marquis of Pizarro, started with Orellana from Zumaque, where they met by accident. Together they descended the River Coca in search of the wondrous El Dorado, which, they had been told, was situated on the banks of a great river into which the Coca flowed. During the voyage they met with innumerable difficulties, and suffered great hardships, especially from the want of provisions.

Several of their followers fell ill; and at last Pizarro constructed a brigantine, and embarked his invalids on board, with two hundred thousand livres in gold. He gave Orellana the command, and remained behind with the rest of the adventurers; desiring Orellana, if successful, to return with supplies. The latter, having entered at last a broad river, whose shores were so distant from each other that the waters seemed like those of an inland sea, was certain he had almost reached El Dorado.

On the last day of December, 1540, he resolved not to turn back;

110

so, letting himself go with the current, he abandoned his comrades under Pizarro to their fate. At the mouth of the Nayho, Orellana was cautioned by an old Indian chief to beware of the warlike women. At the River Canuriz, between the mouth of the Xingu and the Rio Negro, he encountered a hostile tribe of Indians who opposed his landing. Blows were exchanged; several fell on each side. Amongst the slain were several women, who had fought quite as bravely as the men. Orellana was, of course, the victor, and lived to carry home to Europe an account (improved and embellished) of a nation of Amazons who lived in South America, and made war on the Indians.

Thenceforth a legend existed among the European adventurers that a nation of female warriors dwelt somewhere on the South American continent. The river, hitherto called the Marañon, from its first discoverer, was re-christened as the Amazons' river; and a large tract of country, with indefinable limits, was set down in the maps under the somewhat vague denomination of Amazonia.

Whether the natives first told the Europeans, or whether the latter, with a view to increase the wonders of the New World, invented the story and told it to the natives, none can tell; but even before the voyage of Orellana, a tradition existed amongst both natives and colonists that a nation of armed women dwelt somewhere in America. Christopher Columbus was told that the small island of Mandanino, or Matinino (Montserrat), was inhabited solely by female warriors.

Since the days of Orellana, there have been found plenty of travellers to confirm the story and add their testimony to its truth. Hernando de Ribeira, a follower of Cabega de Vega, the Conquistador of Paraguay, asserted in 1545 that he had been told of a nation of Amazons who lived on the western shore of a large lake poetically termed "The Mansion of the Sun," because that orb sinks into its waters every evening. Father d'Acugna, in his *Discovery of the River Amazon*, declares that the various tribes of Indians (amongst others, the Toupinambous) dwelling around the Amazon, assured him again and again that a republic of female warriors did exist in that region; several chiefs said they themselves had been in the country of the Amazons on a visit.

If, says d'Acugna, the tradition is not true, it is certainly the greatest of all the fables invented about the New World. The Indians all believed that the Amazons possessed vast treasures, sufficient to enrich many kingdoms; but no one dared to attack so warlike a nation, to whom liberty was dearer than all the riches in the world, and who knew how to send their poisoned shafts straight to the heart.

D'Acugna fixes the residence of the Amazons on the banks of the Canuriz, on lofty, almost inaccessible mountains, he says:

> When their neighbours visit them, at a time appointed by themselves, they receive them with bows and arrows in their hands, which they exercise as if about to engage with enemies. But knowing the object of their visitors, they lay these weapons down, and welcome as their guests the strangers, who remain with them a few days.

André Thevet, in his work *Les Singularités de la France Antarctique,* Paris, 1558, makes the arrival of the Amazons' guests the subject of a pictorial illustration.

In 1595, Sir Walter Raleigh, wishing to make a fortune in a hurry, undertook an expedition to Guiana to seek for the golden city of Manoa. Most probably he had read Thevet's work, an English translation of which, by Bynneman, appeared in 1568; and he made the most careful enquiries after the Amazons. But, like his predecessors, he was doomed to disappointment.

He says, in his book *The Discourie of the Large, Rich, and Bewtifvl Empire of Gviana:*

> I made inqvirie, amongst the most ancient and best traueled of the Orenoqveponi, and I had knowledge of all the riuers betweene Orenoqve and Amazones, and was uery desirovs to vnderstand the trvth of the warlike women, bicavce of some it is beleeved, of others not; though I digresse from my pvrpose, yet I will set doune what hath been deliuered to me for troth of those women, and I spake with a Casiqve, or lord of the people, that told me he had been in the riuer, and beyond it also, the nations of those women are on the sovth side of the riuer in a prouince of Topago, and their chiefest strength and retraicts are in the Islands scitvate on the sovth side of the entrance, some sixty leagves within the movth of the said riuer.

After entering into some details about the reception of their guests in the month of April, when, he says, "this one moneth they feast, davnce, and drinke," he gives an account of the treatment of children, which bears a suspicious resemblance to the stories related of the ancient Amazons. He further tells us the South American Amazons were "said to be very crvell and bloodthirsty, especially to svch as offer to inuade their territories."

In 1599 an abridged Latin translation of Raleigh's work appeared at Nuremberg, at the cost of Levinus Hulsius, geographer and collector. It was illustrated by five coloured plates; the third representing the joyful reception of the Amazons' visitors, and their subsequent amusements; the fourth showing the treatment bestowed on prisoners of war, who are seen hung up by the heels to trees, where they serve as targets for the skill of their captors, while their ultimate fate is hinted by the figures of several Amazons preparing huge fires.

At the close of the seventeenth century. Father Cyprian Baraza, a Jesuit missionary who went among the South American Indians, gave an account of some Amazonian tribes who dwelt to the west of the Paraquay, in 12° south latitude. M. de Condamine, who read a *Relation abrégée d'un Voyage*, etc., before the Académie des Sciences in 1745, brought forward several testimonies to the existence of the Amazons, whom he described as a society of independent women, who were visited by the sterner sex during the month of April only. Amongst other authorities he mentions Don Francisco Diego Portales, and Don Francisco Torralva, two Spanish governors of Venezuela, who agreed in declaring that a tribe of female warriors lived in the interior of Guiana.

Thirty years later he was supported by a Portuguese astronomer, Don Ribeiro de Sampeio (*Diario da Viegem, no anno de* 1774 *et* 1775) who, however, spoke only by hearsay. Gili, the missionary, was told by an Indian of the Quaqua tribe that the Aikeambenanos ("women living alone") dwelt on the banks of the Cuchinero, which falls into the Orinoco opposite the island of Taran, between Cayeara and Alta Gracia.

Count Pagan, in his *Relation de la Rivière des Amazones*, after testifying to the existence of the nation, observes, in his florid style:

Que l'Asie ne se vante plus de ses comptes véritables ou fabuleuses des Amazones. L'Amérique ne lui céde point cet avantage. . . . Et que le fleuve de Thermodoon ne soit plus enflé de la gloire de ces conquérantes les guerrières.

(That Asia no longer boasts of its real or fabulous accounts of the Amazons. America does not give him this advantage. . . . And that the river of Thermodoon is no longer swollen with the glory of these conquering warriors.)

The Abbé Guyon, in his *Histoire des Amazons* Paris, 1740, expresses great faith in the story of these South American dames; and suggests that they were colonised by the African Amazons, who might, he suggests, have passed from the Old to the New World by the now submerged isle of Atlantis. But his testimony is of little value, as it evidently rests almost entirely upon D'Acugna's report.

Even within the last twenty or thirty years, many Indian tribes have expressed their belief in the existence of the Amazons. Those who dwell on the Essequibo, the Rupunni, and the lower Corentyn, gravely assured Sir Robert Schomburgh, in 1844, that separate tribes of women still lived on the upper part of the Corentyn, in a country called Marawonne; and the narrators went so much into detail that Sir Robert and his companions were almost inclined to believe them. The natives further told them that when they had journeyed some distance above the great cataracts of the Corentyn, at a point where two gigantic rocks (named by the Indians Pioomoco and Surama) rose from either shore, they would be in the country of the Woruisamocos, or Amazons.

Sir Robert, while travelling over the vast savannahs, frequently came upon heaps of broken pottery, which the Macusion Indians said were relics of the Woruisamocos, who had formerly dwelt there. The Caribs were especially persistent in declaring that an Amazonian republic still existed in the centre of Guiana "in those districts which no European had ever visited."

The explorers of the River Amazon were formerly stopped by the great cataracts on the Rio Trombetas, and in many instances, they were murdered by ferocious Indians who inhabit the upper branches. Naturally those parts of the river which remained unexplored were supposed to be the land of the "*bellicose dames.*" In 1842-44 M. Montravel, commander of the French war-ship *La Boulonnaise*, surveyed the Amazon from the sea as high up as the Rio Negro, and heard the same tale in the region of the Rio Trombetas. Thus, from the west as well as from the north, Europeans heard of a nation of Amazons dwelling in the central districts of Guiana.

Humboldt believed to a certain extent in the tradition. His idea was that women, in various parts of South America, have now and then wearied of the degrading condition in which they are held, and occasionally united themselves into bands, as fugitive negroes sometimes do, and that the necessity of preserving their independence has made them warriors.

Southey, in his *History of Brazil*, makes a very trite observation concerning the female warriors of the New World:

Had we never heard of the Amazons of antiquity, I should, without hesitation, believe in those of America. Their existence is not the less likely for this reason, and yet it must be admitted that the probable truth is made to appear suspicious by its resemblance to a known fable.

CHAPTER 10

Lady Offaley (Irish Rebellion, 1641) to Mademoiselle de la Charce

The Abbé Brotier says:

> There are three sorts of things in the world, that know no kind
> of restraint, and are governed by passion and brutality—family
> quarrels, religious disputes, and civil wars.

The truth of these words is undeniable, more especially as the last
is very frequently brought about by its forerunners. The war between
Charles I. and the Parliament was prosecuted on both sides with so
much bitterness, that, in certain instances, the conduct of the officers
and generals savoured more of private feud than public zeal.

The Irish Rebellion of 1641 was one of many unfortunate oc-
currences which precipitated the revolution at home, for not only
did the Republican party take advantage of the king's difficulties to
increase its own power, but the Irish rebels envenomed the bitterness between King and Commons by declaring that they were em-
powered, by Royal Commission, to defend His Majesty's prerogatives
against a Puritanical, levelling Government.

The Irish rebels stormed many a castle belonging to English nobles
or gentry. Amongst others, they beleaguered, in April, 1642, the Castle
of Geashill, in King's County, the residence of Lettice Digby, Baroness
of Offaley. This lady, though upwards of sixty years old, and a widow,
retained all the fire and energy of youth. She closed the gates, and
made a most resolute defence, refusing to hear any proposal for surrender, for the castle, being defended on all sides by bogs and woods,
was very difficult of access. She was at last relieved by the approach of
Viscount Lisle and Sir Charles Coote with one hundred and twenty

116

foot and three hundred horse.

The castle having been provisioned and supplied with ammunition, Lady Offaley chose to remain there for a time; but being again menaced by the rebels, she was relieved by Sir Richard Grenville, in October of the same year, when she retired to her mansion at Coles Hill, in Warwickshire, where she died, December the 1st, 1658.

On the 25th of August, 1642, King Charles raised his standard at Nottingham. He was at once joined by thousands of Cavaliers; amongst others, by the Earl of Arundell, one of his most staunch adherents. The latter made himself so troublesome to the Parliament that they determined to seize Wardour Castle, his mansion. In 1643, they sent orders to Sir Edward Hungerford, commander-in-chief of their forces in Wiltshire, to accomplish this design. He arrived before the castle on the 2nd of May, and as Lord Arundell was absent, the Puritans expected an easy conquest. But Lady Blanche, who had been left in charge, was well supplied with provisions and ammunition: and although the garrison consisted of barely twenty-five fighting men, she resolved to make a brave defence.

Sir Edward Hungerford, on the arrival of Colonel Strode with reinforcements, summoned the castle to surrender, pretending that it contained men and arms, money, and plate which he was ordered, by a warrant from Parliament, to seize. Lady Arundell declined to comply with his demands. Sir Edward immediately ordered up his heavy guns, and commenced a bombardment which lasted from Wednesday the 3rd to the following Monday. The besiegers, moreover, ran two mines under the walls, and so terrific was the explosion that the fortress was shaken to its foundations.

During the siege, Sir Edward offered again and again to grant quarter to the ladies and children if the castle would surrender; but Lady Arundell and the other ladies rejected the proposal with disdain. The latter, too, together with the women-servants, aided in the defence in various ways; they loaded the muskets, and carried round refreshments to their gallant defenders.

According as the garrison, exhausted by the continued struggle, relaxed in its efforts, the Parliamentary soldiers redoubled their attacks. They applied petards to the garden-door, they flung balls of wild-fire through the dismantled windows, causing much damage to the apartments in the castle, destroying valuable pictures, rich carvings, statuettes, costly vases, chairs and couches, mirrors, and various works of almost priceless worth.

After the siege had lasted nine days. Lady Arundell, finding the castle was no longer tenable, demanded a parley. Articles of surrender were drawn up, by which it was stipulated, firstly, that the garrison and all the inmates of the castle should be granted quarter; secondly, that the ladies and servants should have all their wearing apparel, and that sixty serving-men, chosen by the ladies themselves, should be permitted to attend them wherever they might please to retire; thirdly, that the furniture of the castle was to be saved from plunder or destruction.

The Puritans violated, without scruple, the treaty, destroyed or mutilated everything of value in the castle, and left with the inmates nothing but the clothes they wore. Lady Arundell, with the women and children, was carried prisoner to Shaftesbury. Thither, too, five van-loads of costly furniture were borne in triumph as the spoils of the vanquished.

The loss to Lord Arundell by the devastation and plunder of Wardour Castle was estimated at one hundred thousand pounds.

The Parliament, thinking their prisoners were insecure at Shaftesbury, wished to remove them to Bath. But the town was infected with small-pox and plague; and Lady Arundell refused so stubbornly to consent, that her captors left her where she was, but took her children to Dorchester.

Lady Arundell survived the siege only five years; and at her death, she was buried, with her husband, in the chapel of Wardour Castle.

In point of heroic valour, Lady Arundell was outdone by Lady Mary Bankes, wife of Sir John Bankes, Lord Chief Justice of the Common Pleas. In August, 1643, Parliament despatched Sir William Earle with a strong force to reduce Corfe Castle, the family residence of Sir John, in the Isle of Purbeck. Thinking to gain possession by stratagem, Sir William sent a party of forty sailors to demand four field-pieces which were in the castle. Lady Bankes, suspecting their real object, went to the gate, and requested the sailors to show their warrant. They produced one, signed by several Parliamentary Commissioners. Thereupon Lady Bankes retired into the castle; and although there were only five men within the walls, they mounted the field-pieces with the assistance of the female servants, and having loaded one of them, fired it off, and drove the sailors away.

Sir William Earle now tried to starve the castle into a surrender. Lady Bankes affected a wish to treat for the surrender of the guns; but her real object was, that the besiegers, relaxing in their careful blockade, would give greater facilities for introducing fresh supplies to the garrison. The event justified her hopes. She also obtained the help of Captain Lawrence, commanding a company of Royalists.

The Puritans, about six hundred in number, assaulted the castle, and endeavoured to carry it by a *coup de main*. But the brave little garrison, sallying forth, drove away the besiegers and brought back nine oxen. Again, the besiegers tried to take the castle by storm. Dividing their forces, one party attacked the middle ward, which was defended by Captain Lawrence and his company, while the other division assaulted the upper ward, held by Lady Bankes with her daughters, her female servants, and five soldiers, who hurled down huge stones and red-hot coals on the heads of the storming party. At last, after losing one hundred men in the assault, the Parliamentary forces retreated from before Corfe Castle. The blockade had lasted, altogether, six weeks.

Lady Bankes lived to see the Restoration, and died in April, 1661. She was interred in the south aisle of Rislipp church. The following inscription was placed upon her monument by her eldest son:—

To the memory of
The Lady Mary Bankes, the only daughter of Rafe Hawtrey, of Rislipp, in the County of Middlesex, Esquire., the wife and widow of the Honourable Sir John Bankes, Knight, late Lord Chief Justice of his late Majesty's Court of Common Pleas, and of the Privy Council to his late Majesty King Charles the First, of blessed memory; who, having had the honour to have borne, with a constancy and courage above her sex, a noble proportion of the late calamity, and the happiness to have outlived them so far as to have seen the restitution of the government, with great peace of mind laid down her most desired life the 19th day of April, 1661. Sir Ralphe Bankes, her son and heir, hath dedicated this. She left four sonnes—first, Sir Ralphe; second, Jerome; third, Charles; fourth, William (since dead, without issue); and six daughters.

The Earl of Derby was one of the most prominent Cavalier leaders. In 1643, while awaiting a siege at Lathom House, Lancashire, his family mansion, the earl received intelligence that Parliament had despatched troops to annex his miniature kingdom, the Isle of Man. Wishing to preserve the island as a final retreat for his royal master, in case of misfortune overtaking him, he left Lathom House in charge of Charlotte, his countess, and set off to the Isle of Man.

On the 27th of May, 1643, Mr. Holland, governor of Manchester, despatched a messenger to Lathom, commanding Lady Derby either to subscribe to the propositions of Parliament or surrender the mansion. She refused compliance with either alternative; and for nearly a year contrived, though closely blockaded, to keep the enemy from coming to open hostilities. At last, on the 24th of February, 1644, Parliament despatched three colonels to Lathom House. Before their arrival, the countess hastened to lay in provisions and ammunition, and to arm a sufficient number of retainers to serve as a garrison.

The countess determined not to surrender on any terms, and rejected every proposal, said she:

> Though a woman, and a stranger divorced from her friends and robbed of her estates, she was ready to receive their utmost violence, trusting in God for protection and deliverance.

Hostilities having commenced, the Parliamentary army pushed the siege with great vigour. The countess conducted the defence in person; but, though she took the office of commander, she was not unmindful of the spiritual welfare of her people. She was present four times a day at public prayer, attended by her little daughters, Catherine and Mary.

A few days after the opening of the siege, Sir Thomas Fairfax, the Parliamentary general, received a letter from the Earl of Derby, in which the latter, dreading the extremes to which his wife and children might be reduced, requested for them a free pass through the camp of the besiegers. When this was communicated to the countess, she thanked Sir Thomas for his courtesy in forwarding the missive; but replied that:

> She would willingly submit to her lord's commands, and therefore willed the general to treat with her; but till she was assured that such was his lordship's pleasure, she would neither yield up the house nor desert it herself, but wait for the event according to the will of God.

She forwarded a similar message to her husband at Chester.

On the 25th of April, Colonel Rigby despatched a peremptory message, demanding the surrender of Lathom House immediately. The countess refused: and the siege was prosecuted with renewed vigour; while the garrison, animated by the presence of Lady Derby, continued to defend the house with unabated courage. At last, on the 23rd of May, they learnt, to their inexpressible relief, that Prince Rupert and the Earl of Derby were in Cheshire, marching to their aid.

When the Puritans heard of the approach of Prince Rupert, they retreated to Bolton. On the 29th, Prince Rupert "not only relieved, but revenged the most noble lady, his cousin," leaving one thousand five hundred of the besiegers dead on the field, and taking seven hundred prisoners. The next day he presented the countess with twenty-two of those standards which, three days previously, had been proudly waving before Lathom House.

The countess and her children accompanied the earl to the Isle of Man, leaving the mansion in charge of Colonel Rawstone. The latter defended it till the following December, when the decline of the Royal cause obliged him to open negotiations with Fairfax. Before they were brought to a satisfactory conclusion, the house was treacherously surrendered by an Irish soldier.

The earl and countess, in the midst of their devoted adherents in the Isle of Man, defied the threats of Parliament. The earl was one of the first to join the standard of Charles II. in 1651. Captured on the borders of Cheshire, he was carried to his own town of Bolton-le-Moors, where he was beheaded, October 15th. Misfortune never comes unaccompanied. The bereaved countess was betrayed, with her children, by a false friend, and thrown into prison. She regained her liberty at the Restoration; and for the rest of her life dwelt, with her remaining children, at Knowsley, near Lathom, where she died in 1663.

Although the Turks were expelled from Hungary in the sixteenth century, they by no means gave up their ambitious designs on that country. Taking advantage of the cruelty and oppression exercised by Austria towards the Hungarians, they secretly stirred up the nobles to revolt against their harsh masters. In 1678, an able leader was found in Emeric Tekeli, or Tokolyi, who, weary of vainly soliciting the Emperor Leopold to restore his paternal estates, resolved to take them for himself, together with the crown of Hungary. Setting up his standard in Transylvania, he was soon joined by thousands of malcontents. Day by day the revolt gathered strength; and had not the emperor resorted to the arts of cunning and bribery, it is probable the rebellion would have terminated in a revolution.

Tekeli was husband of Helena, widow of Francis Ragotsky (who died in 1667), and daughter of Peter, Count Zrinyi, Ban of Croatia, who, with others, lost his head in 1671 for conspiring against Leopold. Helena was as brave as she was beautiful. By her first husband she had two sons, of whom the eldest, Francis, afterwards took a conspicuous part in the affairs of Hungary.

Tekeli commenced the war in 1678, and in 1682 he entered Buda in triumph, where he was inaugurated Prince of Upper Hungary by the nobles and the Turkish Bashaw. In the following year, the Turks, following up these successes, advanced to Vienna, which would have fallen, but for John Sobiesky and his Poles. Leopold took care to foment the growing jealousies between Tekeli and the Turks; and on the failure of the Hungarian leader in an attack on Cassau, the Bashaw of Great Waradin sent the hero in chains to Constantinople. He was released the following year; but during his imprisonment the Turks were driven from Hungary and the rebellion crushed. Helena continued to defend the rock-fortress of Mongatz (or Munkacs) with great courage for two years after the arrest of her husband; but in 1688 she was overpowered by superior numbers, and reduced to capitulate and throw herself with her sons under the protection of the Emperor.

Helena was thrown into a convent, while her children were educated under the auspices of Leopold. After a time, she was exchanged for an Austrian general, and permitted to join her husband in Turkey. The *Sultan*, Mustapha, conferred upon Tekeli, Widdin, and some other districts, as a sort of feudal sovereignty; but he was afterwards neglected by the Turkish Government, and compelled to start as a vintner in Constantinople, where he died in 1705, in his fiftieth year. Helena, after sharing the misfortunes and vicissitudes of his life, died two years before him, in 1703.

A somewhat ludicrous affair happened at the coronation of William and Mary, April 23rd-, 1689. The champion of England, according to custom, entered Westminster Hall, and throwing down his mailed glove, gave the customary challenge to anyone who should dare to dispute their Majesty's claim to the crown. An old woman came in on crutches (which she left behind her), snatched up the gauntlet, laid her own glove in its place, and made off as fast as she could, before any one was able to stop her. In the glove was found a challenge for the champion to meet her the following day in Hyde Park. This matter occasioned much merriment at the lower end of the hall.

Next day an old woman, similarly dressed, was seen waiting at the appointed ground, and was conjectured by those who saw her, to be a soldier in disguise. The champion, however, wisely declining any warlike contest with one of the fair sex, refused to keep the appointment.

Madlle. de la Tour du Pin Gouvernail, better known as Madlle. de la Charce, heroine of the war between Louis Quatorze and the Duke of Savoy, was the daughter of Pierre de la Tour du Pin, Marquis de la Charce, lieutenant-general of the king's armies.

In 1692 the Piedmontese invaded Dauphiné. Madlle. de la Charce, arming the villagers on her estates, placed herself at their head, and harassed the enemy in the mountains; her mother, meanwhile, addressed the people in the plains, exhorting them to remain faithful. The sister of Madlle. de la Charce caused the cables of the enemy's vessels to be cut. This brave family contributed so greatly towards driving the Duke of Savoy from Dauphine, that Louis XIV. granted Philis a pension, the same as he would have given to a brave general, and allowed her to place her sword and armour in the treasury of St. Denis.

Madlle. de la Charce was fond of literature, and composed some very pretty verses. An anonymous work appeared in 1731, under the title of *Mémoires de Madlle. de la Charce*. This little romance, says Langlet-Dufresnoy, is well written, and contains many historical anecdotes connected with the reign of the *Grand-Monarque*.

Chapter 11

Female Officer in the French Army to Female Sailor on Board Admiral Rodney's Ship

During the eighteenth century there were to be found in nearly every European army, one or more female soldiers. They sometimes held commissions as officers, but more frequently served as non-commissioned officers or privates. Those women and girls who enlisted in the British Army were generally wives or sweethearts of soldiers whose regiments had been ordered abroad, and the women, preferring to encounter the dangers and hardships of a foreign campaign rather than the miseries of separation, disguised themselves in male attire and enlisted in some battalion which was embarking for the seat of war.

Sometimes, indeed, women, deserted by their husbands, resolved to follow their unfaithful spouses all over the world: and, unable to afford travelling expenses, enlisted at the first recruiting depot, and trusted to chance for meeting with or hearing of the object of their search. As no personal examination of recruits took place in those days, either in Great Britain or elsewhere, there was no way of finding out the imposture until afterwards, more especially as the female soldiers behaved themselves quite as manly as their comrades.

Of course, in every country there have been local celebrities whose names even are unknown beyond the frontiers, for a man or woman must perform very great deeds to become famous in foreign lands. Thus, it happens, while we are familiar with the names of many an English female soldier, we know of only two or three women who served during the last century in the armies of France. Yet the world well knows that Frenchwomen are second to none in warlike *esprit*. One of these Gallic warriors was Captain Bodeaux, an officer holding a commission as lieutenant in one of the regiments which went over to Ireland under the command of St. Ruth, to assist James the Second.

This gallant officer distinguished herself at the Battle of the Boyne, July 1st, 1690, where she met with Mr. Cavanaugh, father of Christian Davies. She stopped at the house of that gentleman (who was also fighting for King James) till about three in the morning, when, being alarmed, they fled together precipitately. Christian Davies describes this officer as "a very handsome young French gentleman," though the real sex of Bodeaux was not unknown to her.

At the siege of Limerick, June, 1691, she held Thomond bridge, over the Shannon, with a small body of troops, against the English, till at last she fell, covered with wounds. Such was the bravery of this young French officer that her death was lamented even by the foe. Great was their astonishment when they found their valiant antagonist was a woman.

The most famous woman who has ever served as a private in any modern European army, was Christian (or Christiana) Davies, *alias* Mother Ross. She was born in 1667, in Dublin, "of parents whose probity acquired them that respect from their acquaintance which they had no claim to from their birth." Her father, Mr. Cavanaugh, was a brewer and maltster, employing upwards of twenty servants, exclusive of those engaged on his farm at Leslipp, where his wife and daughter resided. Christiana never liked sedentary work, and in the matter of education never made much progress. She had barely sufficient patience to learn reading, and to become a good needle-woman.

Open air exercises were her delight; ploughing, hay-making, using the flail, and, above all, riding on horseback, she says:

> I used to get astride upon the horses and ride them bare-backed about the fields and ditches, by which I once got a terrible fall and spoiled a grey mare given to my brother by our grandfather.

Mr. Cavanaugh never discovered the offender; but, to purchase the silence of a cowherd who saw her and the mare fall into a dry ditch, she was obliged, for a long time, to give him a cup of ale every night.

In 1685, when the Irish were arming for King James, Mr. Cavanaugh sold his corn and equipped a troop of horse, with which he joined that monarch. After enduring great hardships he was dangerously wounded at the Battle of Aughrim, June 12th, 1691, and died a few days after. His property was confiscated by Government.

Previous to this, shortly after the departure of Mr. Cavanaugh from home, the Roman Catholic inhabitants of Leslipp blocked up the door of the parish church during divine service, with logs of wood, butchers' blocks, and any other heavy articles which came to hand. Christiana was at home when this occurred; but her mother being, with others, blockaded in the sacred edifice, she seized up a spit and ran to the rescue. Being resisted by a sergeant, she thrust the spit through his leg; then removing the things which blocked up the door, set the congregation free. Christiana was arrested for wounding the sergeant, but was afterwards liberated.

After the death of her father, Christian went on a visit to her aunt, the landlady of a public-house in Dublin, who, at her death, left the establishment to her niece. The latter married Richard Welsh, a good-looking young fellow who acted as barman and general assistant. After two boys had been born, her happiness was suddenly blighted by the mysterious disappearance of Richard, of whom nothing was heard for several months. At last, when she had given him up for dead, a letter arrived (the *twelfth* he had written) telling her how, on the day of his disappearance, he had been invited by an old friend on board a transport with recruits on board; the vessel set sail, and they had reached Helvoet Sluys before he could get ashore. Having no way of getting back to Ireland, he enlisted in a foot-regiment.

Christian resolved to follow her husband to Flanders. Letting the public-house, leaving her furniture with different friends, and placing one child with her grandmother and the other with a nurse, she dressed herself in a suit of her husband's clothes, cut her hair short, and went to the "Golden Last," where Ensign Laurence told the new recruit that she was "a clever, brisk young fellow," and enrolled her, under the name of Christopher Welsh, in the Marquis de Pisare's regiment of foot.

The recruits were disembarked at Williamstadt, in Holland. Thence they marched to Gorkhum, where they received their uniforms; and the next day they advanced to Landen, which they reached a day or two before the great battle of July 19th, 1693. Here they were incorporated into their respective battalions. Christian found the drill very easy, as she says:

> Having been accustomed to soldiers, when a girl, and delighted with seeing them exercise. I very soon was perfect. . . . and ap-

plauded by my officers for my dexterity in going through it.

The same night that she arrived at Landen, being on night-guard at the door of the Elector of Hanover (afterwards George I.), Christian was wounded by a musket-ball which grazed her leg, barely missing the bone. She was thus laid up for two months.

During the summer of 1694, Christian being out with a foraging party, was made prisoner, and brought, together with three-score English and Dutch, to St. Germain-en-Laye. When the ex-Queen of England heard that Christian and her companions were English soldiers, she ordered that each man should have a pound of bread, a pint of wine, and five farthings each *per diem*, with clean straw every night. But the Dutch prisoners were not allowed these luxuries. The Duke of Berwick, a Marshal of France, visited the prison, and tried to persuade the British to follow his example and enter the service of the *Grand Monarque*. The chief annoyance which Christian suffered was the fear of being recognised by her cousin, Captain Cavanaugh, a French officer, who visited the prison nearly every day.

About nine days later, the English prisoners were exchanged, and on being set free they waited upon the queen to thank her for her kindness. Her regiment passed the winter of 1694-5 in Gorkhum, where Christian passed her time "very merrily" by making love to the young and pretty daughter of a wealthy *burgher*. After a few weeks' courtship "the poor girl grew absolutely fond" of her military wooer. This *harmless frolic* led to a duel between Private Welsh and a sergeant of the regiment who wished to engage the girl's affections. Having dangerously wounded the sergeant, Christian was ordered under arrest; but the old father, who was in ignorance of the real state of the case, exerted his influence with the authorities, and procured her discharge from the regiment.

Bidding farewell to the girl, under pretence of going to purchase a commission, Christian enlisted in the 6th Dragoons, commanded by Lord John Hayes, and served all through the campaign of 1695, including the siege of Namur. Nothing remarkable happened to her till the Peace of Ryswick, Sept. 20th, 1697, when she was discharged, and went home to Ireland. None of her friends recognised the stalwart dragoon as being identical with Mrs Welsh; so, in place of claiming her property she found other means of support, until the War of the Spanish Succession broke out, in 1701. Returning to Holland, Christian re-enlisted in the 6th Dragoons.

She served through the campaigns of 1701-2, under the Duke of Marlborough, without being wounded. She was one of the captors of Venlo, Sept. 23rd, 1702, which proved a profitable investment for the English, for they found more than thirty pieces of cannon, twenty thousand florins, and a quantity of plate and jewellery. Christian complains that, the Grenadiers having the start of the Dragoons, she "got very little of the plunder." "I got, however," she confesses, "a large silver chalice and some other pieces of plate," which prize was sufficient to console her.

The Dragoons wintered at Venlo, and a night or two after their arrival she was ordered, with others, to escort the Duke of Marlborough along the banks of the Meuse. Christian says:

> During our march by the darkness of the night we mistook our way, and going up the country fell in with a hog-stye where was a sow with five pigs, one of which I made bold with. I was possessed of it sometime. . . . when one Taylor, a corporal belonging to Brigadier Panton's Regiment of Horse, attempted to spoil me of my booty, whereupon some words arising, he drew, and made a stroke at my head, which I warding with my hand, had the sinew of my little finger cut in two; at the same time, with the butt-end of my pistol I struck out one of his eyes.

Pretty discipline for British soldiers!

After serving all through the campaign of 1703, including the Battle of Eckeren, and the sieges of Bonn and Lembourg, she was wounded in the hip at the Battle of Donawert, July 2nd, 1704. The musket-ball lodged so firmly in the bone that the efforts of three surgeons in the hospital near Schellenberg were insufficient to extract it. Christian with difficulty warded off the discovery of her sex.

She left hospital just in time to assist in plundering the Bavarians, she says:

> We spared nothing, burning or otherwise destroying whatever we could not carry off. The bells of the churches we broke to pieces that we might bring them away with us. I filled three bed-ticks, after having emptied them of the feathers, with bell-metal, men's and women's clothes, some velvets, and about one hundred Dutch caps which I had plundered from a shop.

Besides these things she got several pieces of plate, as spoons, mugs, cups, etc.

After the Battle of Blenheim, August 2nd, 1704, in which she was in the midst of the fight, under the hottest of the fire, Christian was appointed one of the guard despatched with the prisoners to Breda. Having halted to refresh themselves with a pint of beer and a pennyworth of bread each (the prisoners being allowed the same indulgence), Christian saw the long-lost Richard Welsh, now a sergeant in the Earl of Orkney's regiment of foot, making love to a Dutch woman. She abused him heartily at first, but she soon forgave him. It was agreed that she should remain in the army and pass as his brother. On her return to her regiment she assisted in the siege of Landau. Nothing of any consequence happened to her during the campaign of 1705.

On the 23rd of May, 1706, was fought the great Battle of Ramilies. When the French were retreating, Christian, who had fought valiantly during the engagement, was struck in the head by "an unlucky shell" fired from a mortar planted on the steeple of the church. Her skull was fractured, and she was carried to the hospital of Meldré or Meldret, where her head was trepanned. During a ten weeks' illness the long-dreaded discovery of her sex was made. The surgeons sent word to Brigadier Preston that his "pretty dragoon" was a woman. The Brigadier, who would at first scarcely believe the news, told Christian that he had always looked upon her "as the prettiest fellow, and the best man he had."

The story soon spread through the regiment, and Christian was visited by Lord John Hayes and all her officers and comrades. Lord John gave strict orders that she should want for nothing, and promised that her pay as a dragoon should be continued till she had quitted the hospital.

Of course, she could no longer stop in the regiment, she says:

Brigadier Preston made me a present of a handsome silk gown; every one of the officers contributed to furnishing me with whatever was requisite for the dress of my sex, and dismissed me the service with a handsome compliment."

Her husband having been questioned relative to their previous acquaintance, it was thought prudent to have them married again; and this second wedding was celebrated with much solemnity, in presence of all the officers, "who, everyone, at taking leave, would kiss the bride, and left me," adds Christian, "a piece of gold, some four or five, to put me in a way of life."

For a short time, she carried on the business of cook to the 6th

Dragoons; but finding the work too heavy, she turned sutler, and was permitted, as a special favour, to pitch her tent in the front of the army, the other sutlers being driven to the rear. She spent much time in marauding; and one day in 1708, being in male garb, she and her mule were taken prisoner. However, she persuaded the French officer to let her go. Shortly before this she hired herself as cook to the head sutler of the British Army, Mr. Dupper, who afterwards kept a tavern on Fish Street Hill, London.

Richard Welsh was slain at the siege of Mons, in September, 1709. Her grief, she tells us, was something terrible. It was on this occasion that she first came to be styled Mother Ross.

> Captain Ross came by, who seeing my agony, could not forbear sympathizing with me and dropped some tears, protesting that the poor woman's grief touched him nearer than the loss of so many brave men. This confession from the captain gave me the nickname of Mother Ross, by which I became better known than by that of my husband.

Eleven weeks after the death of Welsh, his sorrowing widow was persuaded to bestow her hand on Hugh Jones, Grenadier, who was killed at the siege of St. Venant, 1710. During this and the following year Christian held the post of undercook in Lord Stair's kitchen.

On the close of the campaign of 1712 she returned to England, and called on the Duke of Marlborough; but he, being in disgrace, advised her to wait on the Duke of Argyle. The latter told Christian to draw up a petition to the queen. Her majesty received Mother Ross very graciously, and gave her an order on the Earl of Oxford for fifty pounds. But having waited on the earl several times and seen neither him nor the money, she petitioned the queen again. Anne granted a second order for the same sum, payable this time on Sir William Windham, and Christian was also put on the pension list for a shilling a day. Sir William at once paid the fifty pounds; but the Earl of Oxford, without speaking to Queen Anne, cut down the pension to five-pence. On the accession of George I., she succeeded in having it raised again to a shilling; and this pension she retained till her death.

Immediately after receiving the money, Christian returned to Dublin; but being unable to recover either her house or furniture, she set up a beer-shop. She was keeping herself very comfortably, "till my evil genius," she laments, "entangled me in a third marriage."

This time the bridegroom was named Davies, and belonged to

the Welsh Fusileers. His regiment was ordered, soon after the marriage, to England; Christian therefore sold her effects, and returned to London, where she established a shop in Willow Walk, Tothill Fields, Westminster, for the sale of strong liquors and farthing pies. This was in 1715. She prospered so well, that after the return of her husband from Preston (where he had gone to fight the Pretender), she was able to purchase his discharge; but "in two days after his arrival in London, being drunk, he enlisted in the Guards." During the November of this year, Mother Ross kept a sutler's tent in Hyde Park where the Life, and Foot Guards were encamped.

Her husband was a constant source of trouble and vexation. Some friends having obtained his discharge, he spent her money so fast that she was, obliged to give up, successively, public-houses at Paddington and in Charles-street, Westminster. She returned to Dublin, when the Lord-Lieutenant granted her the exclusive privilege of selling beer in the Phoenix Park on review-days. Tiring of this, in less than a year, she returned to England; and after living three years in Chester, she entered Chelsea College as a Pensioner.

She also succeeded in obtaining a sergeantcy in the College for her husband. Here she resided till her death: being supported by the benevolence of several members of the nobility—principally officers who had known her as Mother Ross. She went to Court twice a week to keep herself in the minds of her patrons; she laments:

> But, the expense of coach-hire, as both my lameness and age increases, for I cannot walk ten yards without help, is a terrible tax upon their charity, and at the same time many of my old friends no longer going to Court, my former subsistence is greatly diminished from what it was.

For some months previous to her death Christian Davies's health was undermined by dropsy, scurvy, and other disorders. But the chief cause of her last illness was sitting up several nights by the bedside of her husband. This brought on a severe cold, which threw her into a fever, of which she died, July 7th, 1739. She was interred with military honours in the burial-ground of Chelsea College. Her autobiography, edited by Daniel Defoe, was published in 1740. A second edition came out in 1741, with a vignette frontispiece representing Christian Davies first in her Dragoon's uniform, and then in the dress of a sutler. (Republished by Leonaur in 2011 as *Mother Ross*).

According to the embarkation returns of the 2oth Foot, dated 1st

July, 1702, preserved among the Harleian MSS. at the British Museum, one of the soldiers in Captain St. Clair's Company was found to be a woman. The regiment was embarking to join the expedition against Cadiz.

During the war of the Spanish Succession, Catalonia having declared against Philip, the French claimant to the crown, was invaded and ravaged by the forces of Louis Quatorze. Barcelona, the capital, was invested for several months, and the formidable artillery of France played, almost unceasingly, on the walls. But the people, nothing daunted by the arrival of Marshal Berwick with twenty thousand men to reinforce the besiegers, made a most resolute defence. All who could bear arms flew to aid in the defence; the priests and the women enrolled themselves in the ranks, and fought with the same desperate valour as the rest. Their courage, however, was unavailing; for the city was taken by assault, Sept. 11th, 1714.

Hannah Snell, another British heroine, was born in Fryer-street, Winchester, on the 23rd of April, 1723. Military predilections ran in the family; her grandfather served under King William and the Duke of Marlborough, and was slain in the Battle of Malplaquet. Her father, however, was a simple dyer and hosier. Hannah was the youngest but one of a family of three sons and six daughters.

On the death of her father and mother in 1740, Hannah came to London, and lived for some time in Ship-street, Wapping, in the house of one of her sisters, Mrs. Gray, whose husband was a carpenter. She had not resided in the house very long before she became acquainted with James Summs, a Dutch sailor, whom she married, Jan. 6th, 1743, after a courtship of about two years. Her marriage was not a happy one. After squandering the little property belonging to his wife, spending it in the lowest debauchery, James became heavily involved in debt, and deserted her altogether. Hannah, left without the means of support, was obliged to return to the house of her sister, where, two months after, her child, a girl, was born.

Notwithstanding his vile conduct, Mrs. Summs still dearly loved her husband; and on the death of her child, she resolved to set out in search of the truant. Dressing herself in a suit of clothes belonging to her brother-in-law, which, together with his name, she borrowed, Hannah left London, Nov. 23rd, 1743, and reached Coventry without hearing any news of her missing husband. On the 27th of the same month she enlisted, under the name of James Gray, in General Guise's regiment of Foot (the 6th, or Royal First Warwickshire). After remaining about three weeks in the town, during which she made number-less inquiries about James Summs, Hannah was sent with seventeen comrades to join her regiment at Carlisle.

She was soon very proficient in the drill; but at the same time, she had the misfortune to incur the enmity of Davis, a sergeant in her company, who wished to employ the new recruit in a somewhat dis-honourable affair with a girl who lived in Carlisle. Hannah, however, disclosed the real intentions of the sergeant to the intended victim, and gained the love of the girl, while she made a bitter enemy of Da-vis. The latter, from seeing Hannah and the other very frequently to-gether, grew terribly jealous; he seized the first opportunity to charge his supposed rival with neglect of duty. Hannah was sentenced to receive six hundred lashes. After five hundred had been administered, the officers interceded, and obtained for her the remission of the other hundred.

The tyranny of Davis soon became unbearable; and, to make mat-ters worse, a carpenter from Worcester, who had lodged in the house of Hannah's brother-in-law, enlisted in the regiment, and she was in constant terror lest he should recognise and betray her. To get away without the discovery of her sex was now the great object of her thoughts. She borrowed a small sum of money from the girl in Car-lisle, deserted, and set off on foot for Portsmouth. About a mile from Carlisle she saw several men and women picking peas; their clothes lay about, at a short distance, and Hannah very speedily exchanged her soldier's coat for an old jacket.

At Liverpool she entered a small public-house; and, by affecting to make love to the landlady, made the landlord so jealous that a match of "fisticuffs" ensued. Boniface, however, got the worst of it, and was compelled to keep his bed all next day. Hannah borrowed some mon-ey of the landlady, and made the best of her way to Chester, where she took genteel lodgings in a private house.

It chanced that a pretty young mantua-maker lodged in the same house. Hannah contrived to make the acquaintance of the girl, and speedily won her heart, together with five guineas. The handsome young suitor levanted to Winchester, where, in an attempt on the heart of a widow, she met her match. She speedily quitted the town, with only a few shillings in her pocket.

In about a month from the day she left Carlisle, Hannah reached Portsmouth, where she enlisted in Colonel Fraser's Regiment of Ma-rines. With others of her regiment, she embarked, three weeks later, for the East Indies. The *Swallow* formed part of Admiral Boscawen's fleet. Hannah soon earned the praises of the officers for her dexterity "in washing, mending, and cooking. Mr. Wyegate, Lieutenant of Marines, was so greatly interested in the young private, that he invited her to become one at the officers' mess.

The *Swallow* suffered from some terrible storms, which destroyed almost all her rigging, and reduced the vessel almost to the condition of a wreck. It was refitted at Gibraltar; proceeding thence by the Cape of Good Hope to the Mauritius, which Admiral Boscawen unsuccessfully attacked. Thence the fleet sailed to Fort St. David on the Coromandel coast; where the marines being disbanded, joined the British force encamped before Areacoping. The place surrendered after a siege of ten days. During the siege Hannah displayed so much courage that she received the commendations of all her officers.

The British next laid siege to Pondicherry; but after suffering terrible hardships, they were forced by the rainy season to raise the siege in eleven weeks. Hannah was one of the first body of British soldiers who forded the river, breast high, under an incessant fire from the French batteries. She was also for seven nights successively on duty in the picket-ground, and worked exceedingly hard for upwards of fourteen days in the trenches.

She was dangerously wounded in one of the attacks. During this action she fired thirty-seven rounds, and received in return six shots in her right leg, five in the left leg, and a dangerous wound in the abdomen; the last-named being excessively painful. She was terrified lest these wounds would lead to the discovery of her sex; so, in place of letting the army-surgeons dress all her wounds, she kept silence about the most dangerous of them, though it was at the risk of her life. Entrusting the secret to no one but a black woman who waited on her, Hannah extracted the bullet with her finger and thumb; the negress obtained lint, salve, and other necessaries for dressing, and the wound was soon perfectly cured.

Hannah was removed for the cure of her other wounds to the hospital at Cuddalore; and before her recovery, the greater part of the fleet had sailed. She was sent on board the *Tartar Pink*, and performed all the regular duties of a sailor, till the return of the fleet from Madras, when she was turned over to the *Eltham* man-of-war. On board this ship she sailed to Bombay. The vessel sprang a leak, and they were obliged to stop here five weeks to repair.

One night the lieutenant of the *Eltham*, who commanded in the absence of Captain Lloyd, wishing to pass the time agreeably, asked Hannah for a song. She declined, on the plea of being unwell; but the officer would take no denial. Hannah became obstinate, but soon she had cause to regret her folly. Shortly after, she was accused of stealing a shirt belonging to one of her comrades. The lieutenant, having a grudge against Hannah, ordered her to be put in irons; and after five days' confinement, ordered her to the gangway, where she received five lashes. The shirt was afterwards found in the box of the very man who had complained of losing it.

Returning to Fort St. David, the *Eltham* rejoined the squadron, which departed soon after on its homeward voyage. Hannah was terribly "chaffed" during the voyage because she had no beard; and she became known among the sailors by the name of Miss Molly Gray. But in place of resenting this, Hannah, to show she was as good a man as any of them, plunged headlong into all the amusements and enjoyments of the others, and they soon forgot the old nickname, for which they substituted that of "Hearty Jemmy."

One night, in a house of entertainment at Lisbon, she learned, from an English sailor who had been in a Dutch ship at Genoa, that James Summs, her husband, was dead. He had murdered a gentleman of high position in Genoa, and for this crime he was put into a bag full of stones, and flung into the sea.

The British fleet arrived at Spithead in 1750. Hannah left the *Eltham*, and came to London, where she was cordially welcomed by her sister. The strange story of Hannah Snell soon became generally known; and as she had a good voice, the managers of the Royalty Theatre, Wellclose Square, engaged her to appear before the footlights as Bill Bobstay, Firelock, and other military and naval heroes, and to go through the manual and platoon exercises with a musket. But she did not long remain on the stage, as, in consideration of the wounds she received during the siege of Pondicherry, she was put on the outpensioners' list at Chelsea Hospital.

Her pension was increased by a special grant to twenty pounds a year, and paid regularly to the day of her death. With the assistance of some friends she set up a public-house at Wapping, by which she realized a very good income. On one side of the sign-board there was painted the figure of a jovial British tar, on the other a portrait of herself in her marine's uniform. Underneath the last was inscribed, "The Widow in Masquerade, or the Female Warrior."

Hannah preferred masculine attire, and continued to wear men's clothes for the rest of her life. She lived long to enjoy her prosperity; but during the latter years of her life she became a lunatic, and died, at the age of sixty-nine, in Bedlam. (Her story along with that of another another is republished by Leonaur in *The Female Soldier.*)

Phoebe Hessel (or Hassel) was for many years a private in the 5th Regiment, and served under the Duke of Cumberland in many engagements, amongst others the Battle of Fontenoy. The fatigues and hardships of war certainly did not tend to shorten her days. Born during the reign of Queen Anne, she lived to see the accession of George IV. Indeed, it was through the liberality of the last-named monarch that Phoebe was enabled to live comfortably during the latter years of her life. When the Prince Regent visited Brighton, he saw old Phoebe, who was living there, maintained by some of the more benevolent inhabitants. Having heard her strange story, the prince told someone to ask her what sum she required to make her comfortable.

"Half-a-guinea a week," replied Phoebe, "will make me as happy as a princess."

This annuity was, by order of the prince regent, paid to her as long as she lived.

Phoebe Hessel was a woman of good information, and very communicative. Her stories were always worth hearing. She retained all her faculties till within a few hours of her death, which took place Dec. 12th, 1821. She was buried in Brighton Churchyard, and a tombstone erected over her grave by public subscription. The following inscription was carved thereon:—

> Sacred to the memory of Phoebe Hessel, born Sept. 1st, 1713. She served for many years as a private soldier in the 5th regiment, in different parts of Europe, and in 1745 fought under the Duke of Cumberland in the Battle of Fontenoy, where she received a bayonet wound in the arm; her long life which commenced in the reign of queen Anne, induced his present Majesty George IV. to grant her a pension. She died at Brighton, where she had long resided, Dec. 12th, 1821, aged 108 years.

In August, 1761, as a sergeant was exercising some recruits on board a transport at Portsmouth, he noticed that one of them, who had enlisted under the name of Paul Daniel, had a more prominent breast than the others. When the firing was over, the sergeant sent for Daniel to the cabin, and told him his suspicion that he was a woman. After some evasions the recruit confessed her sex; and said that she had a husband, to whom she was devotedly attached, who, after squandering a plentiful fortune, had reduced himself and her to beggary, and had then enlisted. His regiment had been ordered to Germany in 1759 to serve against the French, and had remained abroad ever since. Not having heard from him for two years, she had resolved to roam the world in search of him. She heard that the British Government were sending more troops to Germany, so she enlisted in one of the regiments ordered thither, thinking to meet her husband. When the discovery of her sex frustrated this design, she declared herself to be inconsolable.

In October of the same year, a young woman aged about twenty, attired in nautical garb, was seized at Plymouth by the Press-gang, and sent to Captain Toby. On her capture she was placed for safety in the town jail. Not relishing her imprisonment, she roundly abused Captain Toby, told him she was a woman, that her name was Hannah Whitney, that she was born in Ireland, and had served on board several British men-of-war for upwards of five years. She concluded by informing the astounded captain that she would never have discovered her sex if they had not placed her in a common jail. Of course, she was immediately released.

There is (or was) a monument in Chelsea church, commemorative of the masculine courage of Anne Chamberlayne, only daughter of Edward Chamberlayne, Doctor of Laws. She appears to have been infected with an ardour for naval glory by her two brothers, who were both distinguished officers on board men-of-war. Putting on the dress of a sailor, she joined the crew of a fine ship, commanded by one of her brothers; and in an engagement with the French, she fought most gallantly for upwards of six hours.

On the 27th of June, 1808, died at Liverpool Mary Ralphson, a Scottish heroine. She was born in Lochaber, June 1st, 1698; and married Ralph Ralphson, then a private in the British army. She followed her husband in all his campaigns under the Duke of Cumberland, and was present with him in several famous engagements. On the breaking out of the war in French Flanders she embarked with the troops, and shared their toils and vicissitudes. Being present on the field of Dettingen during the heat of the conflict, surrounded with heaps of the slain, she saw a wounded dragoon fall dead by her side. She disguised herself in his clothes, and regained the British camp; then returned with her husband to England. After this she accompanied him in his later campaigns under the Duke of Cumberland. She lived to a fine old age, and was supported during her declining years chiefly by some benevolent ladies of Liverpool.

There is just a hint of a loyal Jacobite heroine in a curious old Scotch ballad called "Polly Oliver's Ramble." The song commences:—

As pretty Polly Oliver lay musing in bed,
A comical fancy came into her head;
Nor father nor mother shall make me false prove,
I'll list for a soldier and follow my love.

There is an old song on the Pretender which appears to be a parody on this ballad. This begins:—

As Perkin one morning lay musing in bed,
The thought of three kingdoms ran much in his head.

In June, 1745, Charles Edward Stuart, the young Pretender, landed in Scotland to assert his father's right to the British crown. He was joined by most of the Highland chieftains with their clans, and he sent to all those lairds who had not yet paid their allegiance, to do so without delay. Lochiel, his lieutenant, wrote to Cameron, the Laird of Glendessary, commanding him to appear at headquarters immediately, with as many of his clan, armed, as he could muster in so short a notice.

The laird was a minor, and, moreover, a youth of little capacity; so, his aunt, Miss Jenny Cameron, roused the clan to arms, and marched, at the head of two hundred and fifty claymores, to the camp of Bonnie Prince Charlie. She rode into camp on a bay gelding decked out in green trappings, trimmed with gold. She wore a sea-green riding habit with scarlet lappets edged with gold. Her hair was tied behind in loose buckles, and covered by a velvet cap with scarlet feathers. In her hand, in lieu of a whip, she carried a drawn sword.

A female soldier was a sight not to be seen every day. The prince immediately quitted the lines to receive her. Miss Jenny rode up to him without the slightest embarrassment; and giving the military salute, told him:

As her nephew was not able to attend the royal standard, she had raised men, and now brought them to his highness; that she believed them ready to hazard their lives in his cause; and that, although at present they were commanded by a woman, yet she hoped they had nothing womanish about them; for she found that so glorious a cause had raised in her own heart every manly thought and quite extinguished the woman. What effect then must it have on those who have no feminine fear to combat, and are free from the incumbrance of female dress. . . . . . These men are yours; they have devoted themselves to your service, they bring you hearts as well as hands. I can follow them no farther, but I shall pray for your success.

The clansmen then passed in review before the prince. When this was over, he conducted Miss Cameron to his tent, where she was entertained with the utmost courtesy and hospitality. Prince Charlie gave her the title of "Colonel Cameron," and by this epithet she was distinguished for many years.

Miss Jenny remained with the Jacobite army until it invaded England, and joined it again on its return, in Annandale. She was still in camp in January, 1746, and fought in the Battle of Falkirk on the 23rd; when she was made prisoner, and lodged in Edinburgh Castle. She was ultimately set at liberty, and returned to the guardianship of her weak-minded nephew.

A Highland song was composed in her honour, relating how:

Miss Jenny Cameron,
She put her belt and hanger on,
And away to the Young Pretender.

Anne Sophia Detzliffin, who served four years in the Prussian army, was born in 1738 at Treptow on the Rega. In 1757, during the Seven Years' War, she was excited by a thirst for glory to quit her father's house and go to Colberg, where she enlisted in Prince Frederic's regiment of *cuirassiers*. She remained in this corps for two years, and fought in several actions; in one of which, near Bamberg, she received a sabre-wound in her left arm.

She next fought in the Battle of Kunnersdorff. Her regiment returned some days later to Saxony, where Anne fell dangerously ill, and was sent to the hospital of Meissen. She soon recovered, but having no opportunity for rejoining her regiment, she enlisted in a battalion of grenadiers, which was decimated shortly after in the actions of Strechlin and Torgau, in 1760. In the latter, fought on Nov. 3rd, Sophia Detzliffin received two severe wounds on the head, and was captured by the Austrians, who took her to the hospital at Dresden.

When she had almost recovered, the heroine found means to escape from the hospital. Passing through the Austrian outposts without being discovered, she enlisted (in 1761) with Colonel Colignon, who sent her to a regiment of Le Noble's Volunteers.

After serving in this corps for two months, she was accused on the 14th of July by one of her comrades of robbing him of fourteen-pence. There was not the slightest foundation for the accusation; but a subaltern immediately placed her under arrest. Anne was determined not to submit to such an indignity. Sending for her lieutenant, she told that she was a female, and declared that during four years' service in various regiments she had never once been ordered under arrest, nor even received a blow for neglect of duty. She concluded by telling the officer that after this insult she would no longer remain in the army—which was, however, a needless remark, as she would not have been permitted to stop after her sex was known.

This heroine, when she quitted the army, was twenty-three years old, with strongly-marked features, and a brown complexion.

On the 8th of June, 1758, General (afterwards Lord) Amherst, with an army of twelve thousand men, in which General Wolfe served as a brigadier, landed on the island of Cape-Breton, in Canada, and commenced the siege of Louisbourg. This town was so strongly fortified that the French, believing it to be impregnable, left only two thousand eight hundred men for its defence. The military commander, the Chevalier de Drucourt, was a brave and resolute soldier, and made a gallant defence. The British, however, determined to make up for all their recent disasters, commenced the siege with more than ordinary vigour and energy. The Chevalier was ably assisted in the defence by his wife; who, appearing on the walls among the common soldiers, exhorted them to fight bravely in defence of the town.

And not only did she thus cheer them by encouraging words; she carried round food and ammunition to the exhausted soldiers, and occasionally took her turn at the guns, which she loaded and fired with skill and rapidity. But the efforts of the Chevalier and his wife were of no avail against the superior numbers of the English. Louisbourg surrendered on the 26th of June; and the Chevalier and Madame de Drucourt were made prisoners. However, General Amherst treated his brave captives with the greatest respect and hospitality.

In 1759, when the British were besieging Guadaloupe, the native planters were incited to resist the invaders by M. Dutril, the French Governor. Amongst others, Madame Ducharmy, wife of a planter, armed her servants and negroes, and led them to an attack on the British forces.

Amongst the celebrities of the eighteenth century, none was more famous than the Chevalier d'Eon. Even before the strange question as to his real sex had been raised, the Chevalier was well known in every European court as a skilful diplomatist and a brave soldier. In 1761, having attained the summit of his glory in the political world, he sighed for military renown. As *aide-de-camp* to Marshal Broglio, he distinguished himself most highly against the British and Prussians. Being entrusted with the removal of the military stores from Hoxter, which the French were evacuating, he passed the Weser with several boats, under a heavy fire from the enemy, and saved all the baggage. Shortly after this he was wounded in the head and thigh in a skirmish at Ultrop.

On the 7th September, at the head of the Grenadiers de Champagne and the Swiss Guards, the Chevalier attacked a Highland regiment ("*Montagnards Ecossais*," Broglio styles them in his despatch) near the village of Meinsloff, and after a slight skirmish, drove them back to the British camp. At Osterwick, with about fifty dragoons and hussars, D'Eon charged a Prussian battalion six or seven hundred strong, which was intercepting the communications of the French with Wolfembutel. The Prussians, seized with a panic, threw down their arms, and surrendered. The capture of Wolfembutel by Marshal Saxe was the result of this brilliant action.

The preliminaries of peace in September, 1762, terminated the Chevalier's military career, and he returned to the political world, where he had already made himself so distinguished. He was sent to London, as Secretary of Legation under the Duc de Nivernois, the Ambassador-Extraordinary. On the return of the *duc* to Paris, the Chevalier remained in London first as resident, and afterwards as minister plenipotentiary at the Court of St. James's. At this period his star was at its zenith. Fortune lavished her favours upon him with the most profuse liberality. Suddenly the wheel turned; and, without any reason being assigned, D'Eon was dismissed from all his appointments, and compelled to reside, disgraced, in London.

The French ministers who had negotiated the peace now effected his ruin. The treaty had been considered disgraceful to France, both by the king and the people; and the negotiators, afraid of the Chevalier, who knew too much, found means to disgrace him. Louis XV., however, settled upon D'Eon a pension of twelve hundred *livres*.

During the Chevalier's residence in London, suspicions arose in the minds of several persons that D'Eon was a disguised woman. The notion soon reached the Continent; and both in England and abroad, some very extraordinary wagers were made on the subject. In July, 1777, a trial took place before Lord-Chief Justice Mansfield on an action brought by a Mr. Hayes against a Mr. Jacques, the latter of whom had received several premiums of fifteen guineas, to return one hundred whenever it should be proved, beyond a doubt, that the Chevalier D'Eon was a woman. MM. Louis Legoux and de Morande deposed to this as a fact so thoroughly established, that the defendant's counsel actually pleaded that the wager was unfair, because the plaintiff knew, before it was laid, that the Court of France had treated with the Chevalier as a woman. The plaintiff, however, obtained a verdict, which was afterwards set aside on the ground of the bet being illegal.

Shortly after the conclusion of the trial, the Chevalier d'Eon, for some unaccountable reason, put on female attire, which he contrived to wear until his death.

Everybody now believed that D'Eon was a woman. Several portraits were published representing him in various characters—as an officer of dragoons, as a French minister, as a fashionable lady, etc. Mr. Hooper, of Ludgate-hill, published a *mezzotinto* engraving of the Chevalier as Pallas, a casque on her head, a lance in her right hand, and the *aegis* on her left arm. Round the edge of the shield were the words *At nunc dura dedit vobis discrimina Pallas*. On each side were drums, muskets, pyramids of cannon-balls, heavy pieces of ordnance, and a pair of colours on which were written, *Impavidam serient ruinae*. In the middle distance might be seen a citadel and a camp. The lower part of the engraving contained representations of the principal events of the Chevalier's life, with a eulogy, in English, on his talents and virtues. After rapturously praising the genius, the courage, the personal beauty of D Eon, this eulogy concludes by saying that "her military comrades offer this homage as an eternal monument of their affection."

The breaking out of the French Revolution deprived D'Eon of his pension. He returned to France in 1792 and offered his services to the National Assembly. But they were declined; and on his return to England his name was placed on the list of Emigrants. He was now plunged into the depths of poverty, and supported himself as best he could by giving lessons in fencing. But he depended chiefly on the kindness of Elisée, first surgeon to Louis XVIII., and other friends. He died May the 2ist, 1810, when Elisée assisted in the dissection of his body; and declared that the Chevalier belonged to the male sex.

During the American War of Independence several women donned masculine attire and enlisted in the Revolutionary Army. One of these heroines was named Deborah Samson. Born at Plymouth, U.S., of very poor parents, she was received at an early age into a respectable family, where the members treated her with great kindness. Her education was at first totally neglected, though she remedied this, to the best of her ability, by teaching herself to read and write; later in life she saved enough to pay for her schooling. In 1778, having dressed herself in male attire, she enlisted under the name of Robert Shirtliffe for the whole term of the war.

Deborah was used to all kinds of hardships, so the fatigues incident to her new life had as little effect on her as on her comrades. Her courage and obedience to military discipline, soon gained for her the esteem of the officers. She served as a volunteer in several expeditions, where her regiment was not engaged, and received two severe wounds one in the head, the other in the shoulder. She managed, however, to avoid the disclosure of her sex.

At last Deborah Samson was seized with a brain fever in Philadelphia. The physician who attended her made the dreaded discovery, and sent word to the colonel of her regiment. When her health was restored, the colonel sent her with a letter to General Washington. Deborah saw that the truth was known, and it was with great reluctance she obeyed. Washington read the missive, without speaking a word. When he had finished, he handed Deborah Samson a discharge in which was enclosed some money and a letter containing good advice. (*Deborah Sampson, Soldier of the Continental Army* by Herman Mann is also published by Leonaur).

Some years after her discharge Deborah married Benjamin Garnett, of Sharon, Massachusetts. For her services as a revolutionary soldier, she was presented with a grant of land and a pension for life.

Another American heroine was Molly Macauley, a Pennsylvanian woman, who rose to the rank of sergeant in the national army, and fought bravely in several battles and skirmishes. Nobody suspected that she was other than she seemed to be—a brave, enthusiastic young American patriot. She was tall and stout, rough-looking, with all the manners of a soldier. In the enthusiasm of the moment she would swing her sabre over her head, and hurrah for "Mad Anthony," as General Wayne was styled.

She was wounded at Brandywine, and her sex discovered. She then returned home.

Another woman, whose name was long remembered in American homes, was Elizabeth Canning. She was at Fort Washington, her husband was slain, she took his place at a gun, loading, priming, and firing with good effect, till she was wounded in the breast by a grape shot.

Besides these examples, many women were frequently detected, disguised, in the American armies; and as they endured the same privations, with even less murmuring than the men, there was nothing, save accident, to reveal their sex. The instances are numerous of women and girls who aided in the defence of private houses. Their names, however, have very seldom reached Europe.

When Catherine the Second of Russia was conspiring to dethrone her husband, Peter III., she based her hopes of success almost entirely on the belief that the Imperial Guard would declare in her favour. On the 26th of June, 1762, she was seated in her palace at St. Petersburg, taking a slight repast in company with her early friend and confidant Catherine Romanowna, Princess of Daschkow, or Daschkova. The latter was born in 1744, a descendant of the noble family of Woronzoff, and became a widow at the early age of eighteen. She applied all her woman's wit to place Catherine on the throne.

When their repast was concluded, Catherine proposed that they should ride at the head of their troops to Peterhoff; and to make themselves more popular with the soldiers, the empress borrowed the uniform of Talitzen, a captain in the Preobraginsky Guards, while the Princess Daschkova donned the regimentals of Lieutenant Pouschkin, in which, she says, she looked "like a boy of fifteen."

It chanced by good luck that these uniforms were the same which had been worn from the time of Peter the Great until superseded by the Prussian uniform introduced by Peter III.

On the 29th July the empress and her friend, still in uniform, passed in review twelve thousand soldiers, besides numberless volunteers. As Catherine rode along the ranks, amidst the cheers of the soldiers, a young ensign, observing that she had no tassel on her sword, untied his own and presented it. Thirty years afterwards, this man died a field-marshal and a prince of the Russian Empire. His name was Potemkin.

It is said the princess (though she makes no mention of it in her memoirs) requested, as the reward of her services, to be given the command of the Imperial Guard. The empress refused; and the princess, finding her inflexible, gave up her military aspirations and devoted herself to study. After her return from abroad in 1782, she was appointed Director of the Academy of Sciences, and President of the newly-established Russian Academy. She wrote much in her native tongue; amongst other works, several comedies. She died at Moscow in 1810.

It is a curious fact that no one has been able to say precisely when and where Nelson lost his left eye. Some say that the disaster occurred during the siege of Bastia, in 1793, while others decide that it was at the siege of Calvi. According to Signor D. Liberate Abarca, general in the service of the Nicaraguan Republic, both these accounts are false. He says that it was in the year 1780, when the future "god of the seas," then a post-captain in the Royal Navy, was cruising along the coast of Central America, that he received the wound which added him to the list of one-eyed warriors.

After inflicting every possible injury on the Spanish colonies, Nelson resolved to take the Castle of San Carlos de Nicaragua by assault. He rowed up the river of San Juan, which flows into the Gulf of Mexico, with a flotilla of launches and other flat-bottomed boats. The Spanish commander was laid up in bed with a severe illness; and the garrison, terrified at the imposing preparations of the English sailors, hastily evacuated the fort. Doña Rafaela Mora, the wife or daughter of the commander, was left alone in the castle; and with great—what would at first sight appear to be reckless—daring resolved to drive the enemy from before the place. The guns were pointed towards the river, and nearly all loaded.

Snatching up a burning match which the terrified soldiers had thrown down in their hasty retreat, Rafaela fired all the cannons one after another. One of the balls struck the boat in which Nelson stood; a splinter from the bulwark hit him in the face, just below left the eye. Such was the force of the blow, he was knocked down, and rendered perfectly insensible. This disaster broke up the siege, and the flotilla descended the stream with all speed.

The heroine received by royal decree the brevet of a captain on active service, together with a full suit of regimentals, which she was permitted to wear whenever she pleased. Besides this, a pension was settled upon her for the rest of her life. General Thomas Martinez, Director of the Republic of Nicaragua, is a descendant of Doña Rafaela Mora. General Abarca says the truth of this story is proved incontestably by documents which he has seen in the archives of the city of Granada, in Nicaragua.

During a sea-fight between the British and French fleets, Admiral Rodney observed a woman helping at one of the guns on the main deck of his ship. He asked her what brought her there?

"An't please your honour," said she, "my husband is sent down to the cock-pit wounded, and I am here to supply his place. Do you think, your honour," she added, "I am afraid of the *French?*"

After the battle was over, the admiral sent for the woman, and told her that she had been guilty of a breach of discipline in being on board at all. However, he modified his rebuke by a gift of ten guineas

CHAPTER 12

The Furies to the Chicago Massacre

The Furies were the female warriors of the Reign of Terror. When we think of their ferocious bravery, their barbarous, maniacal cruelty, the ascendency which they held, even over the great Republican leaders, their wild cries and still wilder deeds, they seem more like the weird figures in some hideous German legend than real, living, sentient women, with human hearts. Women, indeed, they could scarcely be termed; Amazons they were, as brave and as cruel as those of the Euxine. Yet, fiends though they appeared, they had often the pangs of hunger to goad them on; and if cruelty such as theirs *can* be excused, starvation is the most reasonable plea that could be advanced.

Though many of the large towns possessed Furies in those days, Paris was their proper home. There they lived on the sight, the smell, the taste of human blood. To picture their history rightly, the pen should be dipped in blood. Blood, since they were denied bread was all they cared for; and when aristocratic heads grew scarce, these fiends turned on one another, like famished wolves, to glut their insatiable thirst. The Guillotine was a central rallying point for the Furies. Round it they danced and sang by day; its steps formed their pillow by night.

There they crowded together—Tricoteuses, Fileuses, Poissardes—shouting, gesticulating, screaming the *"Marseillaise"* or the "Ça *Ira*" with their wild, demoniac voices, as they watched the red cart deposit its living freight at the foot of the National Razor. When hunger pressed them very sore, they would snatch up swords, pikes, or scythes, and rush in crowds along the narrow, muddy, ill-paved streets, beating drums, waving red flags, brandishing their weapons, to demand bread from those who professed to guide the Republic.

There was always some female leader, brave and eloquent, round

147

whom the Furies would rally, and who was, if possible, more blood-thirsty, more ruthless than the rest. The great leaders of the Parisian Women were Rose Lacombe, the actress, and Théroigne (or Lamber-tine) de Méricourt, the Amazon of Liége. These two women, equally beautiful, equally brave, and equally popular, had wholly different reasons for plunging into the seething whirlpool of blood.

Rose Lacombe (who was born in 1768, and was therefore past twenty when the Revolution broke out), appears to have joined in the scenes of atrocity through a love of excitement, a wish to be a leader, that feeling so natural in the breast of an actress. She was a wild, excitable girl, and although not great on the stage, had a certain fiery eloquence, which, though bombastic, exaggerated, even grotesque, was suited to an audience chiefly gathered from the Halles. Théroigne de Méricourt, however, had quite another object in coming forward as a Republican leader; this was an unquenchable thirst for revenge on the entire aristocracy, to one of whom she owed the shame of her life.

Théroigne was the daughter of a wealthy farmer in the village of Méricourt near Liége, and received a finished education. When scarcely seventeen her excessive beauty attracted the notice of a young Belgian noble, who owned a *château* close by her father's home. In those days of the old regime an aristocrat would never have recovered the disgrace of marrying a farmer's daughter; so, the consequences of their mutual passion might easily have been foreseen. Deserted by her lover, Théroigne fled to England, and remained here for some months, in an agony of shame and grief. When Paris rose against the ill-starred Louis Seize, she returned to France, and became acquainted with Mirabeau, and through him she was introduced to the Abbé Siéyes, Joseph Chénier, Brissac, Danton, Marat, Robespierre, Camille Desmoulins, Ronsin, Romme, and others of the Republican party.

Théroigne de Méricourt was barely eighteen in '89, when the first rumblings of the storm were heard. Plunging headlong into the vortex of Revolution, she soon acquired for her daring the names of "the Amazon of Liége" and "the Jeanne d'Arc of the Revolution;" while her surpassing beauty procured for her the title of "*La Belle Liégoise.*" Attired in a blood-coloured silk riding-habit, and a hat surmounted by a magnificent plume of feathers, she made herself conspicuous in all those deadly conflicts between the People and the Royalists. She was first amongst the infuriate mob who burst open the gates of the Invalides and seized the cannon. She was foremost in the storming of the Bastille, June 14th, 1789; and such was her reckless valour on this occasion, that the victors, assembling on the spot, voted her a *sabre d'homme*. Another of the heroines who joined in the attack on the Bastille, afterwards joined the army, and fought against the enemies of the Republic, for which she was made Captain of Artillery. Her husband was a soldier.

On the 5th of October, Théroigne and Rose led eight or ten thousand starving Parisian Women against Versailles. Previous to this, Rose had commanded a body of Furies in the attack on the Hôtel de Ville, August 7th. Théroigne rode to Versailles astride on a cannon. By her side came Cut-Throat Jourdan, the "Man with the Long Beard." The expedition owed its success almost entirely to the Amazon of Liege. The triumph of the people was complete. *Le Boulanger, la Boulangère, et le petit Mitron* were brought to Paris, escorted by a seething, howling mob, preceded (as a hint to the aristocrats) by two pikes, on which were placed the heads of two *Gardes-du-Corps*. Several Poissardes performed the return journey on the backs of cannon.

For a time, the popularity of Théroigne de Méricourt and Rose Lacombe was unbounded; they were estimated by the Parisians as the first of their sex. Rose founded a female club on the same plan as the Jacobins, and became the chief speaker there. Théroigne held a club at her own house, and frequently spoke at the "Old Cordeliers," of which Danton and Camille Desmoulins were the leaders. Speaking of the enthusiasm with which her orations were received, Camille says:

Her similes were drawn from the Bible and Pindar. It was the eloquence of a Judith.

One evening Théroigne proposed that the Temple of the Representatives of the People should be erected on the site of the Bastille, the scene of their first triumph.

She said:

To found and embellish this edifice, let us strip ourselves of our ornaments, our gold, our jewels. I will be the first to set the example.

And with these words she tore off all her jewels and flung them on the table.

Her power increased every day. She was appointed commander of the 3rd corps of the army of the Fauxbourgs; and so great was her ascendancy over the mob, that she could by a single word acquit or condemn a victim. She thus became both feared and hated by the

Aristocrats. One day when she was at the zenith of her power, she recognised her faithless lover. He sought to avert his impending fate and humbly implored her forgiveness; but Théroigne had not the generosity to save him. He perished in the September massacres, 1792.

A fearful doom was reserved for the beautiful and unfortunate Théroigne de Méricourt. Like Robespierre, she believed that her power was such that she could at any moment arrest the progress of the Revolution. Only a few months after the death of her seducer, the very Furies whom she had commanded, by whom she had been almost worshipped, suspecting her of being a Girondist, turned against their Amazon leader with all the fury they had formerly displayed against Marie Antoinette. They surrounded her on the terrace of the Tuileries, May 3ist, 1793, stripped her naked, and subjected her to a public flogging.

Abandoned and despised by all, the beautiful amazon became a raving lunatic. Years crept on. The Directory superseded the Convention, the Consulate the Directory, the Empire the Consulate, and the Restoration the Empire, and still, in a cold grated cell of the Bicêtre, in Paris, a gibbering, white-haired, wrinkled hag crawled on all fours to and from the bars of the window, whence she shrieked forth warlike orations to phantom meetings of Republicans; again, and again calling for the blood of Suleau, the Royalist author. From the day of her fall till her death in 1817, she refused to wear clothes. Her only covering was her long white hair.

Rose Lacombe terminated her career more happily than her sister-in-arms. True, she also had her downfall, but it did not terminate so horribly. She fell violently in love with a young nobleman who was imprisoned in one of the dungeons of the Republic. With her usual wild impetuosity, she tried to save him; but so far from rescuing him, she very nearly shared his fate. From this day Rose Lacombe's power was gone. Her voice was no longer listened to as it had once been. Jacobins and Cordeliers no longer strove to gain her support. Taking a more sensible view of the matter than one would expect, she retired from public life, and became a small shopkeeper. In this capacity she ended her days, selling petty articles over a counter all day long. The date of her death is unknown.

The citizens of Lyons, unlike those of Paris, were devoted to the Royal cause. At last the Convention resolved to tolerate this no longer; and General Kellermann was despatched against the city in August, 1793. The people made a gallant defence; never did the female sex show greater bravery. The city fell on Oct. 8th; and, furious at having been resisted, Collot d'Herbois, Couthon, and the other emissaries of the Convention tried to stamp out the very existence of Lyons. Wholesale massacres were perpetrated daily; and the friends of liberty were if possible more enraged against those brave women, who so nobly aided in the defence, than they were against the male leaders.

One of the most intrepid female soldiers, named Madame Cochet, when she was on her way to the guillotine, addressed her countrymen from the tumbril, and upbraided them with their cruelty, and their cowardice in tamely submitting to the Terrorists. The crowd at first followed in silence; at last a cry of "Mercy," was heard: but the falling of the National Razor cut short the appeal.

Another heroine of Lyons was Marie Adrian, a young girl of seventeen, whose features bore a strange resemblance to Charlotte Corday. She fought desperately by the side of her brother and her lover in one of the batteries. After the city had fallen she was made prisoner.

"What is your name?" demanded the judges, struck by her youth and beauty.

"Marie," she replied. "The name of the mother of that God for whom I am about to die."

"Your age?"

"Seventeen. The age of Charlotte Corday."

"How could you combat against your country?"

"I fought to defend it."

"*Citoyenne*," said one of the judges, "we admire your courage. What would you do if we granted your life?"

"I would poignard you as the murderers of my country," was her daring reply.

She was, of course, condemned to the guillotine. She ascended the scaffold in silence, and refused the aid of the executioner. Twice she cried with a loud, clear voice "*Vive le Roi!*" After her death a note was found among her garments; it was the farewell letter of her lover, who had been shot some days previously in the Plaine des Brotteaux.

This letter was written in blood!

The same loyal, unselfish courage was displayed by the Royalist insurgents in La Vendée. The rough, yet kind-hearted Chouans form a striking contrast to the ferocious, bloodthirsty Republicans, far from advantageous to the latter. There was not one Republican leader who could bear comparison with the enthusiastic self-sacrificing young Rochejacquelin, who risked everything for his king.

The most prominent Vendéan leaders, next to Rochejacquelin, were La Rochefoucault de Beaulieu and the Marquis de Lescure. The former was one of the first to raise the standard of Louis XVIII. Scarcely had he called together a few hundred neighbours and their peasant tenantry when he received a visit from Madlle. de la Rochefoucault, a near relative, and at this time only eighteen. She was accoutred *en Amazon*, with a sword by her side and a brace of pistols in her belt. She presented the troops with embroidered standards, worked by her own hands, and declared her resolution to fight personally for the royal cause.

Mademoiselle de la Rochefoucault displayed the greatest possible daring in the numerous encounters between the contending armies. She was always the first to advance and the last to retreat. But though she was so fierce while the battle raged, directly it was over she showed her kind and humane disposition by the care which she took of the wounded. She made no distinction between friends and foes; the unfortunate, whether Royalists or Republicans, were always sure of her sympathy and assistance.

In the disastrous Battle of Chollet, when the superior numbers of the Republicans spread such confusion through the Chouan ranks, Mademoiselle de la Rochefoucault rallied her troops three times successively, and charged the foe. Repulsed a fourth time, she ascended a slight eminence, and addressed seven hundred of her followers in a speech well calculated to rouse their sinking energies. Once more she led them against the foe. This time they returned without her!

But the most famous heroine of this war was Renée Bordereau, commonly called Langevin, known as the "Military Heroine of La Vendée," who afterwards wrote and published her autobiography. She was born in June, 1770, at the village of Soulaine, near Angers, of poor, but honest parents. When the insurrection of 1793 broke out, the Republican troops ravaged and massacred without mercy throughout La Vendée. It chanced that forty-two of Renée's relatives fell victims, successively, to this fury. At last the barbarous murder of her father before her eyes so transported Renée with rage and a thirst for revenge that she devoted herself thenceforth to the royal cause.

She bought a light musket with double sights, and learned privately to load, fire, and aim at a mark. She also practised the military drill; and when she considered herself sufficiently expert, she procured a suit of masculine clothes, and joined a corps commanded by M. Coeur-de-Roi whose name, by the way, was only a *nom de guerre*. She enrolled under the name of Hyacinthe, that of her brother, but her comrades soon gave her the soubriquet of Langevin, a name she never lost.

During a war of six years, the heroine was engaged in over two hundred battles and skirmishes. She usually fought on horseback, but sometimes, to be nearer the foe, she combated on foot. She always solicited to be placed in the most dangerous posts, and never quitted the field till compelled by her wounds, or the toils and fatigues of the battle. Although no one at this time suspected her sex, she was conspicuous all through the country for her bravery. All the Royalists strove to emulate her deeds of valour, but none could ever equal her daring. She had entered on the war with a firm determination to conquer or die, and her resolution never flagged. Her only ambition, her sole passion, was to drive the Republicans from France, and restore the legitimate Church and King.

When Napoleon had subdued La Vendée, he was so afraid of the brave Langevin that he excepted her from the general amnesty, and set the price of forty million *francs* on her head. She was betrayed into the hands of her enemies; and the emperor threw her into a loathsome dungeon, weighting her limbs with iron chains lest she should escape. She remained in the prison of Angers for three years, and in that of Mount St. Michael for two, and was fed on nothing save the coarsest bread, and rainwater which she collected for herself in a basin. Her piety and fortitude, however, never forsook her during these cruel hardships. She was at last set free on the Restoration of that king for whom she had fought so bravely and endured such privations.

The sex of Renée had become known by an accident before her imprisonment; so it was no surprise, at least to her comrades, when her autobiography appeared, to, learn that she was a woman. In 1816, she was presented to Louis XVIII.; but what recompense if any, was awarded, her memoirs do not say. She was still living in 1818.

Madame Dufief, a native of Nantes, was another heroine of this war; and, in reward she received at the Restoration the Ribbon of the Order of St. Louis.

The French Revolution, it must be confessed, aroused throughout the land a feeling of earnest, self-sacrificing patriotism, which no monarchical government, however popular, had ever called forth. A wild, enthusiastic desire spread through France to drive the enemies of the Republic from its sacred soil or perish in the attempt. Young and old were alike infected with the eager longing to die for the Republic. Lamartine says:

Married men dragged themselves from the arms of their wives to rush to the altar of their country. Men already advanced in life, old men, even, still green and robust, came to offer the remainder of their life to the safety of the Republic. They were seen tearing off their coats or jackets, before the representatives, and exposing, naked, their breasts, their shoulders, their arms, their joints still supple, to prove that they had strength enough to carry the knapsack and the carbine, and to brave the fatigues of the camp.

Fathers, devoting themselves with their children, themselves offered their sons to the country, and demanded to be allowed to march with them. Women, in order to follow their husbands or their lovers, or themselves seized with that delirium of the country, the most generous and the most devoted of all passions, divested themselves of the garments of their sex, put on the uniform of volunteers, and enrolled themselves in the battalions of their departments.

The greater number of these brave women and girls left their bones to bleach on the various battlefields of the Republic without their sex being ever discovered. Those who became known were but few. Amongst these latter were the two sisters Félicité and Théophile de Fernig, who held the nominal rank of orderly officers on the staff of General Dumouriez, wearing the uniform, and performing all the duties appertaining to their position. Their father, M. de Fernig, was Captain of Dumouriez's Guides; while their brother was lieutenant in the regiment d'Auxerrois. Thus, the entire family were fighting in defence of the Republic.

The De Fernigs were natives of French Flanders, whence they were driven in August, 1792, by the invading Austrians, who amongst other atrocities, burnt the house of this family. Having no longer a home, they joined the army of Dumouriez which arrived shortly after in the neighbourhood. The girls, whose sex was known to all, when on the march rode near their father or brother; but during battle they acted as *aide-de-camp* to one or other of the French generals.

They entered at once on active service, and marched to the woody heights of Argonne in Champagne, which General Dumouriez was vainly endeavouring to hold against the Austrians. On his retreat to St. Ménéhould the De Fernigs distinguished themselves, September 20th, during the famous cannonade of Valmy by the Duke of Brunswick;

when the superior skill of Kellermann forced the Allies to retreat.

The Convention, informed of the gallant conduct of the Desmoiselles de Fernig, sent them horses and arms of honour in the name of the Republic. Dumouriez, in the camp of Maulde, made a striking example of these two young girls to inspire his soldiers with courage.

In October, Dumouriez returned to Paris, and formed a plan with the Executive Council for the winter campaign. On his return to the army he issued a proclamation calling on the Belgians to rise against their sovereign; and on the 6th of November, he attacked the Austrian camp at Jemappes. In this battle, which was perhaps the most hotly contested of all those fought during the entire war, Félicité, the eldest girl, acted as *aide-de-camp* to the Duc de Chartres, afterwards Louis Philippe, King of the French, while her sister performed the same duty for the brave veteran, General Ferrand, who stormed the redoubts on the heights. Both girls were young and exceedingly pretty—Félicité was scarcely sixteen; and Lamartine observed:

> Their modesty, their blushes, and their grace, under the uniform of officers of the staff, formed a contrast to the masculine figures of the warriors who surrounded them.

Before the battle, while reviewing his troops, Dumouriez pointed out the heroines to his soldiers "as models of patriotism and auguries of victory." Throughout the day they were conspicuous for their reckless bravery, which rendered them of inestimable price in an army composed of raw soldiers. When the regiments which formed the centre of the French Army gave way before the overwhelming masses of Clerfayt's cavalry, the Duc de Chartres and his brother, the Duc de Montpensier, followed by Félicité de Fernig and half-a-dozen *aides-de-camp*, rode, sword in hand, through the Austrian hussars' which separated him from the infantry. The latter were restored to their former courage, partly by the words of the *duc*, but more especially by the reproaches of a fragile girl of sixteen, who, a pistol in each hand and her bridle between her teeth, accused them bitterly of cowardice in flying from dangers which she fearlessly braved.

After the battle had raged for several hours the Austrians were driven from the field. The capture of Mons followed shortly after; and the French entered Brussels, November 14th, after a series of skirmishes between their advance-guard and the rear-guard of the Austrians. During one of these contests, Félicité de Fernig, while bearing the orders of Dumouriez to the heads of the columns, was surrounded by a troop of *Uhlans*, from whom she extricated herself with difficulty. As she was turning her horse's head to rejoin the column, she saw a young officer of Belgian Volunteers, who had just been flung from his horse, by a shot, defending himself desperately against several *Uhlans*. Riding hastily to the spot, Félicité with her pistols shot two of his assailants, and the rest took to flight. Dismounting from her horse, she confided the care of the wounded officer to her hussars, and with their assistance conveyed him to the military hospital of Brussels.

The spring of 1793 saw the popularity of Dumouriez wane rapidly. He was suspected firstly of Girondism, and, worse again, of wishing to rescue Louis Capet, the unfortunate ex-king, whose trial was in preparation, or, some said, he meditated placing Philippe Egalité on the throne. In addition to all these accusations, he had the misfortune to lose nearly as many battles as he had previously gained; and, knowing well that his head was very far from secure on his martial shoulders, he entered into negotiations with Austria. But he mistook the patriotism of his soldiers for personal attachment to himself.

On the 7th April his army was in a state of open mutiny; but hoping to set matters right, he set out for Condé, followed by the Duc de Chartres, Colonel Thouvenet, Adjutant-General Montjoie, eight hussars of ordnance, and his immediate staff, including the sisters De Fernig. On the road he met three battalions of Versailles Volunteers who were marching without orders to Condé. Dumouriez commanded them to halt; but the Volunteers fired on his escort. Dumouriez fled amidst a rain of bullets, sprang, on foot, across a canal which interrupted his flight, and made his escape over the Dutch marshes.

Theophile de Fernig was not wounded, though her horse was slain. Félicité dismounted, and gave her steed to the Duc de Chartres. The two young girls and nearly all their companions reached the opposite shore of the canal safely; when they dispersed in all directions. The girls, who were acquainted with the country, guided Dumouriez to the ferryboat, in which he, they, and the Duc de Chartres passed the Scheldt. On landing they returned to the French camp at Maulde; but very soon the fugitives had to take refuge in the camp of Clerfayt, the Austrian general, at Tournay.

In those days one star eclipsed another so fast, that the soldiers were only too ready to forget their former idols. Of course, when the troops could easily forget the general who had first led them to victory, they could hardly be expected to trouble themselves about two friendless girls. When Vanderwalen, the young Belgian officer, recovered from his wounds, he could not banish from his mind the young Amazon who had saved his life. But neither his brother officers nor the soldiers could give him any information respecting the De Fernig family. Vanderwalen left the army, and wandered all over Germany and northern Europe seeking his preserver. For a long time, his search was vain; but at last, when he had almost given up the search, he found the family buried in the heart of Denmark.

The sisters had resumed "the dress, the graces, and the modesty" of their own sex. The love of Vanderwalen was very soon reciprocated; and they returned, as man and wife, to Belgium. Theophile accompanied her sister to Brussels; where, after spending a few years in the study of music and poetry, she died, unmarried. She has left, it is said, several exquisite poems.

Lamartine says:

These two sisters, inseparable in life, in death, as upon the field of battle, repose under the same cypress—in a foreign land. Where are their names upon the marble monuments of our triumphal arches? Where are their pictures at Versailles? Where are their statues upon our frontiers bedewed with their blood?

Mary Schelienck, or Shellenck, was one of the most remarkable women whose names occur in the roll-call of warriors. She was a native of Ghent, but nothing is known of her early youth. In March, 1792, she entered the Second Belgian Battalion, as a male Volunteer. At the Battle of Jemappes, in the succeeding November, she distinguished herself by her bravery, and received six wounds. Afterwards she entered the 30th Demi-Brigade (Batavian), and made the campaigns of Germany. She was next removed to the 8th Light Infantry, and displayed great bravery at the Battle of Austerlitz. Unfortunately for her, she there received a severe wound on the thigh, and was left for dead on the field, which led to her real sex being discovered. In spite of this, she continued to follow the regiment, and at last presented a petition with her own hand to Napoleon.

The emperor received her with "marked distinction:" he invested her with the cross of the Legion of Honour, giving her the very decoration he had himself worn, and he placed her tenth on the list of lieutenants. In 1807, Napoleon granted her a pension of 673 *francs* (£20). On her return from Italy, Mary Schelienck, in her military uniform, waited on the Empress Josephine. That imperial lady, either in kindness or as an ironical compliment, presented her with a velvet robe. Mary Schelienck's commission of lieutenant, the decoration of the Legion of Honour, and the velvet robe were afterwards (1841) in the possession of William Shellenck, cloth merchant of Ghent. Mary Shelienck died in January, 1841, at Menin, where she was buried. Her funeral was attended by every member of the Legion of Honour belonging to the garrison, and an immense concourse of people.

Thérèse Figueur, better known as "*Le Dragon sans Gêne*," was born, January, 1774, at Talmay, a town six leagues from Dijon. She became a dragoon in the 15th and 9th regiments, and, from 1793 to 1812, served in all the campaigns of the Republic and of the Empire. At this time, she was known to her comrades by the soubriquet of "*Sans Gêne.*"

One day the Comité du Salut Public issued a decree forbidding any woman to remain in the regiments. The commissioned officers and generals of the Army of the Pyrenees, however, begged that an exception might be made in favour of the Citoyenne Thérèse Figueur; and special authorisation was granted, permitting her to remain in the service.

At the siege of Toulon, 1793, Thérèse received an English bullet in her left shoulder. She had the misfortune to be placed under arrest during the same siege by General Bonaparte, for being guilty of a delay of twenty-five minutes in the execution of an order. Some years subsequently, when the former *Commandant d'Artillerie* had become First Consul, he wished to see once more the Dragon sans Gene, who came willingly enough to St. Cloud under the escort of M. Denon. The First Consul made some complimentary remarks to the "Dragon," and added that "*Mademoiselle Figueur est un brave:*" then gaily pledged her in "a glass of something stronger than wine."

Therese Figueur served in the "*Armée d'Italie*" in 1792, and in the army of the Eastern Pyrenees during the 2nd and 3rd year, and in the Army of Italy during the years 4, 5, 6, 7, 8, and 9. Among her exploits were several campaigns in Germany, and she took part in the war in Spain. In July, 1812, she was made prisoner by the Guerillas of the Curé Marino, and sent off to England, where she remained until the Peace in 1814.

She was frequently wounded, and had horses killed under her. At the Battle of Savigliano, she was wounded four times.

A modest pension hardly sufficed for her simple wants, yet being very generous, she constantly helped others poorer than herself. In disposition she was remarkable for piety, delicate tact, singleness of heart, and self-forgetfulness.

About 1840, Thérèse Figueur, then *veuve* Sutter, was admitted into the *Hospice des Ménages*. In that retreat her last years glided calmly away, enlivened by the frequent visits of her many faithful friends, who delighted in hearing her military reminiscences. In June, 1861, her simple funeral passed from the gates of the Hospice.

During the long wars between England and the French Republic, women continued to enlist in the British Army. One of the best known female soldiers of this period was a woman named Roberts, afterwards styled the "Manchester Heroine" from the place of her death. On the 15th November, 1814, a middle-aged woman applied for relief at the Church-Warden's offices in Manchester; and on being questioned, it appeared that she had in days gone by served her king as a soldier. Her romantic story afterwards appeared, in great detail, in the *Manchester Herald*.

The father of this heroine, William Roberts, was a bricklayer, and used to employ his little girl, dressed in boy's clothes, as a labourer. When she was about fourteen years old, being tall of her age, Miss Roberts enlisted in the 15th Light Dragoons. In the course of two months she learned the drill sufficiently for all purposes of parade; and the roughriding master told her she was the best rider in the squad he was teaching. Private William Roberts was promoted in the course of a few years, first to be a corporal, and then a sergeant; and at the expiration of her twenty-one years' service, the colonel tendered her discharge. She demurred accepting it; but being under size, was, with her own consent, transferred to the 37th Foot; which she joined at the island of St. Vincent, in the West Indies.

At St. Vincent the heroine was attacked by the yellow fever; and this being the first time in her life that she was ever laid prostrate by an illness, her sex was soon made known. On her recovery she was obliged to resume (or rather put on) female *habilaments*. But being still enamoured of a soldier's life, she married, in May, 1801, a private in the 37th, named Taylor. She followed her husband through various climates; and in time became the mother of three children. She was imprisoned for two years with her husband in France, and they were only set free at the general peace of July, 1815. Her husband died the same day they landed in England; leaving his widow in great distress.

During the course of her military career, Mrs Taylor visited the East and West Indies, and fought in Flanders, Spain, Italy, and Egypt. She received many wounds, none of which, however, were serious, though they left their scars all over her body. Her head was graced by a sabre-wound, while her leg showed where a musket ball had been extracted. Yet despite the dangers and hardships of war, this woman sighed after the life of a soldier to the very last. She said that the only really miserable part of her life was the two years' imprisonment in France; which, she said, did her constitution more harm than even the terrible march, under a blazing African sun, from the Red Sea to Egypt. Like a brave old veteran, she kept up her spirits even in adversity, "fought her battles o'er again," and loved to "shoulder her crutch and show how fields were won." Like most old soldiers, she was very fond of relating anecdotes about her past career—the battles she had fought in, the wounds she had received, and the various noble or distinguished officers she had seen.

Another of these British heroines was Mary Anne Talbot, who served as drummer-boy in the 82nd regiment when it was despatched to the Netherlands in 1793. The career of this young woman was so romantic, so very much out of the ordinary routine of every-day life, it is strange that her story has not become more generally known—especially as a long and detailed memoir was published, which she was supposed to have written herself. (Republished along with six others by Leonaur in *The Jill Tars*.)

Mary Anne Talbot was born in a house in Lincoln's Inn Fields on the 2nd February, 1778, and was the youngest of sixteen natural children, whom her mother, whose name has not transpired, had by the Earl of Talbot. Until she had reached the age of five, Mary Anne was kept at nurse at a little village about twelve miles from Shrewsbury. Her mother died when she was an infant; and at the death of Lord Talbot, Mary Anne was removed to a boarding-school in Foregate-street, Chester. Here she remained for nine years under the care of her only surviving sister, Mrs. Wilson.

On the death of Mrs. Wilson, Mr. Sucker, of Newport, Shropshire, came forward as guardian of Mary Anne Talbot. He was a harsh man, and treated her so cruelly that she trembled at the sound of his voice. She had not been in her new home very long when Essex Bowen, a captain in the 82nd, appeared at the house; and the girl was commanded by Sucker to consider him as her future guardian, under whose protection she was to finish her education on the continent.

Early in the year 1792 they proceeded to London and stopped at the Salopian coffee-house, Charing Cross; where, taking advantage of the poor girl's friendless situation, Captain Bowen acted the part of a villain. Immediately after this the 82nd was ordered to the West Indies; and the captain forced his victim to dress herself as a foot-boy and follow him. By his directions, too, she assumed the name of John Taylor. They sailed on the 20th March, from Falmouth, in the Crown Transport; and during the voyage her tyrant used her like a slave, and forced her to eat and drink with the common sailors.

Early in the following year the regiment was remanded to Europe, to join the army of the Duke of York at Tournay. Bowen again intimidating the forlorn girl by the threat of sending her up the country to be sold for a slave, compelled her to enlist under him as a drummer, though he plainly told her that this would not release her from her duties as his servant.

When they arrived in Flanders, Mary Anne was obliged to endure all the horrors of war. During the frequent skirmishes which took place between the English and French, she was compelled to keep up a continuous roll of the drum to drown the groans and cries of wounded and dying comrades. On the 2nd of June, the Duke of York besieged Valenciennes; within a few days of its surrender, the female drummer received two wounds—one from a musket-ball which glanced between her collar-bone and breastbone, and struck one of her ribs, the other in the small of her back from the sabre of an Austrian trooper, who mistook her for a Frenchman. Being in dread and fear lest her sex should be discovered, she had the fortitude to conceal her wounds, and cure them herself by the use of some lint, Dutch drops and basilicon.

Captain Bowen had the reward of his villainy and tyranny, by being slain during the attack on Valenciennes, July 25th, 1793. Having no longer the wrath of a tyrant to fear, Mary Anne disguised herself as a sailor boy, deserted from the regiment, and started for the coast. Carefully avoiding all towns or large villages, she reached Luxembourg, which being in the hands of the French, hindered her further progress. She was compelled, through sheer want, to hire herself to the captain of a French lugger. The vessel turned out to be a privateer, and cruised about the Channel for four months. Mary Anne was compelled to do all the rough work. At last the vessel was captured by the British fleet, and the crew were taken prisoners on board the *Queen Charlotte* to be examined by the admiral, Lord Howe. Previous to their capture, Mary Anne was severely beaten because she refused to fight against her countrymen.

Lord Howe questioned Mary Anne as to who and what she was,

and how she had got on board a French ship. She stated, in explanation, that she had been foot-boy to an English gentleman travelling on the continent, that on his death she had been obliged to seek employment, and had taken Le Sage the French captain, for an honest trader. The admiral was satisfied; and the girl was sent on board the *Brunswick* man-of-war, where she was appointed powder-monkey on the quarter-deck. Her cleanly habits, and her quiet respectful demeanour, attracted the notice of Captain Harvey, who raised her to the post of principal cabin boy.

The *Brunswick* having fallen in with a French ship, in June, 1794, a sharp action ensued, in which Captain Harvey was slain, and Mary Anne received a grape-shot in the ankle of her left leg. So severe was the wound that, though she tried three several times to rise, the broken bone protruding through the skin gave her such agony she fell back almost fainting. A few minutes after this a musket-ball pierced her thigh, just above the knee of the same leg. After the engagement she was carried to the cock-pit, and after numberless attempts had been made to extract the grape-shot (inflicting excruciating agony all the while on the sufferer), the surgeons were obliged to leave it where it was, fearful of cutting the tendons of the leg.

When the *Brunswick* arrived at Spithead, Mary Anne Talbot was placed in Haslar Hospital, where she was attended as an out-door patient during four months. She lived meanwhile on the money which Captain Harvey had given her. When she was at last discharged from the Hospital, she went as a midshipman on board the *Vesuvius*, which formed part of Sir Sydney Smith's squadron. After cruising some time on the coast of France the *Vesuvius* sailed to Gibraltar and back again without meeting the enemy until near Dunkirk, where she was boarded and captured by two privateers, after keeping up a running fight for seven hours.

Mary Anne and another middy named William Richards were taken on board one of the privateers, and imprisoned for eighteen months in Dunkirk, where they were treated very harshly—being allowed nothing but bread and water, and a bed of straw which was never changed. An exchange of prisoners took place at last; and Mary Anne Talbot was engaged almost immediately after by a Captain Field to go as ship's steward on a voyage to America.

She sailed from Dunkirk on board the *Ariel*, August, 1796, and arrived in due time at New York. During her stay there she resided in the family of Captain Field at Rhode Island; and the pretty niece of the captain was so absurd as to fall in love with her uncle's steward. Before Mary Anne's departure she was obliged to pay eighteen dollars for a portrait of herself in the uniform of an American officer to give to her affianced as a memento.

The *Ariel* dropped anchor in the Thames in November, 1796; and some days after their arrival, Mary Anne and the mate went on shore, where they were seized by the press-gang. To obtain her freedom she was obliged to reveal her sex.

Mary Anne applied several times at the Navy-Pay Office for moneys due to her for service on board the *Brunswick* and *Vesuvius*. One day she became abusive, and was taken to Bow Street Police Court; whence of course she was very soon discharged. Several gentlemen who were in court made up a subscription, the amount of which was twelve shillings a week, to last until she received her pension from Somerset House.

Mary Anne Talbot wasted her money shamefully at the theatres and at certain public-houses near Covent Garden, where her real sex was not even suspected; all her friends giving her the name of *bon compagnon*. In February, 1797, owing to her fondness for grog, the grape-shot worked itself out of her ankle, and left her leg in so bad a state that she was taken into St. Bartholomew's Hospital. After her discharge she was attended in different hospitals by several medical men, none of whom were able to effect a permanent cure. She became at last so famous that a beggar was sent to the House of Correction charged with passing himself off as John Taylor, the midshipman. In 1799, she became, for the second time, an inmate of Middlesex Hospital.

For some years her principal support was a pension of twenty pounds a year from the Crown; besides this she received frequent presents from the Duke of York, the Duke of Norfolk, and other members of the nobility. She was advised by Justice Bond, the magistrate of Bow Street, to endeavour to find out something about her early life. She went to Shrewsbury and called on Mr. Sucker, in Newport. Being unable to procure an interview while in "coloured" clothes, she returned to Shrewsbury, dressed herself in an ensign's uniform, hired a horse, and rode back to Mr. Sucker's. She sent in word that an officer, a friend of the late Captain Bowen, had an important message to deliver. This ruse succeeded; she declared who she was, and, drawing her sword, demanded an explanation of Mr. Sucker's conduct towards her. He stared as though an apparition had risen from the grave, and, trembling violently, repeated that he was a ruined man. Three days after this he

163

was found dead in his bed.

Mary Anne Talbot lived for many years after this, maintaining herself in various ways. At one time she thought of going on the stage, and joined the Thespian Society in Tottenham Court Road; where she performed the parts of Irene, Lady Helen, Juliet, Floranthe, and Adeline, and sometimes appeared in low comedy as Mrs. Scout, or Jack Hawser. However, she gave up the stage, which was to her more amusing than profitable.

Once she was summoned before the Commissioners of the Stamp Office for wearing hair-powder without a licence. But she was honourably discharged; whereupon she made the observation that "although she had never worn powder as an article of dress, she had frequently used it in defence of her king and country." The clerks were so tickled with her wit that they immediately made up a subscription.

In June, 1796, the British attacked the New Vigie, in the Island of St. Vincent. The Royal Highlanders were conspicuous for their valour, as Highlanders have ever been. Major-General Stewart, at that time a captain in the regiment, relates how one of the men of his company was followed to the scene of action by his wife. He (Captain Stewart) ordered the man to remain behind and guard the knapsacks, which the soldiers threw down preparatory to charging up the hill. The woman, however, perhaps thinking that the family honour was at stake, rushed up the hill, and made herself conspicuous, cheering and exciting the troops. When the British had captured the third redoubt, Captain Stewart was standing at a short distance, giving some directions relative to the storming of the last entrenchments, when he was tapped on the shoulder by the female Highlander, who seized his arm, and exclaimed:

Well done, my Highland lads! See how the brigands scamper like so many deer! Come, lads, let us drive them from yonder hill."

And she charged off again, much to the delight of her Gaelic brothers-in-arms. When the storm was over, she helped the surgeons in looking after the wounded.

During the Irish Rebellion of '98, women very often risked their lives both on the battlefield and in the defence of houses. Amongst the latter was Susan Frost, a Suffolk woman, nurse to General Sir Charles James Napier. During the temporary absence of the Napier family in England, this woman remained at Celbridge House, in Ireland, with a few of the younger children. The "Defenders" having ascertained that this mansion contained a great number of arms, surrounded it one night. The only persons in the house, besides Susan and the children, were a few maids and Lauchlin Moore, an old serving-man. The rebels, who numbered several hundreds, anticipated an easy capture; but the house was strongly built, and, besides, was defended by Susan Frost, of whose obstinate courage they were as yet ignorant. Collecting all the children together in one room, she stationed herself with a brace of pistols outside the door. The "Defenders" called on the little garrison to surrender; but Lauchlin Moore, acting under the orders of Susan, shouted out defiant refusals. Every time he passed a window, volleys of shot whizzed around his head.

When the assailants began to batter the door with a beam of wood, Moore's courage failed him, and he wished to give up the arms. But Susan invariably answered "No! No! Never! Never!" At last the arrival of some men-servants, from a neighbouring mansion, put the rebels to flight.

Another heroine of the Irish Rebellion was Peggy Monro, who fought bravely in the Battle of Ballinahinch, where the rebels were commanded by her brother.

At the latter end of 1797 the French invaded Switzerland, with the ostensible view of spreading liberty, equality, and fraternity. However, in place of being welcomed by the republican Swiss, they were met on all sides by armed peasants who defended every foot of ground before giving way. The women acted with the same courage as the men. The most conspicuous was Martha Glar, a peasant-woman. When the war broke out she was far from young; being then in her sixty-fourth year, and having both children and grandchildren.

In February, 1798, her husband marched with the rest of the farmers and peasants to check the advance of the French. On the last Sunday in the month, Martha collected all the women and girls of the parish in the church-yard, half an hour before divine service, and addressed them in an impressive oration, inciting them to take up arms in defence of their native land.

Two hundred and sixty women, urged by her patriotism, armed themselves, and marched to meet the invaders. In this little regiment were two of Martha Glar's daughters, and three of her granddaughters, the youngest of whom was only ten years old. After exciting the admiration of both friends and foes by their extraordinary bravery, this female corps was decimated in the Battle of Frauenbrun, March 3rd,

1798. One hundred and eighty of them were killed, and the rest carried, more or less wounded, from the field. Martha Glar, together with her husband, her father, her two sons, both her daughters, her brother, and her three grand-daughters were amongst the slain.

In 1806, when Prussia was arming against the "Colossus of Europe," the queen, who was young, beautiful, and fascinating, appeared several times at the head of the troops attired in a military uniform, which, it is said, became her exceedingly well; and in this costume, she made fiery speeches inciting the people to rise against the "Modern Attila;"

Besides this display of martial ardour, the queen, mounted on a superb charger, accompanied the Prussian Army to the field of Jena, Oct. 14th, 1806, and remained in the midst of the fight till her troops were routed. On her head she wore a helmet of burnished steel, overshadowed by a magnificent plume. She wore a tunic of silver brocade, reaching to her feet, which were encased in scarlet boots with gold spurs. Her breast was protected by a *cuirass* glittering in gold and silver. Accompanied by the *élite* of the young Berlin nobility, she rode along in front of the most advanced ranks, whence, the day being clear, she was easily seen by the French. As she approached each regiment, the flags, embroidered by her own fair hands, besides the blackened rags—all that remained of the time-honoured banners of Frederick the Great—were lowered respectfully.

When the battle was over and the Prussians in full rout, the queen remained on the field, attended by three or four equerries, who, for some time, contrived to defend her against the French troops, who had strict orders to capture the queen at all risks. A squadron of hussars riding up at full speed soon dispersed the little escort of Her Majesty. The horse ridden by the queen fortunately took fright, and galloped off at full speed. Had it not been for his swiftness, the royal heroine would inevitably have been captured.

Pursued by the detachment of hussars, who were several times within a few yards of the royal fugitive, she arrived at last within sight of Weimar, and was congratulating herself upon having escaped so imminent a danger, when, to her dismay, she observed a strong body of French dragoons endeavouring to cut off her retreat. However, before they could come near, she was inside Weimar, the gates of which were immediately closed upon the discomfited troopers.

The queen found her costume exceedingly inconvenient during her flight; and it was principally owing to this that she was so very near being made prisoner.

Marie-Anne-Elise Bonaparte, sister of the first Napoleon, was a woman of superior intellect, and shared to a considerable extent her brother's military predilections. When she married Bacciochi, Prince of Lucca and Piombino, it was she who conducted the government, while the prince was kept in a subordinate position. From her fondness for military shows she acquired the title of the "Semiramis of Lucca." Whenever she reviewed the troops, Prince Bacciochi discharged the duties of *aide-de-camp*.

Next to Joan of Arc, the Maid of Saragossa is the most famous female warrior that ever lived. Pictures and statues without number have been exhibited commemorative of this Spanish girl's heroism; and what renders her resemblance even greater to Jeanne is the fact that the Maid of Saragossa was young, handsome, and interesting.

The siege of Saragossa (or Zaragoza), was one of the most extraordinary recorded in modern history. The town was not even properly fortified, but merely enclosed by a badly-constructed wall twelve feet high and three feet in breadth. This was, moreover, intersected by houses, which, with the neighbouring churches and monasteries, were in a most dilapidated condition. The inhabitants numbered only sixty thousand, and amongst these there was barely two hundred and twenty soldiers. The artillery consisted of ten dilapidated old guns.

When the rest of Spain was at the feet of Napoleon, Marshal Lefebvre was despatched in June 1808, with a strong division of the French Army to besiege Saragossa. Never, in our days at least, have the inhabitants of a beleaguered town displayed such courage. Women of all ranks assisted in the defence; they formed themselves into companies of two or three hundred each, and materially aided the men. They were always the most forward in danger, and the great difficulty was to teach them prudence and a proper sense of their own danger.

The French Marshal, astounded at this unexpected resistance, bribed the keeper of a large powder-magazine to blow it up on the night of June 28th. The French immediately pressed forward to the gates, and commenced a vigorous cannonade. The confusion within the walls was fearful. The people, terrified by the explosion, stupefied by the noise of the cannon thundering in their ears, were paralysed with terror. It was at this critical moment, when the French were pouring into the town, already considered it as their own, that Agostina (or Angostina) the Maid of Saragossa performed that heroic action which has made her name famous throughout the world.

According to the popular version of the story current at the time, the deed was unpremeditated, and simply the result of a sudden impulse. She was carrying round wine and water to the parched and fainting soldiers; entering the Battery of El Portillo, she found that all its defenders had been slain. She tore a match from the hand of a dying artilleryman (whom Southey incorrectly supposes to have been her lover) and fired off a twenty-six pounder gun which was loaded. But in Mrs. Rale's *Woman's Record*, and some other biographical dictionaries, Agostina is represented as having gone to the battery with the previous determination of performing great deeds.

Mrs. Hale says:

At this dreadful moment, an unknown maiden issued from the church of Nostra Donna del Pillas, habited in white raiment, a cross suspended from her neck, her dark hair dishevelled and her eyes sparkling with supernatural lustre! She traversed the city with a bold and firm step; she passed to the ramparts, to the very spot where the enemy was pouring in to the assault; she mounted to the breach, seized a lighted match from the hand of a dying engineer, and fired the piece of artillery he had failed to manage; then kissing her cross, she cried with the accent of inspiration—'Death or victory!' and re-loaded her cannon. Such a cry, such a vision, could not fail to call up enthusiasm; it seemed that heaven had brought aid to the just cause; her cry was answered 'Long live Agostina.'

The people, inspired with new courage, rushed into the battery, and blazed away at the French. Agostina swore not to quit her post while the assault continued. The enthusiasm soon spread through the town. Shouts of "Forward! Forward! We will conquer!" resounded from all sides, and the besiegers were driven back at every point.

Marshal Lefebvre saw it would cost too many soldiers to take the town by storm; so, he endeavoured to reduce it by famine, aided by a heavy bombardment. The horrors of war—people dying of hunger, shells bursting in the streets, the destruction of houses—reigned paramount in Saragossa. Agostina risked her life daily to assist the wounded. But she was seen daily working a heavy gun in the battery at the north-western gate.

The French, from their superior numbers and their determined perseverance, soon became masters of nearly half the town. Lefebvre sent to General Palafox, the Spanish *commandant*, requesting him, once more, to surrender. Palafox read this message in the public street. Turning to Agostina, who, completely armed, stood near him, he asked:—

"What answer shall I send?"

"War to the knife!" said she.

And this answer, echoed by all, was sent back to the Duke of Dantzic.

The latter gave immediate orders for his troops to press the siege by every possible means. For eleven days and eleven nights the town was like the crater of a volcano. The Spaniards disputed the possession of every street, every house, sometimes every room in a house. Agostina was seen at all points, wherever there was most danger to be encountered. Running from post to post, she fought almost incessantly. At last the French, thoroughly exhausted, retired from before Saragossa early on the morning of the 17th August, and the brave townspeople had their reward when they saw the legions of France retiring towards Pampeluna.

When General Palafox was rewarding the surviving warriors, he told Agostina to select whatever reward she pleased; for, said he, anything she asked for would be granted. The only favour she asked was permission to retain the rank of an artillery-soldier, and to have the privilege of taking the surname, and wearing the arms of Saragossa. This was at once granted, with the double-pay of an artilleryman and a pension; while she was decorated with medals and crosses by the Spanish *Junta*, and given the additional surname of La Artillera.

During the second siege of Saragossa, Agostina distinguished herself again as a warrior. When the French sat down before the gates, she took up her former station at the Portillo battery, beside the same gun which she had served so well.

"See," said she to Palafox, pointing to the gun, "I am again with my old friend."

Her husband was severely wounded, but Agostina took his duties, while he lay bleeding at her side. Besides loading and firing this famous gun, Agostina frequently headed sallying parties; when, knife or sword in hand, her cloak wrapped round her, she cheered and encouraged the soldiers by her example and her words. Although constantly under fire, she escaped without a wound. Once, however, she was flung into a ditch, and nearly suffocated by the bodies of dead and dying which fell upon her.

When the town capitulated in February, 1809, Agostina became a prisoner. She was too much feared for Marshal Lannes to let her escape. Fortunately for herself, she was seized with a contagious fever then raging in the town, and was removed to the hospital; where, as it was supposed she lay dying, so little care was taken in watching her that she contrived to escape in a few days.

When Lord Byron visited Spain in 1809, the Maid of Saragossa used to walk every day on the Prado at Seville, attired in the Spanish military uniform—retaining, however, the petticoat and skirt, of her sex. Byron devoted half-a-dozen verses of *Childe Harold* to her praises. Sir John Carr, who was introduced to her about the same time, describes the heroine as "about twenty-three," with a light olive complexion.

> Her countenance soft and pleasing, and her manners, which were perfectly feminine, were easy and engaging.

When he saw Agostina she wore the national black *mantilla*; but on the sleeve of one arm she had three embroidered badges of honour, commemorative of three different acts of bravery.

Sir John says:

> The day before I was introduced to this extraordinary female, she had been entertained at dinner by Admiral Purvis on board his flag-ship. . . . . As she received a pension from Government, and also the pay of an artilleryman, the admiral considered her as a military character, and, much to his credit, received her with the honours of that profession. Upon her reaching the deck, the marines were drawn up and manoeuvred before her. She appeared quite at home, regarding them with a steady eye, and speaking in terms of admiration of their neatness, and soldier-like appearance. Upon examining the guns, she observed of one of them, as other women would speak of a cap, 'My gun.' alluding to one with which she had effected a considerable havoc among the French at Saragossa, 'was not so nice and clean as this.'

Agostina lived to the age of sixty-nine, and died at Cuesta in July, 1857; when her remains were interred with all the honours due to her public position as a Spanish patriot.

Although the women of Saragossa had been ordered to leave the town in November, 1808, previous to the commencement of the second siege, most of them remained, and assisted bravely in raising fortifications. During the siege they exceeded even their past valour.

In the short space of two months no fewer than six hundred women and children perished by the bayonets and musket-balls of the French; without reckoning the thousands who owed their deaths to the frequent explosions of powder-magazines and the constant bursting of shells in the streets. A girl named Manuella Sanchez was shot through the heart. A noble lady named Benita, who commanded one of the female corps raised to carry round provisions, to bear away the wounded, and to fight in the streets, narrowly escaped death again and again; and at the last she only survived the dangers of war to die of grief on hearing that her daughter had been slain.

All through the Peninsula women displayed the same Amazonian prowess. Those towns which ventured to resist the Imperial Eagles were as much influenced in their stubborn patriotism by the courage of the women as by the exciting speeches of the priests or the promise of assistance from England. And all those places which were besieged by the French were defended by women as well as by men. In 1810 there was, it is said, a woman holding the commission of Captain in a Spanish regiment.

In 1811, Mrs. Dalbiac, wife of a British colonel, "an English lady of gentle disposition and possessing a very delicate frame," accompanied, or perhaps followed, her husband to the Peninsula, and shared in all the hardships of more than one campaign. At the Battle of Salamanca, July 22nd, 1812, she rode into the midst of the fight, and was several times under fire.

The King of Prussia, unable to shake off the yoke of Napoleon in 1806, when the star of the "Modern Attila" was at its zenith, took advantage of the Emperor's misfortunes in 1813 to call upon the Germans to rise against the tyranny of France. His call was warmly responded to from all parts of the realm; and, like France in the early days of the Republic, almost all who could bear arms hastened to enrol themselves as volunteers, and march away to fight the Gaul. Perhaps the best known rifle-corps was that commanded by Major Lutzow. Young men of the best families, men of genius (amongst others, Korner the poet, who has celebrated it in verse) joined this battalion. In this corps there was a female soldier, who enrolled under the name of Renz. A monument was erected to the memory of this heroine at Dannenberg, in September, 1865. It is in the form of a pyramid, one foot high. Nothing further is known concerning her history, beyond what is told by the inscription on this memorial.

Ellonora Prochaska, known as one of the Lutzow Rifle Volunteers, by the name of Augustus Renz, born at Potzdam on the 11th March, 1785, received a fatal wound in the Battle of Göhrde on the 15th September, 1813, died at Dannenberg on the 5th October, 1813. She fell exclaiming:—'*Herr Lieutenant,* I am a woman!'

In 1869 a young man was received, by the express order of the King of Prussia, as a candidate for an ensign's commission into the second company of the first battalion of the 9th regiment, in Stargard, the same company in which his grandmother had served as a subaltern officer during the war of liberation against the French, and bravely won the Iron Cross and the Russian order of St. George. This lady— Augusta Frederica Krüger—was a native of Friedland, in Mecklenberg. Not content with offering, like many of her countrywomen, her trinkets and her flowing hair on the altar of patriotism, she entered the ranks as a volunteer, under the name of Lübeck, and distinguished herself by her intrepidity on many a hard-fought field. On October 23, 1815, she received her discharge, and her services were mentioned in this document in the most flattering terms.

In January, 1816, being present, dressed in the garments of her own sex, at the festival of the Iron Cross, held at Berlin, she attracted the attention of a sub-officer of lancers, named Karl Köhler, to whom she was married, in the garrison church of Berlin, on March 5, of the same year. The church was densely packed with spectators on the occasion, every one anxious to witness the marriage of two Prussian subaltern officers. The heroic bride appeared in a handsome silk gown, and wore on her breast the orders she had honourably won, which, with her short hair, were the only signs or symbols of her former military career.

Marshal Massena once related how, during an action between the French and Russians at Buezenghen, he observed a young soldier, apparently scarcely more than a child, who belonged to the French Light Artillery, defending himself bravely against several herculean Cossacks and Bavarians. This young artilleryman, whose horse had been slain by the thrust of a Cossack lance, displayed the most determined courage.

"I immediately despatched an officer and some men to his assistance, but they arrived too late. Although the action had taken place on the borders of the wood and in front of the bridge, the artilleryman had alone withstood the attack of the small body of Cossacks and Bavarians whom the officers and men I had despatched put to flight. His body was covered with wounds inflicted by shots, lances, and swords. There were at least thirty. And do you know, *Madame*," asked the Marshal, "what the *young man* was?"

"A woman!"

"Yes, a woman, and a handsome woman too! Although she was so covered with blood that it was difficult to judge of her beauty. She had followed her lover to the army. The latter was a Captain of Artillery; she never left him, and when he was killed, defended like a lioness the remains of him she loved. She was a native of Paris, her name was Louise Belletz, and she was the daughter of a fringe-maker."

It was in 1812 that the Chicago Massacre took place. For more than a year before, the Indian tribes residing near the remote lakes and the sources of the Mississippi had displayed great hostility towards the pale-faces; though for a long time they did not venture to proceed to extremities. But after the declaration of war between the United States and Great Britain, on the 18th May, 1812, the savages came forward in great numbers as the allies of the British, and acted with their customary barbarity. One of their worst deeds was the Massacre of Chicago, August 15th, 1812.

The Fort of Chicago was commanded by Captain Heald. On the 7th August, he received despatches announcing that the Pottawatomie Indians had declared war against the United States, and commanding him to evacuate the place. He marched out on the 15th, accompanied by all the women and children, and had not proceeded very far before they were surrounded by overwhelming numbers of redskins. The Americans defended themselves with their usual bravery; and though hardly more than one to twenty, they sold their lives dearly.

Mrs. Heald, who was in the thick of the fight, received seven wounds. Her horse, a splendid animal, was prized by the Indians, who valued it far higher than its rider, and tried their best to avoid hurting it. A savage was in the act of tearing off Mrs. Heald's bonnet to scalp her, when one of the St. Joseph's tribe ransomed her for ten bottles of whiskey and a mule.

Mrs. Helm, wife of the officer second in command, fought bravely for her life. She was wounded slightly in the ankle, and had her horse shot under her. Being attacked by a young savage who aimed a blow at her head with his tomahawk, she sprang on one side, and the stroke fell on her shoulder, inflicting a severe wound. She seized him round the neck, and endeavoured to snatch his scalping-knife; but another Indian came up and dragged her away. The newcomer proved to be a friend. Plunging Mrs. Helm into the lake, he held her there, despite her struggles, till the firing was over.

After fighting with desperate valour, until only twenty-seven of them were left, the Americans were compelled to surrender. The wife of one of the soldiers, hearing of the tortures which the savages inflicted on their prisoners, resolved to die sooner than let herself be taken. When her companions had given up their arms, the Indians wished to capture this woman; but rejecting all their promises of kind treatment, she fought so desperately that she was literally cut to pieces.

Captain Helm, twice wounded, was sent with his wife and children to Mackinaw on the eastern coast of Michigan, and delivered as prisoners of war to the British general, who received them kindly, and sent them to Detroit. Lieutenant Helm, also wounded, was taken to St. Louis; where he was liberated through the entreaties of Mr. Forsyth, an Indian trader. Mrs. Helm was taken to Detroit, where she was exchanged, together with Captain and Mrs. Heald, sometime after.

CHAPTER 13

Private in the Brazilian Army (War of the Reconcave) to Amazon Corps

Since the first French Revolution, monarchs have not always sat easily upon their thrones. They fancied they had cut down the Tree of Liberty after the downfall of Napoleon, and that it would never grow up again; but in a very short time it brought forth new branches, and has since borne fruit in a way which the most sanguine Republican of olden times would scarcely have ventured to predict. Since the Battle of Waterloo, Europe and America—even parts of Asia and Africa—have been convulsed by rebellions, civil wars, and revolutions, which have often shaken the world to its centre.

The people learnt to hate their rulers; and one nation after another, catching the revolutionary fire from the smouldering brand half stamped out in France, rose in rebellion against the monarch who refused them immediate enfranchisement. Again, and again have the nations been compelled by force of arms to submit; but they rise again whenever they fancy they see a favourable opportunity. Thus, it happened that almost every war, fought in Europe or America since Waterloo up to some ten years since, had its origin in the same cause—the struggles of nations to cast off their rulers.

Amongst those states which took the initiative in raising the standard of revolt, the South American colonies of Spain and Portugal were foremost. Brazil declared its independence in 1821, and elected Don Pedro, the Crown Prince of Portugal, to be Emperor. The latter had a hard struggle to maintain his throne against not only the Portuguese troops, but against the Republicans, who composed a large party in Brazil. His emissaries were despatched all over the country, to the most distant plantations, to raise recruits for the Imperial Army.

One of these messengers arrived one day at the farmhouse of Gonzalez de Almeida, a Portuguese settler in the parish of San José, on the Rio de Pax. The patriot was invited to dinner; and, mindful of his object, he endeavoured to enlist the sympathies of his host for Don Pedro. Almeida listened very attentively; but it awakened no feelings of patriotism in his breast. He was old, and could not join the army himself, nor had he a son to give.

"As to giving a slave," added he, "what interest would a slave have in fighting for the independence of Brazil?"

But though Almeida had no sons, he had two daughters. One of them, Doña Maria de Jesus, was desirous, for many reasons, to leave home and seek employment elsewhere. Her father had married again, and the stepmother and her young children made home exceedingly uncomfortable for Maria. She was much excited by the patriot's words; "So that at last," she said, "I felt my heart burning in my breast!"

She stole from the house, and went to that of her married sister. After recapitulating the stranger's discourse, she expressed a wish that she were a man and could join the Imperial standard.

"Nay," said her sister. "If I had not a husband and child, for one half of what you say, I would join the ranks of the emperor."

This decided the wavering resolution of Dona Maria. Her sister supplied her with a suit of clothes belonging to the husband, so Maria took the opportunity, as her father was going to Cachoeira, about forty leagues distant, to dispose of some cotton, to ride after him; not close enough to be seen, but sufficiently near for protection. When in sight of Cachoeira, she halted; and going a little way from the road, dressed herself in male attire.

She entered the town on a Friday, and by the following Sunday she had enlisted in an artillery regiment, and had already mounted guard. She was, however, too slight for the heavy duties of an artilleryman; so, she exchanged into an infantry corps, in which she remained till the close of the war.

Her real sex was not even suspected till Almeida applied to the commanding officer of her regiment. In the summer of 1823 she was sent with despatches to Rio Janeiro, and there presented to Don Pedro, who gave her an ensign's commission and the Order of the Cross—the latter of which he himself placed upon her jacket.

Maria Graham in her *Journal of a Voyage to Brazil*, gives, as one of the illustrations, Maria de Jesus in her uniform. This traveller says:

Her dress is that of a soldier of one of the emperor's battalions, with the addition of a tartan kilt, which she told me she had adopted from a picture representing a Highlander, as the most feminine military dress. What would the Gordons and Macdonalds say to this? The 'garb of old Gaul' chosen as a womanish attire!

This lady further says that Maria, though clever, was almost totally uneducated:

She might have been a remarkable person. She is not particularly masculine in her appearance, and her manners are gentle and cheerful.

In a census of the population of St. Petersburg, published about 1829, there appears the following curious item:—

Soldiers and Subalterns.

Men.	Women.	Total.
46,076	9,975	56,051.

When the civil war broke out in Spain, in 1634, the town of Eybar, in the province of Guipuzcoa, being attacked by Zabala, the Carlist general, several women and girls assisted the Christino troops in its defence. One of these brave girls, Juana de Anito, at this time barely fifteen, was married six years later to Don Eulogio Barbero Quintero, a young officer in the Spanish Army.

In 1840 he became mixed up in a conspiracy against the government; and on the failure of the plot, attempted to escape into France. He was intercepted on his road, and imprisoned in the citadel of San Sebastian. Directly Juana heard of his capture she resolved to effect his escape; which she accomplished in Nov. 1841, by exchanging clothes with him. Don Eulogio succeeded in reaching the French frontier; but the courage and devotion of his young wife did not avert the wrath of the Spanish Regent, by whose orders she was condemned to imprisonment for life.

It was whilst fighting in Brazil as a rebel against the Imperial Government that Garibaldi first met his beloved wife, Anita. She was a Brazilian by birth, and possessed all the beauty of her countrywomen. Her complexion was a clear olive, set off by piercing black eyes, her figure tall and commanding. She was a fit companion for the brave Garibaldi; being to the full as courageous as he. The general himself said that his wife took part in battle as "an amusement" and "a simple variation to the monotony of camp-life."

Anita accompanied her husband in all his expeditions both on shore and at sea. Ably did she second him in the struggle for Brazilian freedom. Shortly after marriage they were one day at sea, when the Imperial fleet hove in sight, and bore down upon them. Garibaldi entreated his bride to land, and remain on shore whilst the engagement lasted; but she firmly refused, and not only remained during the action, but took a very leading share in it. One of the sailors fell dead at her feet; she snatched up his carbine, and kept up a constant fire on the Brazilians for several hours.

When the battle was at its height, Anita was standing on deck, waving a sword over her head, encouraging the men to resist bravely. Suddenly she was struck down by the wind of a cannon-ball, which killed two men close by. Garibaldi rushed forward, expecting to find that life was extinct; but to his astonishment and delight she rose up unhurt. Again, he entreated her to go below, and remain there till the fighting was over.

"Yes," said Anita. "I will go below; but only to drive out the cowards who are skulking there."

And running down the hatchway, she speedily reappeared, driving before her three men who had gone below to escape the storm.

Anita was also present, on horseback, in a battle fought at a place called Coritibani, where the Garibaldians, numbering scarcely eighty men, half of whom were infantry, were attacked by a large body of Brazilian cavalry. She was not satisfied with being a mere spectator; knowing that the rebels, as they kept up a constant fire, would soon exhaust their ammunition, she went to the baggage-waggons to see that the men were properly supplied with cartridges. She had not been there very long before the baggage-train was attacked by twenty or thirty Brazilian horsemen. Anita was a good rider, and could have saved herself; but she preferred to remain on the spot, encouraging the Garibaldians.

The Brazilians were victorious in this battle; Anita surrounded on every side, received orders to yield. Clapping spurs to her horse, she dashed through the midst of her foes. Several shots were fired after her; one, a pistol shot, went through her hat, cutting off a lock of hair, while another pierced her horse's head. The animal fell heavily to the ground, flinging her with violence from the saddle. Before she could recover her feet, the Brazilian troopers had made her prisoner.

Anita believed that her husband had been killed; so, the Brazilian colonel gave her permission to search the battlefield for his body. She looked through the corpses again and again for several hours, and at last came to the conclusion that Garibaldi still lived, and she determined to rejoin him. That night, when the Brazilians had retired to rest, and when even the sentry began to nod, she succeeded in escaping to a farmhouse a quarter of a mile distant; where she seized a horse, and plunged into the forest, in the direction which she believed the Garibaldians to have taken.

For more than a week, Anita Garibaldi wandered alone amidst the almost impenetrable wilds of the dense Brazilian forests, without food, and exposed to the hourly chances of capture. More than once she was pursued by the enemy placed in ambush at various points. One stormy night, four horsemen, who were stationed at a ford of the River Canoas, believing her to be a phantom, fled in terror. Anita plunged boldly into the stream; and, although it was five hundred yards broad, and swollen by the mountain rivulets till it had assumed the aspect of a roaring cataract, she succeeded, holding on by her horse's mane, in reaching the opposite shore, amidst a shower of bullets from the Brazilians, who had found out their mistake.

After enduring for eight days every kind of danger and privation, she overtook the Garibaldians, and rejoined her husband.

"Yes, yes, gentlemen," added Garibaldi, when he related this anecdote, "my wife is valiant."

There are many more of these anecdotes related concerning the extraordinary bravery of Anita. She afterwards accompanied her husband on his return to Italy, in 1848, and was with him during the insurrection of Lombardy against Austria. In the following year she attended him throughout the siege of Rome. After the fall of the Eternal City in 1849, when Garibaldi was escaping to Venice, Anita, worn out by long suffering, died at Mandriole, a small village in the marshes of Ravenna.

Apollonia Jagiello, a Polish heroine, who acquired no little celebrity for her bravery during the insurrections of '46 and '48, was born in Lithuania, in 1825. She was educated at Cracow, in which city she passed her early life; sometimes changing for a few weeks to Warsaw or Vienna. In 1846 the insurrection broke out in the former city. Apollonia was, at this time, rather more than twenty, of medium height, with a graceful and slender figure. She was a brunette, with big black eyes, and a profusion of dark hair. Her arms and hands, which were more than once admired by those who saw her, were beautiful, and delicately formed. Although her lips were usually compressed, with a resolute expression of one who was not easily daunted, yet she could also smile most sweetly. The *National Era* (an American journal) says:

> In that, the woman comes out; it is arch, soft and winning—a rare and indescribable smile. Her manner is simple and engaging. Her voice is now gentle or mirthful, now earnest and passionate sometimes it sounds like the utterance of some quiet home lyre, and sometimes startles you with a decided ring of the steel.

Apollonia, inspired by that enthusiastic love for her country, which we so often find amongst Polish girls, joined the national army; and, throughout the struggle, which lasted only two or three months, was always found wherever danger was greatest. Mounted on horseback, she was one of those patriots who planted the White Eagle and the flag of freedom on the Castle and Palace of Cracow. She also formed one of that gallant little band which fought the battle near Podgorze against an army ten times their strength.

When the insurrection was suppressed, Madlle. Jagiello, resuming her own attire, remained in Cracow for several weeks without detection. She then removed to Warsaw, where she stayed until the year 1848, the Year of Revolutions. Directly the Cracovians took up arms, she joined their ranks, and displayed the same courage which she had shown two years previously.

The insurrection of '48 proved, if possible, a greater failure than the first. Apollonia fled from Cracow, and reached Vienna just in time to take share in the skirmish of the Faubourg Widen. She remained here only a few days, her object being to join the Hungarian insurgents under Kossuth. With the assistance of some friends she succeeded in reaching Presburg; whence, disguised as a peasant, she was conveyed to the village of St. Paul by those unfortunate country-folks who were compelled to carry provisions for the Austrian Army.

Crossing that part of the country occupied by the German troops, she reached the Hungarian camp, near the village of Ezneszey, on the 15th August, 1848. This was immediately before the battle fought here, in which the Austrians were defeated, and General Wist slain. Apollonia took part in this battle as a volunteer; but such was her courage that the Hungarian general presented her with a lieutenant's commission.

Apollonia, on the urgent solicitation of all, undertook the superintendence of the hospital at Comorn. This post she resigned for a while to join as a volunteer in the expedition of twelve thousand men, commanded by General Klapka, who captured Raab. Returning to Comorn, the heroine resumed her hospital duties, and remained there until the fortress surrendered.

In December, 1849, in company with Governor Ladislaus Ujhazy and his family, Apollonia Jagiello sailed to the United States, where they received an enthusiastic welcome. Here she continued to show that hatred of tyrants for which she had ever been distinguished. One day, when she was at Washington, an album was handed to her, with the request that she would add her autograph to those it already contained. She took it with a smile, but it chanced that on the very page at which she opened, the signature of M. Bodisco, the Russian ambassador, figured prominently. Flinging the album from her, with flashing eyes, she declared that her name should never appear in the same book with "the tool of a tyrant."

While the hatred of Austria was felt by all throughout Hungary, Croatia and Sclavonia were actuated, on the contrary, by feelings of the deepest loyalty to the house of Hapsburg. Baron W., who published his adventures under the title of *Scenes of the Civil War in Hungary in 1848-9, with the personal adventures of an Austrian officer, etc.*, declares that the Croatians joined the Imperial standard by thousands; even the women, moved by an ardent and loyal courage, aided in defending the frontiers against the Bosnians, who, excited by the emissaries of Kossuth, took every opportunity for raids and invasions over the border. While the men were flocking to the banners of Jellachich, the ban of Croatia, their wives and daughters took up arms and repaired to the chain of posts on the Turkish boundary, "that all the men might be able to take the field; and such an eight days' duty as these frontier posts," he adds, "is no trifle, and requires not a little firmness."

Old, half-invalided frontier subalterns, incapacitated for taking the field, were the *commandants*; young, many of them handsome, females composed their troops. "By my faith!" exclaims the baron, "I should have no objection to be the commander of such a corps of Ottochan females myself!"

Numbers of Croatian and Sclavonian women accompanied the Austrian Army into Germany and Italy. The same author says:

We had wives and daughters of frontier soldiers with us in Peschiera and on the march through Hungary, who equalled the men in the endurance of fatigue, and displayed undaunted courage in battle. In Hungary we had with us a young Croatian, the daughter of an old Seressan, who was as daring a rider as the best hussar, and more than once fearlessly joined the men in the charge. A Hungarian *jurat* gave her in an action a cut on the left cheek, which she returned with a severe blow on the arm, seized the bridle of his horse, and took him prisoner. This horse, a grey stallion, she ever afterwards rode, and refused to sell, though I offered her forty *ducats* for him.

The Countess Helene St——, a Hungarian patriot, was the sister of an old comrade of Baron W. The brother, who owned a magnificent estate, was a Magyar to the very core; and directly the insurrection broke out, he took up arms, and fell bravely fighting for his country in February, 1849. His dying agonies were soothed by an unexpected meeting with his early friend, the Baron.

Helene joined the insurgents soon after her brother left home, and served as *aide-de-camp* to his maternal uncle, who commanded a considerable Magyar corps. One cold, moonlight night, a few days after the death of the count, the author of the *Adventures* discovered the corpse of this beautiful girl, dressed in the military uniform of a Hungarian soldier, stretched out at the foot of a tree, her life's blood crimsoning the white snow, he says:

> Forcibly mustering my spirits, I ordered my men to carry the body to the fire. There we examined it more closely, and with extreme anxiety I sought to ascertain whether there was any hope left of reviving her. Vain hope! It was several hours since her spirit had departed; the ball of one of our riflemen had gone through her heart. From the small red wound blood was still oozing in a single drop, which I carefully caught in my handkerchief to be preserved as a relic.
>
> My only consolation was that the deceased could not have suffered long; that she must have expired the very moment she was struck. Those pure, noble, still wondrous beautiful features; on her brow dwelt peace and composure, and the lips almost smiled. There she lay, as if in tranquil slumber, and yet those eyes were never more to open—those lips never more to utter noble sentiments or words of kindness.
>
> My hussars were visibly affected, and thought it a pity that one so young and so beautiful should die so early. Many of them

who had been with me on our first march through Hungary for two days together at St———'s mansion, instantly recognised Helene, and doubly lamented her death, because she had shown such kindness to them.

They dug a deep grave beneath the frozen snow.

The corpse, in full uniform; the *holpack*, with plume of glistening heron's feathers on her head, the light Turkish sabre by her side, was then carefully wrapped in a clean large blanket which we had with us, and so deposited in the grave, which we filled up again with earth. Then regardless of caution, I had a full salute fired with pistols over the grave. I have preserved a small gold ring and a lock of her hair for a memorial.

The baron, it should be added, plainly tells the reader that he was very nearly, if not quite, overhead and ears in love with the beautiful Helene.

One of the hussars, who could do carpenter's work, made a cross of two young, white maple trees, which was placed over the heroine's grave.

The Garde Mobile (which, as an extra battalion to the National Guard, did good service to the people in '48,) when it was disbanded, proved to be half composed of Parisian women and girls.

Louisa Battistati, a heroine of the Lombardian Revolution, was a native of Stradella, in Sardinia, and a *mantua*-maker by trade. She was dwelling in Milan, following this business, when the five days' Revolution broke out. On Sunday, the loth March, 1848, Louisa attacked and disarmed an Austrian cavalry soldier, although he carried a carbine. At the head of a valiant band of young women, she now took up her station at the Poppietti bridge, and defended it all through the 20th, the 21st and the 22nd. At every shot from her musket a Croat fell dead.

In June, 1853, the war between Russia and Turkey broke out. The Turkish government, to swell the ranks of the army, were obliged to beat up for recruits among the semi-barbarous tribes of Asia Minor. The chief of one of the wild tribes in the Cilician mountains having been imprisoned by order of the *Sultan*, his wife, Fatima, a little old woman, about sixty years of age, with a dark complexion, who governed during his absence, exercising the double duty of Queen and Prophetess, raised three hundred of her best horsemen and led them to the Allied Camp at Scutari, in the summer of 1854. Her appearance created no little sensation amongst English and French.

There was very little of the Amazon in her personal appearance, though she bestrode her steed like a trooper, and wore a costume intended to represent the military dress of a chieftain. She was attended by two handmaids, also in male attire. Fatima, apprehensive that her entreaties for the release of her husband would prove insufficient to move the Sultan, thought the best means of propitiating the Turkish Government was to lead a few hundreds of her bravest warriors to fight the frozen Russ. The pay for her troops was to be eighty piastres a month, besides tooth and stirrup money in every village through which they should pass.

When the Allies were storming the Mamelon in June, 1855, Lady Paget (wife of Lord George, and daughter of General Sir Arthur Paget, brother of the famous Marquis of Anglesey) was present on the field, at a short distance from the scene of action. General Pennefather went up to the dead body of a Russian officer, and cut a medal off his coat. He then pinned the medal on Lady Paget's shawl, paying her a handsome compliment to the effect that she deserved a medal as much as anyone present.

Most people can remember the fortitude and courage displayed by the British ladies at Cawnpore, Lucknow, and other Indian cities during the terrible Mutiny. Ladies, some of them mere girls, delicately nurtured, unused to hardships of any kind, endured without a murmur, the most heartrending privations; and so far from giving way to useless repinings or sinking into apathy, they tried in every way to cheer up their brave defenders. They bore provisions and ammunition to the soldiers, loaded the rifles, and more than once took their turn in mounting guard and firing on the rebels.

The heroine of Cawnpore, Miss Wheeler, was one of the prisoners captured by the notorious Nana Sahib on the 26th June, 1857, and all who survived the terrible Massacre bore witness to her unflinching courage. She is said to have shot five *sepoys* with a revolver; that she was then taken away by a *sowar* (trooper) to his hut, when she snatched his sabre, cut off his head, and flung herself down a well. An *ayah*, belonging to an English family, stated that it was in the hut, after killing the *sowar*, that she shot the five *sepoys*.

The romantic conquest of Naples and Sicily, by General Garibaldi in 1860, has already melted into the past and become an almost distant event in European history. It was said at the time that if Francis II. had possessed a particle of the military courage of his queen, it would have been easy for him with his trained battalions to have captured or dispersed the handful of Garibaldian volunteers. When Bombino had taken refuge in Gaeta, the great stronghold of Southern Italy, he fancied himself secure from the attacks of the foe; but the Sardinian troops were soon battering the walls with long-range guns, and all the appliances necessary for a modern siege.

Amongst the besieged, Queen Marie Sophie Amelie was the only leader who encouraged the soldiers to make a brave defence. Standing on the ramparts of Gaeta, she incited the Neapolitan troops to shed the last drop of their blood for the Bourbon cause. Doubtless there was much exaggeration in those marvellous anecdotes published in the newspapers of the time relating deeds of Amazonian valour performed by the queen; but it is certain that she acted the part of king, while her cowardly husband hid away in the darkness and security of bomb-proof galleries.

In December, 1860, and January, 1861, it was remarked by the troops of Cialdini that every morning, at a particular hour, the fire of the Neapolitan batteries slackened for a short time; recommencing, however, with renewed vigour. They soon learned that the queen, dressed in Calabrian costume, visited a particular battery (named after herself the "Queen's Battery") every morning, sometimes on horseback, but generally in a coach; and would assist in the firing of the heavy guns. The artillerymen were ready to sacrifice their lives in the service of their beautiful and courageous queen, while they heartily despised the contemptible Francis.

The chief heroine of the last Polish insurrection (1862-3-4) was Madlle. Pustowjtoff, or, as some have written it, Pustovoydova, *aide-de-camp* and Adjutant to General Langievicz, the Dictator. When the ill-starred rebellion was at its height *cartes-de-visite* of the heroine, in the costume of a Polish officer, were displayed in the shop-windows of the great European and American cities, side by side with all the public celebrities of the day. She was decidedly pretty, though rather childish looking: her features were good, and she had a profusion of fair hair.

Though her family and her proclivities were essentially Polish, Madlle Pustowjtoff was not a native of the country, but was born in Russia of a Polish mother. When the insurrection broke out, she escaped from a convent where she had been placed (probably by her parents) and joined Langievicz, who almost immediately appointed her to be one of his aides. She was present in numberless battles and skirmishes between the Russians and Poles; and finally accompanied

Langievicz in his precipitate—some say cowardly—flight into Galicia, where, being arrested by the Austrian authorities, the fugitives were imprisoned. Madlle. Pustowjtoff was afterwards released on parole, though she was requested not to quit Galicia. In November, 1863, she exchanged the profession of arms for the occupation of companion to a lady in that country; but after the release of Langievicz and his followers by the Austrian Government in the summer of 1865, she resigned this employment, and travelled westwards.

There was many another Polish heroine as brave though not so famous as the female adjutant. When national liberty is at stake, there will always be found women as well as men ready to arm in its defence; and the women of Poland have ever been remarked for more than ordinary patriotism. A writer in *Fraser's Magazine* for December, 1863, speaking of the part taken by the Polish women in the struggles with Russia, relates the following anecdotes of female courage:—

> The following incident of the active heroism of the Polish women, was told me by an officer who had commanded a detachment of cavalry in Lithuania in the early days of the insurrection:—

> One day about twenty of his Cossacks surrounded the house of a lady, living in a retired part of the country, whose daughter was the betrothed of one of the chiefs of bands known to be in the neighbourhood. At that very moment he and several other leaders were in the house, consulting with the two ladies over their plans. Alarmed by the arrival of the Cossacks, the men hastened to escape from the back windows, and fled to the woods; the two women actually protecting their retreat by keeping up a fire from their pistols from the front.

> When the Cossacks at last forced their way into the house, they found only the two women, whom they do not seem to have molested, but contented themselves, after their manner, with filling their pockets with all the portable valuables within reach. On retiring, they pitched their horses a short distance off. yet in sight of the house. Presently the young girl was seen to come out, and proceed to the stables, from which she soon again came forth, mounted, when she set off in the direction her lover had taken.

> One of the Cossacks, having a sorry beast of his own, and admiring that which the girl rode, galloped after her, took hold

of her bridle, and, as good-humouredly as his rough nature allowed, proposed an exchange, observing that as she was going to join the band, she had no need of such a good horse. The reply was a bullet from her revolver which sent the Cossack reeling from his saddle.

Meanwhile his companions, who had followed him, had come up, and seeing the fate of their comrade, surrounded her. The intrepid girl then snapped her pistol at one after the other, and when all the chambers of this one were discharged, flung the empty weapon at the head of the nearest, knocking him from his horse, and immediately drew forth a second. This was too much for the politeness of the Cossacks, of whom three or four were already on the ground; they lifted the poor girl completely off her horse on the points of their lances, and so she perished. As a further example, I will translate an extract from a private letter lately received from an officer serving in the kingdom of Poland: 'Yesterday,' says the officer who wrote it, 'we defeated a band and took nineteen prisoners, one of whom was a woman. There were altogether seven of them belonging to that band, but we do not as yet know if the others were killed or escaped. All the women, our prisoner tells us, were dressed as *chasseurs*, wearing the same uniform of coarse cloth as the men, only without the red epaulette. Their caps, such as are worn by all the Confederates, were *coquettishly* made, and decorated with a white ostrich feather.'

'We captured her by the merest chance. She was a girl from Cracow, finely built, with broad shoulders, and muscular hand and arm, which showed she had been used to gymnastic exercises, while her weather-beaten complexion proved she must have belonged to the band for some length of time. Her features, without being pretty, were regular and agreeable. On our asking her reasons for serving with the band, she confessed she had followed her lover to the woods, adding that, when he was killed, she would have gone back home, but was prevented by her comrades. Somebody asking if she had not served as *aide-de-camp* to C— (the chief of another band), she blushed deeply, and indignantly denied the imputation.

'After this reply, she was very haughty and retired for a time; but, seeing that we were all respectful to her, she gradually became more at home with us and confiding in her conversation.

As she had lost her boots, and was bare-footed, we furnished her with a pair of our long boots and some stockings, for which the poor girl was very thankful. The next day she was released and sent home, her male companions being forwarded on to Warsaw.'

During the war between France and Mexico, several women and girls were discovered fighting in the ranks of Juarez. One of them, a young Indian, aged twenty-two, enlisted with her husband, in the regiment of Zacatecas. She fought so bravely as to speedily gain her epaulettes. Her husband was slain; but the widow remained in the regiment, where her daring courage soon not only procured the esteem of her superior officers, but caused the Mexican generals to promote her to the rank of lieutenant-colonel, May 5th, 1862. When the French captured Puebla, in the summer of 1863, she was made prisoner, and sent to Vera Cruz; whence she embarked in the *Rhône* steam transport for France. During the voyage, though a prisoner, she was treated with all the respect due to a superior officer. She arrived in France in August, 1863, and was seen by many persons, who described the female colonel as rather good-looking, but somewhat unfeminine in outward carriage and bearing.

If we may believe Transatlantic newspapers, the Civil War in America was more productive of female warriors than almost any conflict since the days of the Amazons. The ranks of both Federals and Confederates, from the very commencement of the great struggle, were swelled by numbers of women, who, for various reasons, chose to risk their lives under the Stars and Stripes, or the Stars and Bars. In the summer of 1864, it was said that upwards of one hundred and fifty women were known to be serving in the Army of the Potomac. It was generally supposed that these women had been in collusion with an equal number of men who had been examined by the surgeons; after which the fair ones substituted themselves, and went to the seat of war. More than seventy of the valiant *demoiselles* were, when their sex became known, acting as officers' servants.

Early in May, 1863, a Pennsylvania girl was discovered serving in one of the regiments in the Federal Army of the West, to which she had belonged for ten months. She said that there were many females in the ranks of this army, and one female lieutenant. She had herself, she declared, assisted in burying three female soldiers whose sex was unknown to any but her.

Mrs. Francis L. Clayton, another female Federal, enlisted in 1861, in company with her husband at St. Paul, Minnesota. The husband and wife fought together, side by side, in eighteen battles, till the former was slain in the engagement of Stone River. After his death, the wife did not care to remain any longer in the service, so she went to the general, and told him she was a woman, and was at once discharged. She then returned to Maine. During her military career, Mrs. Clayton was wounded three times, and once was made prisoner.

The following story, "strange if true," appeared in the *Brooklyn* (New York) *Times*, in October, 1863, just after the Battle of Chattanooga:—

About a twelvemonth since, when disaster everywhere overtook the Union arms, and our gallant sons were falling fast under the marvellous sword of rebellion, a young lady, scarce nineteen, from an academy in a sister State, conceived the idea that she was destined by Providence to lead our armies to victory, and our nation through successful war. It was at first thought by her parents—a highly respectable family in Willoughby-street—that her mind was weakened simply by reading continual accounts of reverses to our arms, and they treated her as a sick child.

This only had the effect of making her more demonstrative, and her enthusiastic declaration and apparent sincerity gave the family great anxiety. Dr. B. was consulted, the minister was spoken to, friends advised, family meetings held, interviews with the young lady and her former companions in the academy were frequent, but nothing could shake the feeling which possessed her. It was finally resolved to take her to Michigan. An old maiden aunt accompanied the fair enthusiast, and for weeks Anne Arbour became their home. But travel had no effect upon the girl. The stern command of her aunt alone prevented her from making her way to Washington to solicit an interview with the President for the purpose of getting command of the United States Army.

Finally, it was found necessary to restrain her from seeing any one but her own family, and her private parlour became her prison. To a high-spirited girl that would be unendurable at any time, but to a young lady filled with such an hallucination it was worse than death. She resolved to elude her friends, and succeeded, leaving them clandestinely,—and, although the most distinguished detectives of the east and west were employed to find her whereabouts, it was unavailing. None could conjecture her hiding-place.

This was last April. She was mourned as lost, the *habiliments* of mourning were assumed by her grief-stricken parents, and a suicide's grave was assumed to be hers. But it was not so. The infatuated girl, finding no sympathy among her friends, resolved to enter the army, disguised as a drummer boy, dreaming, poor girl, that her destiny would be worked out by such a mode. She joined the drum-corps of a Michigan regiment at Detroit, her sex known only to herself, and succeeded in getting with her regiment to the Army of the Cumberland. How the poor girl survived the hardships of the Kentucky campaign, when strong men fell in numbers, must for ever remain a mystery.

The regiment to which she was attached had a place in the division of the gallant Van Cleve, and, during the bloody battle of last Sunday, the fair girl fell, pierced in the left side with a Minie ball, and, when borne to the surgeon's tent, her sex was discovered. She was told by the surgeon that her wound was mortal, and advised to give her name, that her family might be informed of her fate. This she finally, though reluctantly, consented to do, and the colonel of the regiment, suffering himself from a painful wound, became interested in her behalf, and prevailed upon her to let him send a despatch to her father.

Here, then, is a short incident of the war, which might read like romance, but to the unhappy family which are now bowed down by grief, romance loses its attraction, and the actual sad, eventful history of poor Emily—will be a family record for generations to come.

In December, 1863, the correspondent of the *Cincinnati Times*, describing a skirmish between the Federals and a detachment of General Bragg's army at Ringgold, near Chattanooga, says:

Several of the fair sex were in the Confederate ranks, and certainly conducted themselves with a great deal of courage. We make no reflection on their taste in entering the ranks with negroes and greasy grey-backs. Rebellion now needs every aid on the earth above or in the caverns under it.

At Timonsville, S.C., is the grave of Mrs. Florence Bodwin, of Philadelphia, Pa. She was a member of a Federal regiment, and as such, being dressed as a soldier, her sex was not discovered until after her death.

The following anecdote went the round of the papers in October, 1865, though the event chronicled must have taken place sometime previously, doubtless before the close of the war:—

At Theresina, a *mulatto* girl, nineteen years-old, cut her hair, bandaged her bosom, and dressed as a man, went to the President to offer herself as a volunteer. The President detected her sex, and supposed at first that she was mad, or had taken this plan to accompany a lover; but finding that she was really actuated by patriotism, he accepted her, and appointed her second sergeant, and she does all the duties of her post, dressed in the proper uniform.

The Maori War in New Zealand, like the conflicts between the Red Skins and the Pale Faces in North America, gave many opportunities for the wives and daughters of settlers to play the heroine. Some of the native women, too, displayed great prowess, both for and against the English. A correspondent of the *Irish Times*, writing from Wanganui, under date of the 7th January, 1866, in describing the native contingent (a force recruited from the Wanganui River Tribes) to which he was Assistant Surgeon, says:

"Numbers of women accompany us, who generally carry the baggage of the men. This is not their only use in campaigning. They fight, and fight well, carrying their gun and tomahawk."

During the Austro-Italian war of 1866, a Florence journal related that, after the Battle of Custozza (June 27th), a surgeon of the Italian Army discovered among the wounded a young corporal of Bersaglieri still alive, notwithstanding three severe injuries in the neck, left arm, and right leg. When about to dress those wounds, the surgeon perceived that the sufferer was a young woman, who then declared her name to be Herminia Manelli, and her age twenty. Just before the opening of the campaign her brother, who was a corporal of Bersaglieri, had fallen ill, and returned home to his family until his recovery.

The sister, whose parents had previously had some difficulty in preventing from joining the Garibaldians, took advantage of that circumstance, and, cutting short her hair, dressed herself in her brother's uniform, and joined his regiment, her resemblance to him enabling her to pass unnoticed. Four hours later her regiment was engaged, and she was wounded on the field of battle. After the discovery of her sex by the surgeon she was taken to Florence, where she died a few days later.

In the summer of 1868, there was a great deal of talk about an army of women which had just been raised by the savage Lopez, Dictator of Paraguay. A correspondent writing from Buenos Ayres under date May 14th, says:—

An army of women confronts the allies! Lopez has enrolled the Amazons of Paraguay, and we have entered upon what may be called for the sake of distinction—the petticoat campaign? Brigadier-General Eliza Lynch commands the main body of the female army, which is encamped midway between the pass of the river and a small inland town. On the road to Villa Rica her right wing, under Mrs. Captain Herrero, has deployed to the left a little, to hang on the allies should they assail the position of Tebiquary, held by Mrs. Lieutenant Colonel Margaret Fereira and her fair brigade of womankind. Can 'stern-visaged Mars' prove unpropitious? . . . According to authentic accounts, relays of women and girls are constantly at the headquarters of the feminine commander-in-chief to whom has been entrusted the guerilla portion of the campaign.

The Brazilian journals were of course indignant at what they termed an outrage on civilization, and alternately sneered and railed at Lopez's petticoat *corps d'armée*. Very little was afterwards heard of these Amazons. Since their first formation, with the exception of a few stray anecdotes related by travellers and adventurers returning to the States or to this country, absolutely nothing transpired concerning the movements of this female army.

Again, we meet with female warriors in the struggle between Crete and Turkey. A writer in a newspaper eleven years ago says:

Whether they have been effectual defenders of their country, or whether their enthusiasm decreased before the stern necessity of a camp, is hardly known, for very little intelligence comes from the mountains of Crete.

However, in January, 1869, a body of about fifty Cretan Amazons, in uniform, was seen at Michali, practising shooting with carbines at a mark. They were, it is said, very good shots, and had been organised into a regular corps, with a regimental flag, which was carried by a *religieuse* who had turned Amazon.

The Philo-Cretan Committee recognised the patriotism of these Lakkoite damsels, by providing them with arms (consisting of a rifle of the English pattern with a sword-bayonet) and handsome uniforms similar to those worn by the Palikares. This costume included the *fez*, a corset embroidered in gold and silver, a short, piquant half-sleeved jacket, a white petticoat and "continuations," and the most charmingly neat buckskin gaiters. A cartridge-box hung to the belt, while a haversack depended from the shoulders. Picturesque sketches of these heroines, in uniform, appeared in the French and English journals of January, '69.

But while a few of the Cretan women have proved themselves heroines, bravery has been the character of those of Montenegro for more than half a century. War against the Mussulman is the object, the engrossing passion of nearly every Montenegrin—men, women, and children, cripples even, rush to the fight with enthusiasm. In truth, the Turkish Government has never been able thoroughly to subdue the Black Mountain. Women accompany their male relatives in all their expeditions against the *infidels*, wives are ever ready to seize up the *yataghan* and pistols of a slain husband, and avenge his death. Various heroic ballads have been sung or recited from time to time in the fastnesses of the Tsernogora relating the martial deeds of some valiant widow who has slain Turkish *Agas*, captured or dispersed, single-handed, whole companies of the foe, or in other ways distinguished their military courage and their hatred of the Moslem.

A singular incident is alleged to have taken place some nine years since on the occasion of a marriage before the chief authorities in Algeria. The official required the consent of the bride's mother, and asked if she was present. A sonorous bass voice answered "Yes."

The mayor looked up and saw a tall soldier before him. "That is well," said he. "Let the mother come here. Her consent and signature are necessary."

To the astonishment of all present, the soldier approached the mayor with long strides,—saluted military fashion, and said "You ask for the mother of the bride. She stands before you."

"Very well, sir," replied the mayor. "Then stand back. I can take no proxy. I must see the mother the mother, I tell you."

"And I repeat that she stands before you," rejoined the soldier. "My name is Maria L——. I have been thirty-six years in the service. I have been through several campaigns, and obtained the rank of sergeant.

Here are my papers—the permission to wear uniform, and my nomination as sergeant-major."

The mayor carefully examined the documents, and found them perfectly correct. There was nothing to be done but to complete the marriage of the young couple. The mother bestowed her blessing fervently with her deep bass voice in a manner which impressed all present, but the company were "more startled than touched."

The Brigand chiefs of Southern Italy are the last representatives of the *Condottieri* who ravaged the land in olden times. But so far from improving with the march of intellect and growing more civilized, the bandits of our days would seem to have very decidedly retrograded as regards the more polite arts of life; indeed, they are nothing but savage beasts, who can handle the carbine or the dagger, and have the passions of avarice and the thirst for gold added to the reckless cruelty of the tiger. These ferocious brigands are almost invariably accompanied in their adventurous journey through life 'by some beautiful fiend, either the wife or the mistress of the redoubtable chief. These women are often the most abandoned and worthless of their sex, without even the virtue of mercy—the tigress is not uncommonly worse than the tiger.

Amongst those brigand captains who, though almost unknown in Western Europe, have earned a terrible renown in the South of Italy, none was more feared and respected some seventeen or eighteen years ago than Monaco. His deeds of violence and daring audacity rendered him famous throughout the Neapolitan provinces. His wife, Maria Oliveiro, a remarkably handsome woman (about twenty years old in 1864), was his constant companion in all his marauding expeditions. She was unmistakably brave, but her nature was so ruthless that the sight of blood rendered her half mad. Monaco was at last slain in a desperate encounter with the Italian troops near Rossano.

Maria was severely wounded; but without losing her courage or presence of mind, she planted one knee firmly on her husband's corpse, and continued to load and fire with extreme rapidity, exciting the admiration even of her opponents. At last she received a severe wound in the leg, and was made prisoner. She was tried by court-martial at Cattanzaro, and condemned to be shot; but this sentence was commuted to thirty years' penal servitude, and she had not been very long in gaol before the gaoler fell desperately in love with her, and they fled together.

At a short distance from Cattanzaro they were met by her brothers, also brigands. They immediately slew the gaoler, who was of no further use, and Maria formed a new band of brigands, of which she was made captain, and commenced ravaging the tract of mountainous country lying between Cattanzaro and the River Crati. The reckless, useless acts of cruelty excited the indignation of the people for miles round. She sacked the villages of Spinelli, Cotzenei, and Belvedere; and in spite of the exertions made by the Italian Government of the province, who, in the autumn of 1864, despatched two battalions of the line in pursuit of the band, the rural population were in such dread of Maria that the soldiers could do nothing.

Another locally famous brigand, Crouo Donatello, was accompanied in his campaigns by his *inamorata*, who was as brave as he. In an encounter with the royal troops in August or September, 1863, Donatello, compelled to fly, left behind him this woman, who fought desperately before letting herself be taken.

In 1866, in a skirmish between the Papal troops and the brigands in the neighbourhood of the Eternal City, two of the latter were slain. One of the corpses proved to be that of a large, good-looking peasant woman, about thirty years of age, armed and dressed like her comrades. She was subsequently recognised as the wife of the bandit chief Cedrone; and the latter was inconsolable for the loss of his brave spouse, being seen for days and days to weep bitterly, though his followers surrounded him, proffering empty consolations.

The famous Brigand Pietro Bianchi, some eighteen or nineteen years since the terror of the district of Nicastro, in the Calabrian mountains, was accompanied in nearly every expedition by a girl named Generosa Cardamone (aged about seventeen in 1861, the chief himself being then twenty), who might frequently be seen on horseback at the head of the band, encouraging them in the fight. In point of ferocity and ruthless courage she was worthy of her lover—nay, she far surpassed him, and is said to have repeatedly cooked human flesh, and served it up to him and his followers.

Bianchi loved the young and beautiful demon most passionately, and was madly jealous of her. One day a bandit kissed her, but his audacity was instantly punished by a score of dagger-stabs dealt by the unerring hand of his chief. Generosa was deeply religious after a fashion, and marvellously superstitious; when she was arrested, in 1867, a religious book and a Madonna were found upon her, which she carried, through a blind idea that they rendered her invulnerable.

In March, 1867, a lieutenant of *gendarmes* discovered the cave of

Bianchi at Soveria, and with his own men, aided by a detachment of the line, forced the brigand and his mistress to surrender, after they had been the terror of the country for seven years.

De Martino, for some time the worst and most ferocious bandit in the Abruzzi, was likewise accompanied by his paramour, who had the character of being more cruel than he was himself. For months the Royal troops were engaged constantly hunting them up and down the woods. At last, in August, 1869, they discovered and surrounded the lurking place of De Martino. The brigand, firing upon the carabineers, by mishap set the dry twigs of the hut in a blaze, and was burnt alive, together with the partner of his crimes.

Duke Ernest of Saxe-Coburg Gotha, on the occasion of the 25th anniversary of his accession, February, 1869, founded an Order of Decoration to recompense courage in women.

The Franco-Prussian War, and the subsequent Communist Insurrection, proved that the military spirit was not extinct in the hearts of women, and that modern female warriors were as ready and as eager for the fray as any of their ancestresses. But the numerous newspaper anecdotes and reports were in many instances more or less creations of fancy, often false, frequently written in haste, as a rule full of gross exaggerations, whether emanating from French or German quarters, consequently always unreliable.

One of the most remarkable and best authenticated female warriors of the period was Minna Hänsel, of Berlin, who, in the early days of the war, before the Germans had swept all before them, raised an Amazon corps, all ready equipped and full of military ardour. These warlike women were much ridiculed by the Berlinese, but the Fräulein Hänsel, disregarding the adverse criticism which, she said, was "of course only to be expected in these frivolous days of ours," addressed a letter to the governor of the city, General Von Falkenstein, asking him in what place the services of the corps would prove most effective. The general—purposely, perhaps—delayed returning an answer till the closing days of August, 1870, when Miss Hänsel, although her offers of service had by no means been rejected, considered that the "rapid and victorious progress of the war" put an end to any necessity for her corps being employed, and accordingly disbanded her troop.

A wounded soldier in November, 1870, passed through Berlin, and was the object of general attention. This soldier was a young woman only twenty-four, carefully educated, but imbued with a strong bias in favour of masculine dress and an active life. She passed the ensign's examinations, and, with good recommendations, entered the army under the name of Weiss. She distinguished herself by the recovery of a Prussian standard, which had been taken by the enemy, and was presented with the Iron Cross. Having received four shot wounds, she was sent for recovery to her native place, Tilsit.

But the hurried, fragmentary mention of either French or German "heroines" is hardly worth serious record or investigation. To ascertain the truth or the falsity of any one anecdote would be now clearly impossible. That noble spirit and patriotic ardour glowed on both sides throughout the desperate struggle is without a doubt; and in the universal enthusiasm women shared as freely as their fellow-countrymen, and were ready to spend life and treasure in the service of their native land and national honour.

CHAPTER 14

India

The early history of India is involved in such deep obscurity that we have no reliable information before the invasion of Alexander the great. True, we read of a nation of Indian Amazons, mentioned by Nonnus, but we have no details on the subject. Amongst the sovereigns who opposed the invincible Macedonian, was Cleophes, Queen of Massaga, whose capital city was said to have been impregnable. While reconnoitring the fortress, Alexander was wounded in the leg. But without waiting for the wound to heal, he commenced battering the walls with various military engines of the most redoubtable aspect; which so terrified the queen, who had never even heard of anything like them, that she speedily tendered her submission. Alexander, who merely conquered cities for the sake of glory, permitted her to retain all her dominions in peace.

In Martin's *History of Eastern India* we read of a warrior-queen named Moynawoti. She was married to Manikechandro, brother of Dhormo Pal, a King of Kamrup, and on the death of her husband, she made war on the king, who was defeated and slain on the banks of the Tista. Gopichondro, son of Moynawoti, succeeded his uncle on the throne, but he left the management of state affairs to his mother, and gave himself up to a life of pleasure. When he grew up, however, the young king wished to take an active share in the government, but his mother persuaded him to dedicate his life to religion, and he ever after practised the utmost humility and self-denial.

It was during the *caliphate* of Walid that the Mahommedans made their first conquests beyond the Indus. About the year 711 *A.D.*, an Arab ship having been seized at Dival, or Dewal, a port connected with Scinde, Hejaj, the Moslem Governor of Bosra, demanded its restitution. Daher, Rajah of Scinde, refused; and this led to the invasion of India by six thousand followers of Islam. Daher marched at the head of fifty thousand men to oppose the invaders, but in the battle which ensued he was slain, and his troops routed with terrible slaughter.

Daher's widow, with a courage worthy her deceased lord, raised fifteen thousand men, and offered battle to the conquerors. They declined the challenge, and she retired within the walls of Adjur. The Moslems closely invested the city; and the garrison, reduced to the last extremities, sacrificed their wives and children on the burning pile formed by their gold and treasures, and, headed by the royal widow, attacked the besiegers in their own camp. They all fell, fighting gallantly to the last.

On the death of Altumsh, Emperor of Hindostan, in 1235, he was succeeded by his son, Prince Feroze. The latter was an effeminate, luxurious monarch, who thought of nothing but spending on dancing-women, comedians, and musicians, the treasures accumulated by his father, and he left the affairs of state to be ruled by his mother. Her cruelty, and the indifference of Feroze, caused several of the *omrahs* to revolt. The emperor marched against them with a vast army; but he was deserted by his *vizier*, a great portion of his army, and seven of his principal nobles. The latter returned to Delhi, and placed Sultana Rizia, the eldest daughter of Altumsh, on the throne. When this news reached Feroze, he hastened back to Delhi; but the new empress marched out to meet him, and he was delivered into her hands. He died in confinement sometime after.

The *sultana* possessed every quality proper for a ruler; even detractors could find no fault, save that she was a woman. During her father's lifetime she had entered heartily into state affairs and was Regent for a short time during the absence of Altumsh on an expedition against Gwalior.

Rizia was not long left in undisturbed possession of the throne. The *omrahs* who had conspired against her brother now marched from Lahore, and encamped before Delhi; but she contrived to sow dissensions amongst them, and each was compelled to retreat to his own province. Some of them, pursued by the empress, were captured and put to death. The *omrahs* finally tendered their submission and the empire enjoyed peace for a time. But the promotion of Jammal, who had once been an Abyssinian slave, to the post of Captain-General of Hindostan, gave such umbrage to the nobles as to ruin the cause of Rizia. The viceroy of Lahore threw off his allegiance in 1239; but the empress, collecting her forces, marched against him, and the viceroy was compelled to accept peace on the most humiliating terms.

Scarcely was this revolt quelled, when Altunia, governor of Tiberhind, raised the standard of rebellion. Rizia immediately marched against him; but when she had gone about halfway, all the Turkish chiefs mutinied. A tumultuous scene ensued, the Abyssinian general was slain, and the Empress sent prisoner to Tiberhind. The imperial troops then returned to Delhi; and set Byram, the Empress's younger brother, upon the throne.

Rizia married the Governor of Tiberhind, and by their joint influence they raised a great army, and marched to Delhi. They were defeated near the city, by the troops of Byram, and the empress with difficulty escaped to Tiberhind. Soon, however, she rallied her scattered forces, and marched once more towards the capital. But she was again defeated at Keitel, and, together with her husband, made prisoner, and barbarously put to death. Thus, died Sultana Rizia, after a brief reign of three years six months and six days. Indian historians agree that she was worthy of a better fate.

One day the Emperor Alla-a-Deen Khiljy was boasting that no *rajah* throughout Hindostan would dare to oppose his power. Nehr Dew, Rajah of Jalwur, "in the plenitude of his folly," exclaimed, "I will suffer death if I do not raise an army that shall defeat any attempt of the king's troop to take the fort of Jalwur."

The emperor, in a rage, commanded the *rajah* to quit Delhi. Hearing, shortly after, that Nehr Dew was raising forces, he ordered a division of his army to besiege Jalwur. This was in 1309. To signalise his contempt for the *rajah*, he placed the troops under the command of a slave girl of the palace, named Gool Behisht, or, "the Rose of Heaven." She displayed great courage during the siege, and had almost effected the capture of Jalwur, when she was seized with a mortal illness. On her death the command was given to her son, Shaheen. Nehr Dew made a sortie, defeated the imperial forces, and slew Shaheen with his own hand. The emperor, enraged at this defeat, sent reinforcements to renew the siege; Jalwur was taken, and Nehr Dew, with his family, and the whole of the garrison, put to the sword.

In 1510 Ismail Adil Shah ascended the throne of Bijapur. Being too young to rule the state, the administration was entrusted to Kumal Khan Deccany, the most powerful noble in the land. The latter soon made up his mind to usurp the throne; and in the following year he found himself in a position to make the attempt.

He was warned by the astrologers that certain days in the present month were unfavourable to his designs; and recommended to avoid approaching any one of whom he had suspicions. The regent, acting on their advice, committed the charge of the citadel to his own adherents, and shut himself up with his family in a house close by the royal palace.

Booboojee Khanum, the queen-mother, now resolved by a bold stroke to get rid of the regent. Affecting uneasiness about his health, she despatched one of her adherents with secret instructions for the assassination of Kumal Khan. The plot succeeded, though the murderer was immediately cut to pieces. The regent's mother, with great presence of mind, commanded the attendants to keep silent, and sent orders to Sufdur Khan, the son of Kumal Khan, to seize the king at once. Sufdur closed the gates of the citadel and advanced with a strong force to the palace.

The queen-mother would have submitted, but for Dilshad Agha, the king's foster-aunt, who declared that in such a crisis valour was better than submission. She ordered the palace gates to be closed, and sent out to the Persians, on duty in the outer court of the seraglio, entreating them to assist their king against his enemies. The foreign generals declared their readiness to defend the young prince. Dilshad Agha and the queen-mother came out on the battlements, clad in armour, with bows and arrows in their hands. They were accompanied by Ismail Adil Shah, who had the yellow umbrella of his father held over his head by a Turkish girl named Murtufa.

Sufdur Khan tried to force open the gates, but was met with volleys of arrows; the king, his mother and aunt, and Murtufa using the bow with considerable effect. The brave little band were reinforced presently by fifty Deccany matchlock-men; and several score of foreigners from the city; but though the besiegers were thus kept in check, their force was so considerably superior in numbers that they continued the assault with the utmost fury, fully confident of ultimate victory.

Dilshad Agha, with a veil thrown over her face, fought with bow and arrow in the ranks of the soldiers, encouraging them by exciting speeches and promises. Sufdur Khan at last made a desperate attack with five hundred men, bringing cannon to batter the walls; and the royal adherents fell in great numbers. Some fled ignominiously, while the rest, concealing themselves behind the parapet, remained perfectly still. The enemy, believing that all the garrison had taken to flight, burst open the outer gate; but while he was endeavouring to force the inner door, Dilshad Agha gave orders for her troops to discharge a volley of shot and arrows, which committed fearful havoc in the enemy's ranks, and pierced the eye of Sufdur Khan. The latter ran under the terrace on which the royalists stood; and the king, rolling down a heavy stone, crushed his enemy to death.

The death of Sufdur put an end to the rebellion. The insurgents, giving themselves up for lost, opened the gates of the citadel, and fled. By the advice of Dilshad Agha, the heads of the regent and his son were displayed through the streets of the city.

During the reign of Akbar, the Great, Emperor of Hindostan, that part of the Deccan which now comprises Orissa and Bundelcund, was known by the name of Gurrah, and was governed by a warlike queen, named Durgautti, equally distinguished for her beauty, her accomplishments, and the talented manner in which she conducted the affairs of her kingdom. She succeeded to the throne on the death of her husband. The country was about one hundred and fifty crores in length and about fifty in breadth; yet so prosperous, that it contained upwards of seventy thousand towns and villages, closely populated.

About the year 1564, Asaf Khan Hirvys, an Indian noble, was raised by the emperor to the rank of an *omrah* of five thousand, and appointed governor of Kurrah and Mannichpoor. The new *omrah* at once began a series of predatory incursions into Gurrah; and very soon he invaded the country with an army of about twelve thousand foot and five or six hundred horse. Durgautti assembled eight thousand horse, fifteen hundred elephants, and a few hundred foot, and advanced to meet the invaders. Clad in armour, a helmet on her head, a lance grasped in her right hand, a bow and a quiver lying by her side, she led her troops to battle, riding in a *howdah* on the back of an elephant.

Though the men were totally unaccustomed to war, the love of liberty and the example of the queen raised their courage to such a pitch that, in their eagerness to fight, they marched too rapidly, and would speedily have become an undisciplined mob. But Durgautti, perceiving the cause of their disorder, commanded a halt; and after re-forming their broken ranks, she gave them strict orders to march slowly, as compactly as they could, and not to engage the foe until they saw the signal displayed from the elephant of the royal standard.

A sanguinary battle then ensued, in which Durgautti displayed the greatest courage. After a long and obstinate conflict, the Mahommedans were routed, with a loss of eight hundred slain. The queen pursued the flying enemy till night put an end to the contest. She then halted, and gave orders for the soldiers to wash and refresh themselves, preparatory to a night attack on the camp of Asaf Khan; but her *vizier* and the remainder of her generals refused to aid in a night assault, and seditiously demanded permission to inter their fallen comrades. She unwillingly consented; and when the bodies of the slain had been burned, she entreated the chiefs, one by one, to assist her in an assault on the Mogul camp. But all in vain. Not one would second her in this daring enterprise.

Asaf Khan, seeing what kind of enemy he had to do with, advanced next morning with the heavy guns, which, on account of the bad state of the roads, he had not been able to use in the previous action. Durgautti posted her men at a narrow pass, and prepared to meet the enemy once more. Asaf, with his cannon, soon opened a lane into the open ground beyond, where the forces of Gurrah were drawn up. The Rajah Beir Shaw, Durgautti's son, a young man of great promise, displayed great bravery in a charge. Twice he repulsed the Moguls; in the third attack he was severely wounded. He was falling from his horse when the queen, who was in the front of the battle, mounted on her elephant, perceived that her son was expiring, and called to some of her attendants to carry him to the rear.

Several crowded round him, glad of some excuse to quit the field. The death of this young man and the retreat of so many of her soldiers struck terror into the queen's army. Durgautti was soon left with only three hundred men on the field; yet she held her ground, determined to conquer or die. At last her eye was pierced by an arrow. She tried to extricate it, but it broke off near the end, leaving a piece of the steel barb sticking in the wound. At this moment another arrow pierced her neck. This she pulled out; but a mist swam before her eyes, and for a few moments she was seen to rock to and fro in her *howdah*.

Adhar, a brave officer of her household, who drove her elephant, repulsed numbers of the enemy. Perceiving that the day was irretrievably lost, he entreated the queen to let him take her from the field, but Durgautti would not hear of it. She begged of him to stab her to the heart. He refused, and Durgautti, suddenly leaning forward, snatched a dagger from his belt, plunged it into her heart, and immediately expired.

With her death the triumph of Asaf Khan was complete. The queen's youngest son, a mere infant, was trodden to death soon after, at the capture of Chouraghus, and the whole country submitted to the Moguls.

About this time, another warlike queen, Khunza Sultana, was Regent of Ahmednuggur. During the minority of her son, Murtuza Nizam Shah, she transacted the affairs of the state, while he was engaged in amusements suitable to his age.

In 1566, Ally Adil Shah, King of Bijapur, having invaded the neighbouring state of Bijanuggur, Venkatradry, the Hindoo chief of that country, applied for assistance to Khunza Sultana. She marched at the head of a large force against Bijapur, and obliged the king to return and defend his own dominions. However, peace was soon re-established between the two Mohammedan states, and a league formed against the Peishwah of Berar. The united forces of Ahmednuggur and Bijapur entered that country, plundered it, and marched home again, laden with booty. On the homeward march, Ally Adil Shah treacherously endeavoured to seize the young King of Ahmednuggur. But Khunza Sultana, learning his designs, decamped during the night, and a river, which intervened, having swelled, the two armies were effectually separated before morning.

The *sultana*, however, gave great umbrage to the nobles by providing for her own relations at the expense of more deserving men. In 1567, several *rajahs* formed a conspiracy against her, and induced the young king to join them. But the latter, afraid of his mother's ire, betrayed the plot to her, and the ringleaders were all seized.

In 1569, the dowager queen, with her son, marched against Kishwur Khan, the Bijapur general, who had invaded the state of Ahmednuggur. When they reached D'hamungam, Murtuza Nizam Shah resolved to free himself from his mother's trammels, gained over the principal nobles, and sent one of them to inform her that it was his royal will she should no longer meddle in public affairs. Furious at this unlooked-for audacity, Khunza assembled her attendants, threw a veil over her face, and rode out of the palace on horseback, armed with a sword and dagger. She was seized after a short struggle, and her people took to flight. Thenceforth, Khunza Sultana lived in retirement, never again interfering in public matters.

In 1594 died Burhan Nizam Shah, King of Ahmednuggur. His son, Ibrahim Nizam Shah, who succeeded him, was slain in battle, and the *vizier*, Meean Munjoo, raised to the throne a boy named Ahmed, said to belong to the royal family. The nobles refused to acknowledge the new king, and besieged the *vizier* in the capital. Unable to contend with them, the *vizier* solicited aid from the Moguls, promising to put the fort of Ahmednuggur into their hands.

The Moguls had long sought an excuse to interfere in the affairs of

Ahmednuggur; so, Murad Mirza, son of the Emperor Akbar, marched thither with great expedition, being joined on his road by several *rajahs* and generals with their troops. But Meean Munjoo, having suppressed the rebellion, in place of surrendering the fort, resolved to defend it in case he was called upon by the Moguls to fulfil his promise. After laying in a store of provisions, he gave the command to the Princess Chand Beeby, daughter of a former King of Ahmednuggur, and departed with the young Prince Ahmed towards the Bijapur frontier.

Chand Beeby was one of the ablest Indian politicians of her time. She had been for some years queen and dowager-regent of Bijapur. She now took the entire direction of affairs into her own hands; in a few days she had raised her own nephew, Bahadur Nizam Shah, to the throne, though he was at this time a prisoner in a distant fortress, and seemed likely to stay there.

The Moguls, seeing that it was useless to conceal their hostile intentions, prepared openly to besiege Ahmednuggur. On the 14th December, 1595, the first shots were exchanged. The siege was pressed with the utmost vigour. Mounds were raised, trenches opened, battery after battery erected, mines sunk; and on the morning of February 17th, 1596, eighty feet of wall were blown down by the explosion of a mine. Chand Beeby, though many of her principal officers had taken to flight, was not dismayed. She put on armour, covered her face with a veil, and, grasping a drawn sword in her hand, rushed to defend the breach. This intrepidity shamed the fugitives, and re-animated the panic-stricken soldiers.

Recovering from their first terror, the soldiers calmly awaited the approach of the Mogul storming-party. An obstinate conflict ensued at the foot of the breach. Again, and again did the Moguls press onward—again and again they were driven back by a galling fire of shot and rockets. The ditch was soon more than half filled with dead and dying warriors. Although fresh storming parties succeeded one another from four o'clock in the afternoon till dark, they were all repulsed with fearful slaughter. At last the Moguls withdrew, discomfited, to their camp.

Deccan traditions say that, during the storm, the shot of the garrison having become exhausted, Chand Beeby ordered the guns to be loaded, first with copper coins, then with silver, and at length with gold; and all the coins being likewise used up, she fired away her jewels.

The valour of Chand Beeby formed the chief subject of conversation round the camp-fires and in the tents of the Moguls; and, after this memorable day, her title of Chand Beeby, "the Lady Chand," was changed by common consent to the grander one of Chand Sultana.

The want of provisions, and the approach of seventy thousand men from Bijapur, compelled the Moguls to retreat a few days after the storm. Bahadur Shah was now brought from the fort of Chawund, where he had been held prisoner, and was placed on the throne. But the ambition and duplicity of the Ahmednuggur nobles brought about a second siege in 1599. Chand Sultana, afraid to trust any of them, applied to Humeed Khan, an officer of high rank, who recommended her to defend the place to the last extremity; but Chand declared that so many chiefs had acted treacherously, it was plain no reliance could be placed on them, and she proposed that they should negotiate with the besiegers. Humeed Khan rushed into the streets, crying out that Chand Sultana was treating with the Moguls to surrender the fort. The ungrateful and short-sighted mob, believing him, and forgetting the former services of the heroine, rushed to the private apartments of Chand Sultana, and murdered her in their fury.

It is satisfactory to know that the ungrateful people got the reward they so richly merited. For, a few days after the death of Chand, the Moguls captured the fort, giving little or no quarter.

Mher-Ul-Nissa, or Nour Mahal, the "Light of the *Harem*," sometimes styled Nour Jehan, the "Light of the World," was the favourite *sultana* of Jehanghire, the "World subduing Emperor" of Hindostan. A romantic story is told of her strange birth, her desertion by her parents, and how, like Moses, she was entrusted to the care of her own mother by her kind preserver, and how, by the benevolence of the latter, the family rose from poverty and obscurity to the government of the greatest empire in Asia. The beauty of Nour Mahal was famous throughout the East; Moore, in his "Feast of Roses," has painted her portrait most exquisitely. Her personal charms were rivalled by her mental powers; and her political talents were speedily seen by the numerous reforms and improvements effected throughout the empire.

Nour Mahal was a widow when, in 1611, she became the bride of Jehanghire, and it is said that she took for her second husband the murderer of her first. Her influence over the emperor soon became paramount. They had many tastes in common, amongst others the passion for hunting; Nour Mahal was as fond of the chase as Zenobia. In company with Jehanghire she would slay tigers and other savage beasts of the jungle, charming her lord by the adroitness with which she handled the bow or the more unwieldy matchlock.

206

It was strange that a haughty, overbearing, courageous woman like Nour Mahal should never have taken command of an army. We read of only one battle in which she was personally engaged. Her policy was to choose able generals to conduct all her wars. However, one of these chieftains was near causing her ruin. This was Mohabat Khan, the most talented Indian warrior of his time. She had the folly to quarrel with this man, and he, seeing that his ruin was determined upon, took the initiative, and seized the emperor in his own camp. He soon saw that it would have been wiser to arrest the empress; but on returning to remedy this fault, he found she had fled to the camp of her brother, on the other bank of the river—the Chenab.

Next morning the empress led a party across the river to rescue Jehanghire. She was armed with a bow and two quivers of arrows, and sat in a *howdah* on the back of an elephant. In fording the stream, hundreds were swept away by the force of the current. Those who escaped drowning were weighed down by their armour and their wet clothes, and had their powder spoilt. In this disastrous condition they were obliged to fight hand to hand with the rebels before a landing could be effected. Nour Mahal, with her brother and a handful of the bravest chiefs, was amongst the first who reached the shore; but this little band could make no impression on the ranks of Mohabat Khan, whose soldiers poured volley after volley, shot, arrows, and rockets, upon the men struggling in the water. The ford was soon choked up with men, horses, and elephants, dead or dying.

The contest raged fiercest round the elephant of Nour Mahal, who never quailed before the infuriated rebels who sought her life. Her gallant defenders fell one after another, fighting manfully to the last; but she herself appeared to bear a charmed life amidst the perfect hail of bullets and winged shafts, though her infant granddaughter, who sat close beside her, was wounded, the driver of her elephant was shot, and the beast himself received a cut across the trunk. Half-maddened with pain, the animal plunged into the river, and was carried away by the stream. When at length the elephant struggled up the bank, Nour Mahal was discovered calmly extracting an arrow from the wound of her grandchild, as cool and collected as though she had been a spectator at a review in place of the leading actor in a fierce encounter. The *howdah* was saturated with blood.

The failure of this rash, though gallant attempt, proved that Mohabat was too strong to be subdued by open force; Nour Mahal therefore resolved to lull his suspicions, and trust to chance for some expedient to crush him. Next day she went to his camp and surrendered herself a prisoner. For a time Mohabat Khan ruled paramount throughout the empire; but in a few months Nour Mahal, partly by cunning, partly by appealing to the loyalty of the *omrahs*, rescued her husband from the clutches of this man, whose power thenceforth ceased for ever.

Jehanghire died on the 28th of October, 1627.

Although Nour Mahal survived him for twenty-four years, she held aloof from politics. She was buried in a splendid tomb at Lahore, close by the monument of Jehanghire.

Spontini has chosen the story of Nour Mahal as the subject for one of his best operas.

In 1688 the Mogul Army, commanded by Azim Shah (son of Aurengzebe) was engaged in the siege of Bijapur. The troops were much distressed for want of provisions, as their supplies had been cut off by the enemy. Aurengzebe, hearing of this, ordered one of his generals to take twenty thousand bullock-loads of grain to the camp of Azim Shah. The enemy made a desperate attempt to seize this convoy on its road; but after a fierce encounter with the Moguls, they were driven off. During the action, the Princess Janee Begum, who was proceeding with the convoy to join her husband, Azim Shah, rode on the back of an elephant into the midst of the fight, and encouraged the soldiers by her presence.

Juliana is perhaps the only European woman who ever took a leading part in the politics of the court of Delhi. She was born in Bengal in 1658, and her father was a Portuguese gentleman, named Augustin Dias D'Acosta. Early in life she gained the favour of Aurengzebe, who made her superintendent of his Zenana, and governess of his son, Bahadur Shah.

In 1707 Aurengzebe died, and Bahadur Shah ascended the throne. His right was disputed by his brothers, and he was compelled to defend his throne by force of arms. A battle was fought near Agra; Juliana, mounted on an elephant, by the side of Bahadur Shah, aided him by her advice, and cheered him with inspiring words; when his troops began to give way, she exhorted him not to despair. To her presence indeed was he indebted for the ultimate victory gained by his army.

Juliana was created a princess, and given the rank of wife of an *omrah*, together with innumerable honours and riches showered upon her. The Great Mogul held her in such estimation that he used to say:—

If Juliana were a man, I would make her my *vizier*.

Jehandur Shah, who ascended the throne in 1712, entertained the same respect for Juliana. She experienced some persecutions when this emperor was deposed in 1713 by his nephew Ferokshere; but the death of this tyrant, in 1719, restored to her all her influence, which she retained till her death, in 1733

During the latter half of the eighteenth century, the native princes of India finding, by dearly bought experience, that Indian discipline was ludicrously inferior to the European system, determined to introduce the latter into their own battalions. With this view they offered high rewards to European officers who would accept the command of their troops and teach them how to fight. Hundreds of adventurers— British, French, German, Swiss, Portuguese—soldiers of fortune, in short, from every part of Europe, took service under the various *rajahs* and princes, and many of them attained to high rank and honours. It was not uncommon for the widows of these officers to be given the post left vacant by their deceased husbands; and these female commanders led their troops to battle, or stopped at home, as they pleased.

One of these soldiers of fortune was Colonel Mequinez, a Portuguese, who commanded a regiment of Topasses in the service of Hyder Ali Khan, Sultan of Mysore. At his death, Hyder Ali gave the widow (also a Portuguese) the command of her husband's regiment, to hold it till the adopted son of her husband had attained his majority. Madam Mequinez never went into action; she left the duty of leading the Topasses in the field to the officer next in command. But in every other respect she fulfilled the duties of colonel; the colours were carried to her house, at the door of which a sentry paced up and down: she received the pay for the entire corps, and caused the deductions for each company to be made in her presence, and she always inspected the regiment herself.

Madam Mequinez was excessively avaricious, besides having a character for immorality. Having been detected in a plot to cheat the Provincial Father of the Mysore Jesuits out of a large sum in *rupees* and jewels, she was excommunicated, and sentenced to undergo public penance. Some months later she finally disgraced herself by marrying a "mongrel Portuguese sergeant" belonging to her regiment. But she was very much surprised when the *bacsi* informed her that the *Sultan* had reduced her pay to that of a sergeant, because she had brought shame on the memory of her first husband, who had been a great favourite with the Sultan, Hyder Ali.

One of the most thoroughly unprincipled European adventurers of these days was Somroo, a German soldier, who, after serving as private in the French and English armies, and in those of various native chiefs, became general in the army of the Great Mogul. His name was Gualtier Reignard, or Reinehard, but when he enlisted in the French Army (in Europe) he assumed the *nom de guerre* of Summer, which his comrades, on account of his saturnine complexion, altered to Sombre; this, the Hindoos changed to Somroo, and he was afterwards best known by this last name. He will ever remain infamous as the murderer of two hundred English prisoners at Patna, in 1763. While in the service of Shah Aulum, the emperor, he commanded a body of cavalry and several disciplined battalions of *sepoys* officered by Europeans. To maintain this army, the emperor assigned him, as a *jaghire*, the fertile district of Serdhauna, in the Dooab.

Somroo married twice; his second wife was, some say, the daughter of a Mogul noble who had fallen into great distress, though others aver she was a Cashmerian dancing-girl. He persuaded the *begum* to renounce Mohammedanism and become a Roman Catholic. At Somroo's death, in 1778, the Vizier Nujeef Khan gave the widow the *jaghire* and the military post. She was a great favourite with the emperor, who had the highest respect for her talents. He bestowed upon her the name of Zul Al Nissa, which means "Ornament of her sex." Under the government of this talented woman the "small but fertile" town of Serdhauna improved rapidly. A fort standing a short distance from the town served as a kind of citadel, and contained a barrack, an arsenal, and a foundry for cannon. Her five battalions of *sepoys* were officered from nearly every country in Europe, and she had a body of five hundred European artillerymen, armed with forty guns of various calibre.

George Thomas, afterwards the most famous of all these European soldiers of fortune, accepted a commission in the *begum's* service; and her keen eyes quickly discerned his superior military talent. He soon rose to high favour with the *begum*, whose esteem he merited by courage, zeal, and untiring activity. So greatly was her revenue and authority increased by his talents, that he was for many years her chief counsellor and adviser.

Begum Somroo enjoyed the respect of the leading ministers at the court of Delhi; the Viziers Nujeef Khan, Mirza Shuffee, and Afrasiab Khan placed the most implicit trust in her judgment on military matters. When Scindiah, the Mahratta chief, attained to the rank of *vizier*, he not only confirmed her in the *jaghire* of Serdhauna, but added a grant of territory south-west of the Jumna. Her generalship was not confined to occasional reviews; she took an active part in the wars and insurrections which disturbed the reign of Shah Aulem. During the war with Pertaub Sing, the *begum* was stationed with her troops at Panniput; which being an important post, proves Scindiah's belief in her military capacities.

In 1787, during the insurrection of Gholaum Cadir Khan, Prince of Sehraurunpore, Begum Somroo displayed the utmost coolness and determination. Previous to his open declaration of hostility, Gholaum, by the most artful speeches, endeavoured to gain the *begum's* alliance; well aware of her influence at court, he offered her an equal share in the administration if she would assist him in seizing the reins of government. The proposal was tempting, but the *begum*, well acquainted with the perfidious nature of the wily Rohilla chief, rejected all his offers, and repaired to the palace, where she announced her resolve to sacrifice life itself, if necessary, in defence of her sovereign.

Her arrival infused new courage into the Imperial party; and some of the generals having assembled their forces, Gholaum Cadir opened a heavy cannonade on the palace. This was answered from the fort of Delhi; and after the bombardment had lasted for several hours, the rebel chief receiving intelligence that a large force was marching to relieve the Emperor, judged it most prudent to tender an apology, which Shah Aulem thought fit to accept.

In the following year, 1788, Shah Aulem left Delhi with a large army, partly made up by three battalions of sepoys, commanded by the Begum, and commenced a tour through the provinces. Although most of the *rajahs* and *nabobs* were secretly disaffected, they were, with few exceptions, easily prevailed upon to tender their submission. One of those who openly declared themselves rebels was Nujuff Cooli Khan, a powerful chief, who, having possession of the almost impregnable fort of Gocul Ghur, peremptorily refused to submit. His head-quarters were situated at a village about a mile from the fort, and only a portion of his army had been stationed in Gocul Ghur.

The emperor himself, with the main body of the army, invested Gocul Ghur, while two of his principal generals erected batteries against the rebel headquarters, which they bombarded most vigorously. The village would have speedily been taken, but for the disgraceful conduct of the besieging force, both officers and men, who gave themselves up to riot and excess. Nujuff Cooli Khan, taking advantage of this, attacked the Mogul entrenchments one night, when nearly all the soldiers were fast asleep. Carrying all before them, the rebels perpetrated an indiscriminate slaughter before the others had time to arouse themselves. This news rapidly spread to the main body and threw the whole camp into dire confusion. To increase the consternation, Munsoor Khan sallied out from Gocul Ghur, and opened a tremendous cannonade on the rear of the camp.

The entire Imperial Army, together with Shah Aulem and his family, would probably have fallen into the hands of the rebels, but for the courage and presence of mind of Begum Somroo. She was encamped with her *sepoys* to the right of the camp, and her troops not having been infected by the panic, waited, drawn up ready for action. Perceiving the disorder which prevailed, the Begum sent a respectful message to Shah Aulem, entreating him to repair for safety to her quarters. Then, stepping into her *palanquin*, she proceeded at the head of one hundred *sepoys* and a six-pounder (the latter commanded by a European) to the ground occupied by Munsoor Khan. She ordered her *palanquin* to be set down, and ere long drove the rebels from the field by a well-directed fire of grape, supported by volleys of musketry from the *sepoys*.

This gallant exploit gave time for the Imperial troops to rally. In their turn they now attacked the rebels, and after a short sharply contested engagement, the latter were defeated. Nujuff Cooli Khan, disheartened by this reverse, entreated the *begum* to intercede for his pardon; which was granted at last, after he had paid a large sum of money into the Imperial treasury.

In 1791, Nujuff Cooli Khan again broke into rebellion. Ismail Beg was despatched to arrest him; but when the latter reached Rewari, where the rebel chief had set up his headquarters, he learned that Nujuff was dead. However, the widow of Nujuff Cooli, a woman akin to Begum Somroo, of a masculine spirit, possessing, moreover, considerable military abilities, took command of deceased's forces. Knowing that Ismaeel Beg was courageous, talented, and ambitious, she proposed an alliance, which he accepted; and throwing himself into the town of Canoor, defended it against the Mahrattas. The *begum* displayed the utmost courage throughout the siege, and invariably joined in all the sorties made by the garrison.

Unfortunately, this brave woman was slain in a skirmish by a cannon-ball, and her death broke up the rebel camp. It was resolved by the garrison to deliver up Ismaeel Beg to the Mahrattas; but he was beforehand with them, and surrendered the town.

General Thomas, in his zeal for the Begum Somroo's interests, raised up enemies for himself in the principal French and German officers. They took occasion to poison the *begum's* mind against him by foul accusations; and in 1792 he was compelled to withdraw to Anopsheer, one of the frontier stations of the British Army. Early in 1793, he took service under Appakandarow, a Mahratta chieftain. Le Vaissaux, or Levasso, a German adventurer, commanding the *begum's* artillery, had always been Thomas's deadly foe, and was the leading man in driving him away. He possessed great military talents, and had rendered considerable services to his mistress; but he was a man of haughty, overbearing mien, and hated by all his brother-officers. Great was their indignation, though they were scarcely surprised, when the *begum*, disregarding their remonstrances, and the advice, the all but commands, of the emperor, surrendered her hand and heart to the German artilleryman, in 1793.

Begum Somroo, instigated by her husband, now determined to crush poor Thomas; and at the head of four battalions of foot, four hundred horse, and twenty pieces of cannon, she marched towards Jyjur, where he was stationed. But the Mahratta chiefs, who had long been jealous of her influence over Shah Aulem, stirred up a mutiny amongst the troops left in Serdhauna, and compelled her to return thither with all speed. The officers, to give a sanction to their proceedings, offered the *jaghire* to Zuffer Yab Khan, son of Somroo by a former wife. He was a young man of worthless and turbulent character; since his father's death he had lived in Delhi, receiving a handsome allowance from his stepmother.

It was only a few days after the marriage that this mutiny broke out. Zuffer, with a body of troops, rushed into Serdhauna, seized the town, and was proclaimed Jaghire Dar. The *begum* vainly endeavoured to pacify her soldiers. She was arrested, together with her husband, and thrown into prison; and Le Vaissaux, too proud to sue for mercy, put an end to his own life.

In the course of the following year, the *begum*, who had been ever since kept in durance vile, besought the assistance of George Thomas, for, said she, the hourly dread of assassination was driving her mad. Thomas was not deaf to her entreaties; he persuaded Bappoo, a Mahratta chief, to aid him with his forces, and together they marched upon Serdhauna. The Mahrattas were won over, partly by the prayers of Shah Aulem, and partly by liberal promises; and Zuffer having been expelled, the Begum was restored to power.

Begum Sumroo was a good friend to the English, with whom she was always exceedingly popular on account of the great hospitality with which she entertained those who visited her neighbourhood. However, she fought against them, as an auxiliary of Scindiah, in 1803. She took part in the Battle of Assaye; and at the defeat of the Mahrattas, she fled to Northern Hindostan, and hastily made peace with the Marquis Wellesley, on condition that her principality should revert to the British Government of India after her demise, while her personal property remained at her own disposal.

When the British became masters of Delhi, the Begum frequently visited their camp, dressed in European costume, with a hat and veil, sometimes in a palanquin, sometimes on horseback, sometimes on an elephant. At this time, she appeared to be about fifty-five, was of middle height, with a beautiful complexion. Her ancient friendship for the Mahrattas, and an intercepted letter which she was believed to have written to Jeswunt Rao Holkar, caused her to be suspected by the British when they were at war with that chief in 1805. However, she succeeded in clearing herself of the accusation. The exact year of her death is not known.

Although Begum Somroo left no children of her own, she had adopted the daughter of Somroo by his first wife, a Mahratta woman. This girl wedded Mr. Dyce, a half-caste, son of Captain Dyce of the East India Company's service. The *begum* had intended to make him her heir; but in her old age she detected him in a conspiracy, and so she left her property to his son, instead. This latter was the notorious David Ochterlony Dyce-Sombre. About the year 1838, this eccentric gentleman came to England, whither he had been preceded by the renown of his fabulous wealth. His arrival caused considerable excitement in London; he was *fêted* and invited everywhere as the lion of the day.

In 1840, he married the Hon. Mary Ann Jervis, daughter of Viscount St. Vincent; but the husband and wife did not agree—a separation was speedily followed by legal proceedings against Mr. Dyce-Sombre, by which the wife's relations sought to prove the Anglo-Indian to be a lunatic. For months and months this great trial was a matter for public gossip; and the unfortunate *nabob* was compelled to live on the Continent for several years to escape the decision of the Court of Chancery. He returned to London in 1851, to petition against their decree; but was seized with a painful illness, of which he died on the 1st July of that year.

When Lord Lake was in India, fighting the Mahrattas, there was a Sergeant W——, of the artillery, who served in nearly all the battles of his illustrious chief. This sergeant owned a Hindoo slave, belonging to the lowest dregs of the pariahs; but through the earnest labours of a Baptist missionary, she was converted to Christianity, and the sergeant made her his wife. She accompanied him in all his campaigns, and followed him into battle. When he was tired, she would lend a hand at the guns. In one action the sergeant was struck down by a bullet which passed through his shako and struck his forehead just above the temple carrying in its course the brass hoop from the shako and forcing it into his skull. He fell, to all appearance, dead; but his wife, determined not to leave his body to the tender mercies of the foe, seized it up, and bore it from the field, amidst a rain of bullets.

The principal leaders in the terrible Indian Mutiny were Nana Sahib, Tantia Topee, and the Ranee of Jhansi. They were equally ferocious: they detested the British, and the motives which induced them to rebel were almost precisely similar. According to the laws and usages of Hindostan, a native prince, in default of sons, could adopt a strange boy and make him his heir; seldom was a dissentient voice raised against the succession of the adopted child till within the last thirty-five or forty years, when the East India Company constituted itself heir-apparent to all the thrones in the country.

The city of Jhansi is situated in Bundelcund, to the south of the river Jumna. Previous to 1857, it was the strongest and most important place in the entire of Central India. The people were nearly all Brahmins, a religion held in common with their *rajahs*. In the days when the Peishwa was still a person of importance in Hindostan, the ruler of Jhansi was merely a wealthy *zemindar*, or land-owner, and he rendered such good service to the British that Lord William Bentinck (Governor-General from 1828 to 1835), raised him to the position of Rajah.

On the death of this man, he was succeeded by his brother, Gungadhur Rao. The latter, having no children, made a will some weeks before his death, publicly adopting a little boy nearly related to himself, and at this time six years old. Lukshmi Baee, the *rajah's* wife, was to be the guardian of this boy and Regent of Jhansi till he had attained his eighteenth year. Gungadhur gave due notice of this to the British Governor-General; and in presence of the British Resident and his assembled subjects, took the child in his lap, as a public declaration of adoption.

215

Gungadhur Rao died in 1854. Lord Dalhousie, the Governor-General, refused to acknowledge his right to adopt an heir, and the little province of Jhansi was annexed to British India. The young *rajah* and the *ranee*, his mother by adoption, were pensioned off; the latter receiving six thousand a year, paid monthly. Her troops were disbanded, and replaced by a few regiments of *sepoys* and *sowars*.

The *ranee* was powerless to resist; she could only bide her time. She had not long to wait. Three years later, India was in a blaze. The Bundelcund Sepoys were amongst the first to mutiny. On the 14th of June, the native troops at Jhansi broke into rebellion, murdered several of their officers in the cantonments; and seized the "Star Fort." Some few English escaped to Nagoda, but the rest, numbering fifty-five men, women, and children, barricaded themselves in the "Town Fort."

But after a brave resistance of four days, the mutineers burst open the gates on the 8th; and the English, having been promised life and liberty, laid down their arms. Thereupon a massacre commenced, which for barbarity, almost equalled that which took place shortly after at Cawnpore. Nineteen ladies, twenty-three children, twenty-four civil service *employés*, two non-commissioned officers, and eight officers were butchered in a manner familiar to all who can remember the Indian Mutiny.

It was generally believed at the time that this massacre took place by order of the *ranee*, who is said to have stood by while the heads of ladies were chopped off, and the brains of babies were dashed out upon the flags. Nay, some have declared she laughed aloud when some deed of atrocity worse than the rest came under her notice.

Shortly after this massacre, the *ranee* took the field at the head of some hundreds of *sepoys*, and marched towards Gwalior, where Scindiah, the descendant of our old enemy whom we routed at Assaye, remained faithful to the British. But little was known of her movements during the rest of 1857; in August of that year, a female, dressed in a green uniform, was captured at Delhi, while leading on a party of *sepoys*. This woman was at first supposed to be the terrible *ranee*, and a rumour sped through the British Camp that she was leading the Gwalior rebels; but it was afterwards found that Lukshmi Baee still remained in the territories of the *Maharajah*. The prisoner was described as "an ugly old woman, short and fat." She was a species of prophetess, held in high estimation by the rebels around Delhi.

In January, 1858, Sir Hugh Rose (Lord Strathnairn), commanding the second brigade of the Central India Field Force, set out against the rebels south of Delhi; his chief object being the capture of Jhansi. Having been joined by Brigadier Stuart, they invested the fortress on the 2ist of March following.

The city of Jhansi measured about four miles and a half in circumference. It stood on a level plain, surrounding the east, north, and part of the south sides of an elevated rock on which the fort stood. Altogether it was a fine specimen of modern fortification; and since the first outbreak of the Mutiny, its strength had been considerably added to by the *ranee*, who took care to arm the batteries with heavy ordnance of long range. On the 25th a tremendous cannonade was opened from the British lines. Throughout the siege the intrepid *ranee* tried every means to defend the town; all through the day she remained in the fort directing the fire of the artillerymen, save when she visited the different points of defence, watching and planning to strengthen the weak parts of her entrenchments.

Tantia Topee marched to the relief of Jhansi with twenty or twenty-five thousand men, and an obstinately contested battle was fought on the 1st of April.

But Tantia Topee, after proving himself to be a brave man and an able general, was totally routed with the loss of all his ordnance.

Next day a general assault was made on the city; under a murderous fire the British forced their way through the streets. When they had more than half conquered it, the news of the *ranee's* flight put an end to all further resistance on the part of the rebels. It was then found that the brave old tigress, utterly disheartened by the defeat of Tantia Topee, had fled during the previous night, under cover of the darkness. Followed by about three hundred rebels, she joined Tantia Topee at Koonch.

Sir Hugh Rose, as soon as he had settled matters in Jhansi, directed his march towards Calpee. He was intercepted at Koonch by the *ranee* and her ally; when a spirited action took place on the 9th of May. The mutineers were driven from their entrenched camp, with great loss, and the town fell into the hands of the victors. Tantia Topee and the *ranee* fled to Calpee, where they were besieged on the 16th by Sir Hugh; Calpee fell on the 23rd, the *ranee* and Tantia having previously retired towards Gwalior. The *Maharajah*, refusing to join the rebels, was driven to take refuge in the British cantonments at Agra.

On the approach of Sir Hugh Rose, Tantia Topee fled, leaving the *ranee* to defend the city. But she was not a woman easily dispirited. She disposed her forces (chiefly composed of the Gwalior Contingent) most skilfully, so as to command all the roads leading to Gwalior. She was scarcely ever out of the saddle; dressed in a *sowar's* uniform, and attended by a picked, well-armed escort, she rode from post to post, superintending all the operations.

Sir Hugh Rose reached the Moorar cantonments on the 16th of June, and carried them with but slight loss. To intercept his reinforcements, the *ranee* marched to the banks of the little River Oomrar. Brigadiers Smith and Orr, who were marching from Antree to join in the attack on Gwalior, reached Kota-ki-Serai, on the banks of this stream, on the morning of the 17th. Between this village and Gwalior, from which it is distant about three or four miles, the road winds through a succession of hilly ranges.

Some rebel pickets were observed in front of and below the first range; a squadron of the 8th Hussars immediately crossed the stream to reconnoitre, when they were fired upon from a masked battery. Two troops of the same regiment were ordered to charge; and riding at full speed through a narrow ravine, they captured a battery armed with three guns. Thence they pressed on to the rebel camp, where the enemy was driven to bay. The Ranee of Jhansi and her sister, both in the dress of *sowars*, fought desperately, and lost their lives in a gallant charge made to check the British troopers.

The *ranee's* death was caused either by the bullet of a British rifleman, or by the fragment of a shell which pierced her breast. Her body was never found; it was said to have been burned by her followers immediately after the battle.

Upon her death the rebel hosts melted like snow before a sunbeam. The British infantry speedily carried the first range of heights; and the enemy, after losing about four hundred men, and seeing their camp in flames, were compelled to fly. The British, after losing about fifteen men (ten of whom died from sunstroke and fatigue), and spiking three rebel guns, resumed their march; and the same evening rejoined Sir Hugh Rose. The combined forces now advanced on Gwalior, routed the *sepoys* in the Battle of Gurrowlee, June 19th, and recaptured the city, June 20th, when Scindiah was restored to his throne.

The death of the *ranee* excited very little interest in this country. The newspapers of the time, with but one or two exceptions, barely chronicled the event, without making any comments; but it was universally felt by every British soldier serving in India that, with the death of Lukshmi Baee, we had lost the foe who was able to do us most injury. For courage and military skill, she was acknowledged to be far superior to any of the other rebel chiefs. The message flashed along the wires announcing that the *ranee* had fallen, added that "the deaths of Moulvie and the *ranee* were more gain to us than half-a-dozen victories."

The exact age of the "Indian Boadicea" was never accurately determined. While one journal styles her "this girl, barely twenty years of age," another assumes her age to have been at least thirty. An *employé* of the East India Company who visited Jhansi in 1854, and accidentally caught a glimpse of this oriental heroine, describes her as:

> A woman of about the middle size—rather stout, but not *too* stout. Her face must have been very handsome when she was younger, and even now it had many charms—though, according to my idea of beauty, it was too round. The expression, also, was very good and very intellectual. The eyes were particularly fine, and the nose very delicately shaped. She was not very fair, though she was far from black. What spoilt her was her voice, which was something between a whine and a croak.

All agreed as to the extreme licentiousness and immorality of her habits; and the rooms in her palace are said to have been hung with pictures "such as pleased Tiberius at Capri."

It was formerly the custom with many of the native princes to maintain female warriors to guard their *zenanas*. The tyrant Ferokshere, who was murdered in 1719, kept up an Amazon corps at Delhi, composed of Abyssinians, Cashmerians, Persians—in short, drawn from every nation whence slaves could be easily procured. They were armed with matchlocks, bows and arrows, spears and targets, and other weapons, according to their nationality. When the emperor took refuge from his assailants in the *zenana*, the female guards held the entrance bravely for some time, and exchanged shots with the rebels; but they received more wounds than they gave, and were so easily driven away.

In the *harem* of the Nizam, at Hyderabad, there was, so lately as the time of the Mutiny, a regiment of Amazons who wore scarlet tunics, green trousers, and red cloth hats, trimmed with gold lace and mounted with a green plume. Their arms were the customary musket and bayonet. Whenever a distinguished foreigner visited the palace, the female guard received him with military honours. "The extreme youth, and delicate appearance of these interesting warriors," says Prince Soltykoff, "at once attracted attention." Though, despite these feminine attractions, he says their aspect was so decidedly military, he would never have known they were females but for their long hair and the fulness of their bosoms. Their hair was tied in a knot, though in place of concealing it under their caps, they let it fall over the collar of their tunics.

An interesting sketch of the female *sepoys* at Lucknow is given in the *Private Life of an Eastern King*.

Of the living curiosities of the palace, there were none the account of which will appear more strange to European ears than the female *sepoys*. I had seen these men-like women pacing up and down before the various entrances to the female apartments for many days before I was informed of their real character. I regarded them simply as a diminutive race of soldiers with well wadded coats. There was nothing but that fulness of the chest to distinguish many of them from other *sepoys*; and one is so accustomed to see soldiers in England with coats stuffed so as to make their wearers resemble pouter-pigeons, that I took little heed of the circumstance.

These women retained their long hair, which they tied up in a knot on the top of the head, and there it was concealed by the usual shako. They bore the ordinary accoutrements of *sepoys* in India—the musket and bayonet, cross-belts and cartridge-boxes, jackets and white duck continuations, which might be seen anywhere in Bengal. Intended solely for duty in the palace as guardians of the *harem*, they were paraded only in the court-yards, where I have seen them going through their exercise just like other *sepoys*.

They were drilled by one of the native officers of the king's army, and appeared quite familiar with marching and wheeling, with presenting, loading, and firing muskets, with the fixing and unfixing of bayonets; in fact, with all the detail of the ordinary barrack-yard. Whether they could have gone through the same marches in the field with thousands of *mustachioed sepoys* around them, I cannot tell—probably not. They had their own corporals and sergeants; none of them, I believe, attained a higher rank than that of sergeant.

Many of them were married women, obliged to quit the ranks for a month or two at a time, occasionally. They retained their places, however, as long as possible. . . . . of these female *sepoys* there were in all two companies of the usual strength, or weakness, if the reader will have it so. Once, during my residence at Lucknow, they were employed by the king against his own mother.

This act of Nussir was rendered all the worse, because many years before, when Ghazi-u-deen, the late King of Oude, wished to disinherit his son and put him to death, the *begum* armed her retainers, and fought for Nussir with the courage of a lion. After many had fallen on each side, the British resident interfered, and put an end to the contest. Nussir, after he became king, wished to act towards his son as Ghazi would have done towards him; but the old *begum* now fought as stoutly for her grandson as she did previously for her son. The king sent his female *sepoys* to turn her out of her palace, but she armed her servants, fought the *sepoys*, and put them to flight. Fifteen or sixteen of the *begum's* adherents were left dead on the field. The resident again interfered, and guaranteed the life and succession of the child.

But Nussir succeeded in cheating his mother after all, by declaring the boy illegitimate. In vain the old *begum*, after the death of Nussir, surrounded the British Residency with her troops; the Englishman was not to be intimidated. Troops were ordered up from the cantonments, and a few discharges of grape quickly dispersed the *begum's* adherents. One of Nussir's uncles was then placed on the throne, and the brave old *begum* was compelled to submit.

There is a similar guard of female warriors in the palace of the King of Siam, at Bangkok; and the Paris papers of September, 1866, speak of a regiment of female *Zouaves*, armed with rifles, which was then being raised in the first-named city.

As lately as 1873, we read of Amazonian soldiers in Bantam. Says a newspaper of that date, describing the condition of the sexes in that kingdom:—

Although tributary to Holland, it is an independent state, politically without importance, yet happy, rich, and since time immemorial governed and defended by women. The sovereign is indeed a man, but all the rest of the government belongs to the fair sex. The king is entirely dependent upon his state council, composed of three women. The highest authorities, all state officers, court functionaries, military commanders, and soldiers are, without exception, of the female sex. The men are agriculturists and merchants. The bodyguard of the king is formed of the female *élite*. These amazons ride in the masculine style, wearing sharp steel points instead of spurs. They carry a point-ed lance, which they swing very gracefully, and also a musket, which is discharged at full gallop. The throne is inheritable by the eldest son, and in case the king dies without issue a hundred elected amazons assemble, in order to choose a successor from among their own sons. The chosen one is then proclaimed law-ful king.

CHAPTER 16

Savage Africa

The great African continent has contributed but little to the pages of history. Centuries before America was discovered, northern Africa was one of the centres of commerce, its people were amongst the most civilized in the known world; yet America has been explored in almost every part, from north to south, and its history is as well-known and almost as full of interest as that of Europe or Asia, while Africa, until within the last three-quarters of a century, remained, geographically and historically, almost as much a mystery as it was in ancient times. Rightly has it been styled the Dark Continent.

Ethiopia, renowned in distant eras for its stately cities adorned with lofty temples and spacious palaces, and inhabited by learned men, is a sad picture of fallen greatness. Its haughty palaces have crumbled to decay long since, and their sites are occupied by the mud cabins of a savage race, who, only for being Christians, differ very little from their fellow-men who dwell on other parts of this great continent. People took but small interest in Abyssinia till the war with King Theodore, and even then, we learned very little more about that strange land than our grandfathers told us.

Scarcely more than a bare outline of Abyssinian history has been preserved; yet we find that, since the days of the Queen of Sheba, women have more than once taken an active part in the politics of this kingdom. Bruce has given us the story of a beautiful Jewish women named Judith, who, with the aid of her co-religionists, usurped the throne in the 10th or 11th century. She was the wife of Gideon, the governor, or, as he might be called, the feudal sovereign, of a small district called Bugna. He was also a Jew, as were all his subjects. Judith at last grew so powerful that she resolved to overthrow the Christians. She accordingly surprised the almost impregnable rock Damo, where

223

the royal princes were kept for safety, and slew them to the number of four hundred. Del Naad, the king, at this time a mere child, was saved by some of the nobles, who carried him into the loyal province of Shoa. Judith then mounted the throne, and not only reigned over Abyssinia for upwards of forty years, but transmitted the throne to five successive descendants. After that, the line of King Solomon and the Queen of Sheba, as represented by the descendants of Del Naad, was restored.

Even in these degenerate days, women sometimes come forward as leaders in Abyssinia. After the fall of Magdala, Lord Napier was visited by the two Gallas queens, Workite (gold), and Mastrat (looking-glass), who had a race as to which should first congratulate the British general on his victory. These rival queens, who have been fighting one another for years past, professed great delight at the reception which they met with, and both gave and received presents in token of friendship. The *Times* Correspondent in Abyssinia gave a lively and amusing description of them:—

> I am told on good authority, that they go into battle, and handle spear, sword, and gun right manfully; there is even a story, probably mythical, that Mastrat with her own hand wounded the mighty Theodore. But usually they go about so muffled up, and looking so like a bundle of shawls moved by mechanism, that, except in their method of riding, their appearance is anything but amazonic. Workite kept herself closely wrapped up, and hidden during her stay in camp, but Mastrat boldly threw aside her rich royal robe of crimson, speckled with gold, and came out of her tent, and before the soldiers if Her Majesty will pardon the expression like a man,—to have her photograph taken. Her complexion was a very pale olive—fairer than that of many Europeans—and her expression, though the features were large, and scarcely, like those of Theodore's widow-in-chief, of the thoroughbred type, were essentially queen-like and commanding. She looked quite capable of leading an army anywhere.

The natives of Congo, in Lower Guinea, have ever been notorious for their ferocity and love of shedding human blood; and such very savages are they, that what slight improvements have been made in their beloved pastime—war,—are due entirely to those Europeans who have visited the coast. The women are as ferocious as the men; and as the Salic law is either unknown, or neglected, there have from time to time been female sovereigns renowned for their military prowess.

One of these royal Amazons was Shinga, or Zingha, Queen of Matamba, in Congo, who ascended the throne on the death of her brother about 1640. She determined to be queen in her own dominions, and set herself up as a stern opponent of Christianity. She thereby offended the Portuguese priests (who had been established in the country since 1487), and they stirred up her nephew to rebellion. After losing three battles, Shinga was obliged to seek safety in flight.

After proceeding one hundred and fifty miles up the country, Shinga established a new kingdom; and by making war on the Jagas, or Giagas, the Arabs of Western Africa, she became sufficiently powerful once more to take the field against Portugal. But she was again routed, and her two sisters remained in the hands of the victors. At last, in 1646, she recovered her throne, and concluded an honourable treaty with the Christians.

Her long struggle with Portugal had so accustomed Shinga to a military life that she cared for nothing but war. She was almost constantly engaged in a campaign against the neighbouring kingdoms. Before starting on an expedition, she used to sacrifice the handsomest man she could find as a war offering to some African deity who required to be appeased. On such occasions she appeared in military costume, her bow and arrows in her hand, a sword hanging from a collar round her neck, an axe by her side. After going through a warlike dance, singing a martial song, accompanying it on two iron bells, she would cut off the victim's head as a declaration of war, and drink a deep draught of his blood.

The Jagas, at all times feared on account of their ruthless ferocity and cruelty, rose to the height of their glory under King Zimbo, who has been styled the "Napoleon of Africa." Donji, one of Zimbo's captains, was governor of Matamba; his wife, Mussasa, was a warrior like himself, and they trained their daughter, Tembandumba, to the same mode of life. After the death of Zimbo, his vast empire, like that of Alexander, was divided amongst his captains; and Donji, more skilful than the rest, conquered many of the surrounding states. After his death, Mussasa, who possessed military talent equal to her husband,—tarnished though it was by gross cruelty—continued to fight and to conquer the neighbouring chiefs.

Tembandumba received the education of a soldier. Trained, while yet a child, to the use of arms, she took naturally the trade of war. As a girl she accompanied her mother on all her campaigns; fighting side by side at the head of their troops, Mussasa and her daughter were always foremost in battle and last in a retreat. The valour and prudence of Tembandumba soon became so well known that her mother gave her the command of half the army. But when she had gained a few victories, the Amazon was not disposed to remain longer in a subordinate position. Throwing aside the authority of her mother, she assumed the title of Queen of the Jagas; and drew up a code of laws so extravagantly savage and bloodthirsty that only for the high respect, or rather terror, in which the young girl was held, even her subjects would have rebelled.

It was the ambition of Tembandumba to revive the Amazonian empire which had once existed on the African continent. In pursuance of this object, she declared war on the whole race of man; all the male children were to be slain by their mothers, and made into ointment called *"Magiga Samba,"* which when smeared over the human body would render the latter invulnerable. The adult males throughout her dominions were to be converted into food for the women; and to prevent the tender hearts of the women causing them to evade these laws, she commanded that every other food, animal or vegetable, should be destroyed. Had her statutes been obeyed to the letter, Western Africa would soon have been a hideous wilderness, devoid of human habitations, birds, beasts, trees, plants, or even grass.

Having promulgated these laws, together with many others of minor importance, in a speech delivered before a select committee of her female subjects, she concluded by seizing her own child, who was feeding at her breast, and hurling it into a large mortar, where she beat it to a jelly. Throwing this into a large pot, she compounded an oleaginous preparation with leaves, roots and oils, which she rubbed all over her body, telling her subjects to follow the example. Such quantities of *"Magiga Samba"* were manufactured that travellers declare there are still some pots of it to be found among the Jagas. But after the first burst of enthusiasm was over, maternal love prevailed, and Tembandumba, after vainly endeavouring, by the appointment of inspectors, to enforce obedience, was obliged to repeal the law, and permit children taken in war to be substituted to make the precious ointment.

For many years this female devil reigned triumphantly; she kept the Jagas so constantly engrossed by martial glory, they had no time to sigh for liberty. Kingdom after kingdom fell before her legions;

wherever she turned her footsteps, a track of desolation remained to mark her progress.

But Tembandumba, after all, was not above the weaknesses common to her sex; all her passions were exaggerated, and, like many another heroine, she owed her final overthrow to the God of Love. As a rule, she caused her husbands to be treated as Schahriar, in the *Arabian Nights*, used his wives; but at last she fell really in love with Culemba, a private in the army. Culemba was young, strong, and decidedly good-looking—for a negro. He possessed insinuating manners, and succeeded for a time in gaining some influence over the queen. But in time she wearied of him, as she had grown tired of her former lovers.

Culemba, knowing by experience that she had an unpleasant fancy for dining off her lovers, was determined to be beforehand with her. He was a cruel, ambitious man,—equally crafty as Tembandumba. He invited the queen to a sumptuous banquet; such an invitation being the highest compliment one Jaga could pay to another. The entertainment was magnificent, the wine delicious; but while drinking a bumper of Lisbon wine from the skull of an old enemy, the Queen of the Jagas fell down dead.

Culemba was—of course—inconsolable. With difficulty could he be prevented from slaying himself on the corpse. The funeral was conducted with all the splendour customary at the interment of a native African sovereign; the dead queen was buried in a large vault excavated on the top of a high hill. The corpse was placed in a commanding attitude on a throne, surrounded by skins, stuffs, mats, ostrich feathers, and all her favourite dishes and liquors.

Dahomey or,—as it is now fashionable to style it, Dahomé—may with truth be called one of the greatest curiosities of the Nineteenth Century. It seems so strange that a large, closely populated country, the monarch of which is anxious to cultivate the friendship of Europe, should be sunk in such gross barbarity. The chief features of its government are the Slave-Trade, the "Customs," or religious festivals, at which the notorious human sacrifices are offered, and the Amazons; and the last are by far the greatest curiosity. Very few rulers, in ancient or modern times, have authorised the keeping up a standing army of women; and none of the native tribes along the coast seem at all inclined to follow the example of Dahomey.

But the female sex in Dahomey is, they say, vastly superior to the male; the women are tall—upwards of six feet high, and powerfully built—the men, on the contrary, are, as a general rule, round-limbed and sickly-looking. Captain Burton suggests that it was this physical superiority which originated the custom of employing women-soldiers.

The Amazonian division of the army numbers twelve thousand women, ready at an hour's notice for active service. They are officered by females, and have a female commander-in-chief, who is entirely independent of the "*Gau*" or male commander-in-chief. To denote her rank, this female general wears a silver horn, hammer-shaped, projecting from her forehead, similar to a unicorn. The officers are distinguished by a white head-cloth, and by the superior make and material of their clothes; and when on the march, they are attended by what Captain Burton styles an "esquiress" or slave-girl, who carries the musket of her mistress.

The honorary captaincy of each corps is presented by the king to one of his sons, after whom it is sometimes named; though the companies are as frequently styled by the name of the district to which they specially belong. Sometimes the king presents some distinguished European traveller whom he wishes to compliment, with a honorary command.

The Amazons are not remarkable for any superfluity of muscle, but as a rule they are lithe and active. As they grow older, many become extremely stout. "Some of them" remarks Captain Burton "are prodigies of obesity." The commander-in-chief, he says, was "vast in breadth." Beauty is scarce in Dahomey, and what little there is, has not fallen to the lot of the Amazons. Captain Burton, who "expected to see Penthesileas, Thalestrises, Dianas," was sadly disappointed when he beheld "old, ugly, and square-built *frows*, trudging 'grumpily' along, with the face of 'cook' after being much 'nagged' by the 'missus'." They do not, however, as was once supposed, condemn themselves to single-blessedness; on the contrary, many have husbands and children.

They are very careful of their weapons—an English "Tower-marked" firelock, a short falchion, or dirk, and a large razor for cutting off heads. The musket is guarded by numerous charms, and when not in use is protected from the damp by a black, monkey-skin case; the barrel is polished bright, and sometimes adorned with a long tassel. Their skill in the use of these weapons is such as to render them exceedingly formidable adversaries.

Their uniforms are very showy. That of the Royal Guard—which, numbering rather more than a thousand women, is always stationed about the king's person—consists of a sleeveless tunic, surtout, or waistcoat of different colours, buttoning down the front, a pink, blue, or yellow loin-wrapper, or kilt, reaching to the ankles, a sash, generally white, tied round the waist, and folding down in two long ends on the left side, and a fillet of blue or white cotton round the head. The arms are left bare.

A black leather belt, with cartridge box—or "*agluadya*"—forms a girdle, with holds the surtout tight to the figure. This belt is sometimes ornamented with cowrie shells; on it are hung bandoleers, which contain, in separate compartments, twelve, sixteen, or even twenty wooden powder-boxes. Each cartridge contains about four times the quantity of powder used in English cartridges, and the bullet is not placed in it as in Europe; a small leather ball-bag hangs from the shoulder by a strap which passes through the belt. When the Amazons are loading, they pour the powder into the barrel without any wadding, and then drop in a bullet, or a few slugs.

Shaving the head is a general, though not a universal fashion. Those who do so, leave only a small tuft of hair like a cockade; others, however, who do not follow this custom, shave a narrow strip, two inches in breadth, from the forehead to the crown of the head.

When the Amazons are on the march, the privates are obliged to carry an immense number of articles absolutely necessary for a campaign under the scorching sun of Africa. Packs, containing their bed-mats, a change of clothes, and food for a fortnight—said food consisting of toasted grains or bean cakes spiced with pepper—small stools with three or four legs, two cartridge-boxes, water-gourds, fetish-sacks, powder calabashes, bullet wallets, fans, wooden pipe-cases, leather tobacco-bags, hats made of felt or straw, and palm-leaf umbrellas, are just a few of the things carried by them on the march.

The King of Dahomey is very proud of his female soldiers, whom he frequently passes in review. He regards these Amazonian field-days with a pride akin to that of Frederick the Great at one of the Potzdam Reviews, or Napoleon at a review of his Old Guard.

These grand reviews are very showy, effective sights. Although the discipline is not very exact, yet the evolutions performed are executed with a vigour and heartiness which almost atone for the lack of that neatness observed in more civilized armies. The king seats himself under a canopy in some public place, generally the market-place of the town, and the various corps of Amazons march on to the open ground in front; each regiment being preceded by its band, playing the most discordant music on fantastically shaped instruments made of elephants-trunks, bullock's-horns, and triangular iron tubes (which, when struck, emit a sound similar to a sheep-bell), and beating a large war-drum in a truly deafening manner.

This drum, ornamented with twelve human skulls, is carried on the head of one Amazon, while another walks after, beating it. Each corps possesses a similar drum, adorned with a like number of skulls. Every company has, likewise, six or seven standards, the top of each being surmounted by a human skull. In the more disciplined regiments, there is always an advance-guard of nine women, followed, at a short interval, by fifty supports.

The ceremony of passing them in review is so elaborate that one corps has occupied as much as two or three hours before being disposed of. According as each corps arrives within a short distance of the Royal canopy, a halt is ordered, and the women lie down, or squat down, to await their turn to appear before his majesty. The captain then introduces the officers by name, and all kneel down, throwing up the light red dust in showers over themselves. Their deeds of valour are recounted, and when any warrior has especially distinguished herself, the king graciously bestows his royal praises.

After all have been noticed, the officers fall into their proper places, and, together with the privates, burst into a complimentary song in honour of their ruler. It is usual for various Amazons, on the conclusion of this song, to step one after another to the front, and declare their loyalty. Then the entire corps kneels down, with the butt ends of their muskets resting on the ground, and the barrel slanting back over the shoulder. After covering themselves once more with dust, they poise their muskets horizontally in both hands, and, still on their knees, pour forth a lusty cheer. Then springing to their feet with another hearty cheer, they slope arms, and set off at the double-quick march, each trying to outstrip the rest.

This part of the review having at last concluded, the Amazons march on to an open space where sham entrenchments have been constructed. These mock fortifications usually consist of two or three great piles of green briar, armed with the most dangerous kind of prickly thorns. This thorny briar is much used in Africa, and formerly was employed in Asia, to entrench villages or towns. The clumps are about seventy feet wide and eight feet high, standing perhaps three hundred yards in advance of several pens, or yards, the latter surrounded by a strong wall about seven feet high, defended by dense masses of thorns, thickly matted with reeds. To defend this mock entrenchment, a few dozen royal slaves are placed within the enclosure.

Each corps, as it marches on to the ground, headed by the officer appointed to lead the attack—who wears a sword of a different shape from the others—halts about two hundred yards from the nearest pile, and shoulders arms. Directly the signal is given, they charge over the thorns, regardless of their bare feet, and in less than a minute the mimic fortress is captured. At intervals of twenty minutes, the other corps have captured the remaining piles, and they all return in triumph, each leading a slave by a rope. On reaching the royal canopy, each Amazon presents a scalp supposed to have been taken during the sham fight.

Sometimes the Amazons are rehearsed in volley-firing and target-practice. They load and fire quickly, singing all the time. Their target-practice is moderately good. Several thousand goats are tied to stakes in a large field surrounded by a mud wall about ten feet high. Most of the goats are killed before the day is over; which, when we take into account the indifferent quality of their powder, and the careless manner in which they load, speaks very well for the Amazons as markswomen.

The King of Dahomey is almost always engaged in some war, whether foreign or domestic; therefore a few hundred Amazons are constantly on active service. Like the Old Guard, the services of these female warriors are never brought into use save in cases of dire necessity, or when considerable opposition is expected. As the Amazons always strive not only to behead, but to scalp their enemies, they are pretty sure of having one or more of these ghastly trophies to show the king on their return from a campaign. Scalps, however, do not accumulate so fast as one might suppose; six or seven in a year is considered rather a large number, for the Amazons are frequently obliged, after slaying a foe, to pass on without securing his topknot.

The slave-trade provides very constant exercise for the Amazons; because, whenever the king requires slaves, it is necessary to go to war with some neighbour—though of course, His Majesty easily finds a *casus belli*. But the great thorn of vexation in the royal side for the past thirty years and more has been the republic of Abbeokuta. The influence of this free state, in destroying the slave-trade, very naturally brought down the hatred of the King of Dahomey, who is the largest dealer in human flesh on the African coast.

More than once he has tried to conquer this sturdy little city. On the 3rd of March, 1851, he appeared before the walls of Abbeokuta at the head of a great army—male and female. A furious attack was made to gain the ramparts, but the rapid, murderous fire of the Egbas drove back the Dahomans with fearful slaughter, and put them to rout. The Amazons led the attack; many were slain—nearly all the slain Dahomans were women—and one or two made prisoners.

The king undertook a second expedition against Abbeokuta in March, 1864. At the head of ten thousand picked warriors, and three brass six-pounders, he arrived before the walls on the 16th. The Amazons formed the column of attack, and displayed their accustomed bravery. Directly the signal was given for the assault, they scaled the wall like furies, and for a time threatened to carry everything before them. One Amazon having her right hand cut off, clung to the parapet and killed her adversary with her left, before being hurled back into the ditch.

The Egbas received the Amazons with a murderous fire, which thinned their ranks terribly. They were obliged to seek safety in flight, and their example was speedily followed by the whole Dahoman Army. The Egbas, sallying forth, pursued the retreating foe, massacring the stragglers without mercy. In this congenial task they were joined by the neighbouring tribes, who turned out in great numbers and joined heartily in the carnage.

The King of Dahomey experienced a most disastrous rout, with the loss of three thousand of of his best soldiers, one thousand being slain, and two thousand taken prisoners.

LEONAUR

ALSO FROM LEONAUR
AVAILABLE IN SOFTCOVER OR HARDCOVER WITH DUST JACKET

A DIARY FROM DIXIE *by Mary Boykin Chesnut*—A Lady's Account of the Confederacy During the American Civil War

FOLLOWING THE DRUM *by Teresa Griffin Vielé*—A U. S. Infantry Officer's Wife on the Texas frontier in the Early 1850's

FOLLOWING THE GUIDON *by Elizabeth B. Custer*—The Experiences of General Custer's Wife with the U. S. 7th Cavalry.

LADIES OF LUCKNOW *by G. Harris & Adelaide Case*—The Experiences of Two British Women During the Indian Mutiny 1857. A Lady's Diary of the Siege of Lucknow by G. Harris, Day by Day at Lucknow by Adelaide Case

MARIE-LOUISE AND THE INVASION OF 1814 *by Imbert de Saint-Amand*—The Empress and the Fall of the First Empire

SAPPER DOROTHY *by Dorothy Lawrence*—The only English Woman Soldier in the Royal Engineers 51st Division, 79th Tunnelling Co. during the First World War

ARMY LETTERS FROM AN OFFICER'S WIFE 1871-1888 *by Frances M. A. Roe*—Experiences On the Western Frontier With the United States Army

NAPOLEON'S LETTERS TO JOSEPHINE *by Henry Foljambe Hall*—Correspondence of War, Politics, Family and Love 1796-1814

MEMOIRS OF SARAH DUCHESS OF MARLBOROUGH, AND OF THE COURT OF QUEEN ANNE VOLUME 1 by A. T. Thomson

MEMOIRS OF SARAH DUCHESS OF MARLBOROUGH, AND OF THE COURT OF QUEEN ANNE VOLUME 2 by A. T. Thomson

MARY PORTER GAMEWELL AND THE SIEGE OF PEKING *by A. H. Tuttle*—An American Lady's Experiences of the Boxer Uprising, China 1900

VANISHING ARIZONA *by Martha Summerhayes*—A young wife of an officer of the U.S. 8th Infantry in Apacheria during the 1870's

THE RIFLEMAN'S WIFE *by Mrs. Fitz Maurice*—*The Experiences of an Officer's Wife and Chronicles of the Old 95th During the Napoleonic Wars*

THE OATMAN GIRLS *by Royal B. Stratton*—The Capture & Captivity of Two Young American Women in the 1850's by the Apache Indians